Modularity in Syntax

Current Studies in Linguistics
Samuel Jay Keyser, general editor

1. *A Reader on the Sanskrit Grammarians*
   J. F. Staal, editor

2. *Semantic Interpretation in Generative Grammar*
   Ray Jackendoff

3. *The Structure of the Japanese Language*
   Susumu Kuno

4. *Speech Sounds and Features*
   Gunnar Fant

5. *On Raising: One Rule of English Grammar and Its Theoretical Implications*
   Paul M. Postal

6. *French Syntax: The Transformational Cycle*
   Richard S. Kayne

7. *Pāṇini as a Variationist*
   Paul Kiparsky, edited by S. D. Joshi

8. *Semantics and Cognition*
   Ray Jackendoff

9. *Modularity in Syntax: A Study of Japanese and English*
   Ann Kathleen Farmer

Modularity in Syntax: Ann Kathleen Farmer
A Study of Japanese
and English

The MIT Press
Cambridge, Massachusetts
London, England

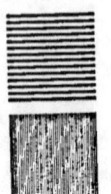

MIT Press
0262060876
FARMER
MODULARITY IN SYNTAX

© 1984 by
The Massachusetts Institute of Technology

All rights reserved. No part of this book may be reproduced in any form or by any means, electronic or mechanical, including photocopying, recording, or by any information storage and retrieval system, without permission in writing from the publisher.

This book was set in VIP Times Roman by Village Typographers, Inc., and printed and bound by Halliday Lithograph in the United States of America.

Library of Congress Cataloging in Publication Data
Farmer, Ann Kathleen.
  Modularity in syntax.

  (Current studies in linguistics series; 9)
  Bibliography: p.
  Includes index.
  1. Grammar, Comparative and general—Syntax.
2. Japanese language—Syntax. 3. English language—Syntax. 4. Japanese language—Grammar, Comparative—English. 5. English language—Grammar, Comparative—Japanese. I. Title. II. Series.
P291.F27 1984   495.6′5   83-16285
ISBN 0-262-06087-6

For Mike

Contents

Series Foreword xi

Preface xiii

Introduction xv

Chapter 1
Defining the Base 3

1.1 Hierarchical Structure 3

1.2 Defining the Base: A Historical Perspective 7

1.3 An Alternative: The Category-Neutral Theory 11

1.4 Ramifications of the Category-Neutral Theory 19

1.5 Consequences for Japanese and English 21

1.6 Other Questions 24

Chapter 2
Japanese Syntax: Prevailing and Alternative Analyses 25

2.1 A Review of Major Issues in Japanese Syntax 25

2.2 Prevailing Analyses 32

Contents

viii

2.3
An Alternative: Predicate Argument Structures, Linking, and Evaluation 45

2.4
Summary and Conclusions 71

Chapter 3
Extending the Modular Theory: Japanese 76

3.1
The Investigation 77

3.2
Results of PS Rules and Case Linking 78

3.3
Another Case-Marking Problem 80

3.4
A Modular Account of Related Constructions 81

3.5
Anaphora 99

3.6
Overgeneration 105

Chapter 4
Extending the Modular Theory: English 109

4.1
Aspects and Components of the Grammar 109

4.2
A Modular Analysis of English 116

4.3
Defining the Base: Problems of Constituency and the Content of the S-Node 152

4.4
Final Remarks 160

Contents

Chapter 5
Consequences for Anaphora in English   161

5.1 Anaphora and Coreference   161

5.2 Anaphora: A Modular Account   165

5.3 The Status of Empty Categories   182

5.4 Accounting for the Properties of NP-Trace and PRO   187

5.5 Summary   193

Chapter 6
Implications for Language Typology   195

6.1 Some Differences between English and Japanese   195

6.2 Speculation on Certain Typological Differences   196

Notes   199

References   223

Index   233

Series Foreword

We are pleased to present this book as the ninth volume in the series Current Studies in Linguistics.

As we have defined it, the series will offer book-length studies in linguistics and neighboring fields that further the exploration of man's ability to manipulate symbols. It will pursue the same editorial goals as its companion journal, *Linguistic Inquiry,* and will complement it by providing a format for in-depth studies beyond the scope of the professional article.

By publishing such studies, we hope the series will answer a need for intensive and detailed research that sheds new light on current theoretical issues and provides a new dimension for their resolution. Toward this end it will present books dealing with the widest range of languages and addressing the widest range of theoretical topics. From time to time and with the same ends in view, the series will include collections of significant articles covering single and selected subject areas and works primarily for use as textbooks.

Like *Linguistic Inquiry,* Current Studies in Linguistics will seek to present work of theoretical interest and excellence.

Samuel Jay Keyser

Preface

In Farmer (1980) my goal was to "develop a theory of the interaction of morphology and syntax in Japanese based on the hypothesis that all derivational word formation is accomplished prior to lexical insertion." This position entailed questioning some basic assumptions concerning the role of the phrase structure component. Concurrently, Hale (1980), Lapointe (1980), and Whitman (1979), among others, also suggested that a reassessment of the role of the phrase structure rules was in order. This book will elaborate a theory of phrase structure in the general spirit of the works just cited, building on some ideas while discarding and modifying others. I will discuss both Japanese and English, carrying over assumptions to English settled upon during the analysis of Japanese.

Among the more recent works that have influenced my thinking are Chomsky (1981b), Stowell (1981), Williams (1980), Marantz (1981b), Hale (1983), and Bresnan (1982).

I have profited immensely by being at the Linguistics Department at the University of Arizona, and would like to thank my colleagues at large for providing a stimulating environment for learning and teaching. In particular, I would like to thank Adrian Akmajian and Chisato Kitagawa for their extensive comments on this work. Mike Harnish has been very generous with his time and has taught me the value of developing a theory of pragmatics, showing me that it is essential to understanding what it is I'm doing and what it is I'm *not* doing.

Ken Hale, Noam Chomsky, and Sylvain Bromberger have all been helpful by discussing many of the points brought up in this book, and challenging them all.

I would like to express my appreciation to the Farmer family, Joanne

Farmer Suppes, Mary Hotvedt, Bonnie Stephens, and Myles and Peggy Brand, who have all been supportive these last several years.

Finally, I would like to thank Theresa Huard-Lentz for an outstanding job of preparing the manuscript for this book.

Introduction

The theory to be constructed here is based on the hypothesis that the language system is modular in nature. Given this view, a theory of Language (a "language system") will be construed as a system of rules and representations factorable into independent but interacting subsystems. My approach, which I will term *Modular Grammar,* is thus an instance of what Pylyshyn (1980, 121) characterizes as "an extremely general scientific maxim, namely, that a central goal of explanatory theories is to factor a set of phenomena, a problem, or a system into the most general and perspicuous components, principles, or subsystems."

This conception of the language system involves pragmatics that is modular in the following sense: the structure of an expression, which is defined by the grammar (narrowly construed), plays a crucial role in determining its literal and direct interpretation. I will be assuming, in other words, that principles delimiting the literal and direct interpretation of an expression form a part of the language system (see Bach and Harnish (1979) and Harnish (1983)).

In this work I will be principally concerned with the syntactic and lexical levels of representation, the properties that individuate these levels, and the properties of the rules and principles that mediate between them.

Chapter 1 discusses several well-known ways of defining the base, pointing out their inadequacies and then motivating a system of "impoverished" phrase structure "rules." The first part of chapter 2 presents an overview of some of the major issues in Japanese syntax that will be of interest. The second part develops an account of the case particles for simple and morphologically complex verbs (specifically, passive and causative verbs). Chapter 3 elaborates the framework sketched in chapter 2, extending the theory to account for aspects of the topic construction, *tough* sentences, and indirect passives, and modifies the application of the case-linking rules. This chapter also examines the status of anaphora in Japanese. Chapter 4 brings to bear on English the theoretical perspective developed for Japanese. The goal is, once again, viewed as one of apportioning certain tasks to certain domains. An account of so-called NP-movement and Control is developed that does not posit entities referred to in the literature as "NP-trace" and "PRO." Redefining the status of such entities entails reconsidering the question of anaphora in general. Chapter 5 addresses the consequences of merging the notions "NP-trace" and "PRO." It is the anaphora issue that critically involves recognition of a modular pragmatics, requiring that a distinction be made between (intended) speaker reference and linguistically triggered referential presumptions in order to handle many heretofore problematic cases of anaphora.

The final chapter speculates that the "typological" differences observed between Japanese and English are, according to the theory of Modular Grammar, in part a function of the nature of the rules and principles that mediate between the syntax and the lexical structure. I am not, then, assuming that parameters, in the sense of Chomsky (1981b, 1982) and Hale (1981b, 1983), play a role in accounting for "typological" differences among languages.

Modularity in Syntax

Chapter 1
Defining the Base

1.1 Hierarchical Structure

In *Syntactic Structures* the following tree diagram is offered as a way of representing a derivation of the sentence *The man hit the ball* (Chomsky (1957, 27)):

(1.1)

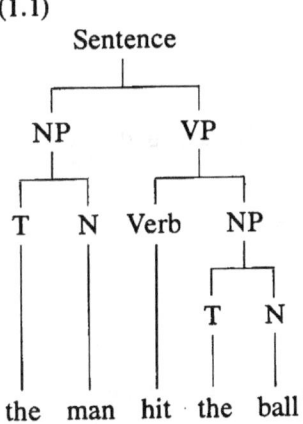

the man hit the ball

While the tree diagram imparts less information than the derivation, "the diagram ... retains just what is essential ... for the determination of the phrase structure (constituent analysis) of the derived sentence 'the man hit the ball' " (p. 28). These hierarchical representations have become more than simply a convenient way of representing certain aspects of the rewrite rules used in the derivation of a sentence. The structure has achieved a certain importance of its own. Constituent analyses of type (1.1) have played an important role in characterizing some cases of ambiguity; moreover, some rather important relations have been defined over hierarchical structures, most notably, the

Modularity in Syntax

"command" relation. In this chapter we will be concerned with two aspects of hierarchical structures: first, are they necessary? and second, how are they defined?

1.1.1 Ambiguity

Strings like those in (1.2) and (1.3) have motivated the hypothesis that different syntactic structures underlying each of these strings account for the ambiguity and not some semantic difference, because the meaning of the words does not vary from reading to reading.[1]

(1.2)
from Akmajian, Demers, and Harnish (1979, 139)
The mother of the boy and the girl will arrive soon.
a. The mother will arrive soon.
b. The mother and also the girl will arrive soon.

(1.3)
from Radford (1981, 55)
very old men and women
a. the women and the very old men
b. the very old men and the very old women

These strings can be assigned the following hierarchical structures:

(1.4)
The mother of the boy and the girl will arrive soon.
a. structure for reading (1.2a)

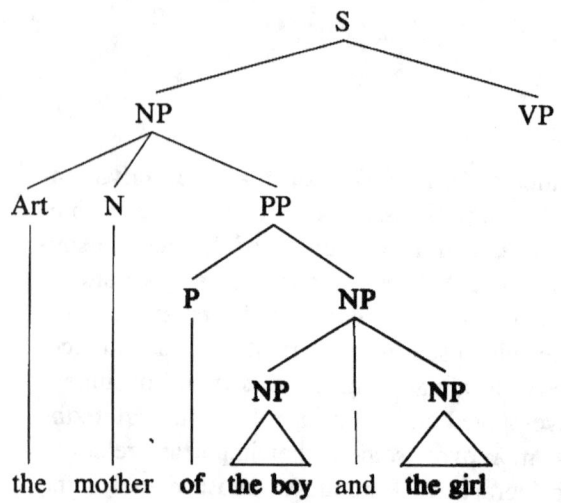

Defining the Base

b. structure for reading (1.2b)

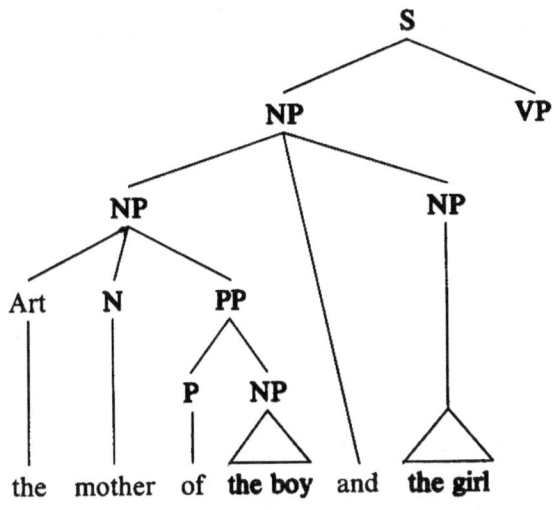

(1.5)
very old men and women
a. structure for reading (1.3a) (from Radford (1981, 55–56))

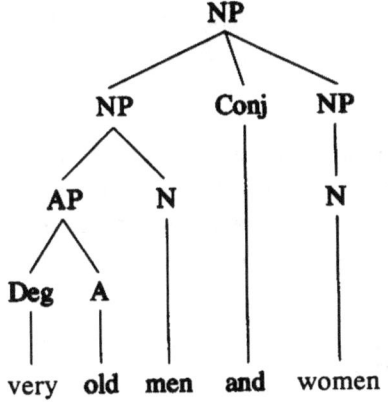

b. structure for reading (1.3b)

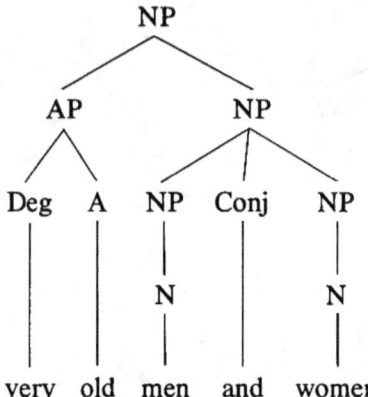

very old men and women

These structures characterize the ambiguity in (1.2) and (1.3). For example, the AP in (1.5a) is represented as modifying only *men*, whereas the AP in (1.5b) modifies both *men* and *women*. To answer our first question, then, it appears that hierarchical representations are *sufficient* for characterizing certain scope relations. This does not entail that hierarchical structures are *necessary* for expressing such relations, however, since one could imagine other ways of representing this kind of information.

1.1.2 Command

Another example of the role hierarchical structure has played in linguistic theory involves anaphora. In order to account for the contrast between (1.6) and (1.7), many linguists have proposed versions of a condition that is sensitive to structural configurations. These examples are taken from Langacker (1969, 166).

(1.6)
*He is much more intelligent than *Ralph* looks.

(1.7)
The woman who is to marry *him* will visit *Ralph* tomorrow.

In both sentences the pronoun precedes *Ralph*, but the coreference possibilities differ: *he* and *Ralph* in (1.6) cannot be coreferential, whereas *him* and *Ralph* in (1.7) can be. To account for this difference, Langacker offers the following condition, which he calls the *Precede and Command Condition*.[2]

(1.8)
An NP A may serve as the antecedent for a pronoun B (which agrees with A in the relevant features, including person, number and gender) if and only if either:
   (a) B follows A in the discourse, or
   (b) A and B are in the same sentence, and B does not command A.
A node X is said to command a node Y if every S dominating X dominates Y.

Such a condition has been proposed in order to govern both a "pronominalization" rule and rules of indexing; it also plays an important role in the Binding Conditions of Government-Binding (GB) theory. Thus, no matter what rules or principles are being used to describe anaphoric relations, structural conditions seem to be important. Once again, hierarchical structure has some utility. However, its utility does not allow us to conclude that it is necessary for every conceivable account of anaphoric phenomena. The theory to be developed here will utilize hierarchical structures to define the domain of application of certain rules. Assuming a syntactic level of representation that is hierarchical does not entail committing oneself to any particular type of mechanism for defining the structure. I now turn to this question.

1.2 Defining the Base: A Historical Perspective

Given a theory that utilizes hierarchical structure to characterize or encode certain types of information, there still remains the question of *how* this structure is to be defined. In *Aspects of the Theory of Syntax*, Chomsky offers a set of phrase structure (PS) rules that, coupled with a transformation, yields a structural analysis of a string. Chomsky entertains two alternatives for introducing lexical items into the tree, the *matching* format and the *substitution* format. Chomsky discusses the matching format at considerable length and the substitution format only briefly, even though in subsequent work he never uses the matching procedure. Both formats differ from the *Syntactic Structures* model in that "the categorial component of the base generates no lexical items in strings (though it may introduce grammatical morphemes)" (Chomsky (1971, 97)); that is, there was no lexicon in *Syntactic Structures*. Both formats utilize a transformation for the purposes of lexical insertion. The matching format utilizes the following "lexical rule" (from Chomsky (1965, 84)):

(1.9)
If Q is a complex symbol[3] of a preterminal string and (D, C) is a lexical entry, where C is not distinct from Q, then Q can be replaced by D.

At this stage, the grammatical properties of formatives no longer need to be represented in the rewrite rules, as in *Syntactic Structures;* the theory now has a lexicon where these properties can be stated. In the matching format subcategorization is both in the rewrite rules and in the lexicon, whereas in the substitution format it is only in the lexicon. Another difference is that in the substitution format a lexical category, A, rewrites as Δ, where Δ is a fixed dummy symbol. The categorial component is defined (p. 123) "... as the system of rewriting rules of the base—that is, the system of base rules exclusive of the lexicon and the subcategorization rules that we, for the present, regard as belonging to the lexicon." The system of rewrite rules is therefore responsible for defining hierarchical structure. These rules have two functions: "they define the system of grammatical relations, and they determine the ordering of elements in deep structures" (p. 123). The rewrite rules are a statement of the "is a" relation, capturing the various categorial dependencies.

The next stage in the development of the rules that define hierarchical structure concerns the attempt to capture cross-categorial generalizations and to rule out certain types of PS rules, i.e., the rules that define structures like those in (1.10).

(1.10)
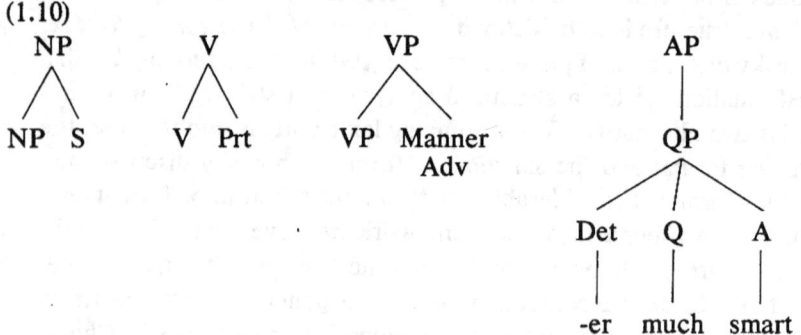

In "Remarks on Nominalization" Chomsky introduces *X-bar theory*— a response to the need for cross-categorial generalizations previously

Defining the Base

captured, in part, by certain syntactic derivations (e.g., nominalization transformations) that, he argues, are now ruled out.[4]

One of the major innovations of X-bar theory is that it provides a simple definition of the notion "head." In addition, structure acquires a certain amount of autonomy from categories. Now, in principle, exocentric structures (structures that are defined by category-switching rules like NP → S) are not allowed. The lexical node, X, is supposed to be projected up to its maximal projection and not be changed on the way. (One question that has been extensively argued is whether S is or is not a projection of V. Jackendoff (1977) and Marantz (1980) argue that it is; Chomsky, Hornstein (1977), Stowell (1981), and Bresnan (1982) argue that it is not. I will examine this issue further in a later section.) Jackendoff (1977) departs from this general view by lifting the ban on exocentric structures. For example, gerundive nominals, which behave internally like a sentence and externally like an NP, are given an analysis that yields an exocentric structure (example from Jackendoff (1977, 223)):

(1.11)
PS rule: 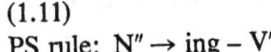 N″ → ing – V″

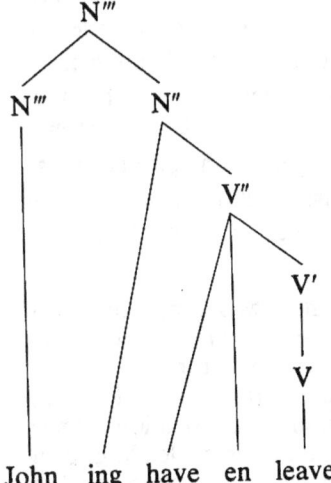

After Affix Hopping the following structure results:

(1.12)

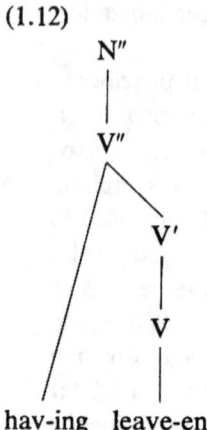

hav-ing leave-en

N″ directly dominates V″, and N″ has no head. This would appear to open the door that Chomsky and others had tried to close.

The problem just discussed is particular to Jackendoff's system and not necessarily an inherent problem of rewrite rules. Farmer (1980) responds to this problem by stripping the rewrite rules of their categorial content. In other words, if the rewrite rules themselves don't have access to the vocabulary of categories, then they can't be used as a device for switching them. Farmer (1980) develops a theory of the base for Japanese founded on the idea that the rewrite rules only define hierarchical structures and neither state categorial dependencies nor determine linear order among complements of the head. Stowell (1981) develops a theory of the base for English using the same ground rules, within the framework of GB theory. Chomsky (1981b) confronts the earlier conception of the role of the PS rules in the context of the Projection Principle. He notes (pp. 31–32) that

Consideration of the projection principle illuminates a conceptual deficiency of theories of UG [universal grammar] of the type considered in Chomsky (1965). . . . The categorial component of the base is sometimes described as a specification of redundancy rules of the lexicon, i.e., as an explicit formulation of the class of subcategorization frames that are found in the lexicon. But this formulation is misleading; as a specification of redundancy rules, the categorial component does no work. . . . But the rules of the categorial component do not have this effect [i.e., do not act like true redundancy rules]; even when these rules are explicitly formulated, each lexical item must still contain a full specification of its subcategorization frames. . . . Apart from order, the rule of the categorial component serves no function as a redundancy rule; as for order, I will suggest below that this specification too is probably unnecessary in this case, [i.e., referring to NP $\bar{S}$ order], and in quite a few others.

We see, then, that attempts are being made on many theoretical fronts to capture dependencies formerly captured by the rewrite rules, via other means. The means are, of course, theory dependent.

1.3 An Alternative: The Category-Neutral Theory

There are many ways that one can proceed from here, while still sharing the assumption that the PS rules are more impoverished than previously conceived. I will outline my alternative theory of the composition of the base by looking at Japanese and English. In section 1.3.1 I will discuss Japanese. In section 1.3.2 I will outline a general approach to PS rules in English.

It should be noted that Hale's work on "nonconfigurational" languages has played an important role in exploring alternatives to the traditional PS rules. See especially Hale (1980, 1981a, 1983).

1.3.1 The Japanese Phrase Structure System

1.3.1.1 Phrase Structure Rules Phrase structure rules have always had the role of defining the structure of categories—that is, relating supercategories, X', $X''...X^k$, where X is some lexical category, to X. The head of the phrase is identified as X^{n-1}, or as X if it is the terminal node.[5]

For Japanese, I will propose a PS rule that only specifies depth of structure and indicates the location of the head (X^{n-1}). The PS rule itself does not project categories (N^n N^{n-1}). Instead, it projects node-markers, X, which do not have any categorial content,[6] but which are associated with an exponent representing the level of structure. The head in each expansion is identified by the reduction in the exponent. (For typographical reasons, primes replace the traditional bars of X-bar notation throughout this book.)

(1.13)
a. $X' \rightarrow X'^* \ X$
  where X is the head
b. $X \rightarrow \Delta$

(See Hale (1983) for discussion of this rule, and Chomsky (1981a,b) for another version of it.)

I should emphasize that the Xs in the above rule do *not* stand for variables that range over categories. They are to be interpreted as node-markers. Thus, (1.13) should not be understood to mean that each instance of X must be the same category. The following are possible structures defined by these rules:

(1.14)

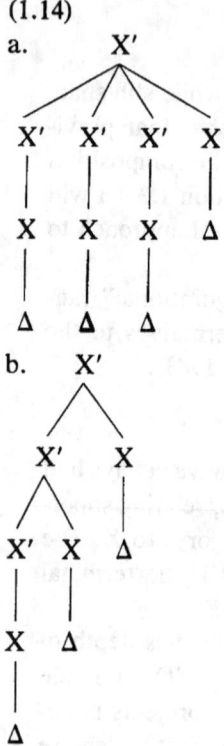

These structures correspond to (1.15a,b), respectively:

(1.15)
a. Taroo wa Hanako ni hon o ageta.
   'Taro gave Hanako the book.'
b. Hanako ga yonda hon o
   'the book which Hanako read'

1.3.1.2 The Role of the Lexical Item In a theory incorporating a PS component that projects only categorially unspecified nodes, the lexical item itself plays an important role in defining the nature of its constituents.[7]

Defining the Base

The following examples show some relevant aspects of lexical entries.

(1.16)
HON 'book'
(i) [$_N$ ____] (i.e., category affiliation)

TABE 'eat'
(i) [$_V$ ____]

AGE 'give'
(i) [$_V$ ____]

-SASE verbal suffix (causative)
(i) $_V$] ____ $_V$]

This lexical representation figures quite importantly in the interpretation of the string.

1.3.1.3 Context-free Lexical Insertion I am proposing that lexical insertion is context free. Since the PS rules do not provide any categorial information, the only available contexts are the dominance relations of the unlabeled nodes. (The numbers associated with the Xs are for ease of reference and have no theoretical significance.)

(1.17)

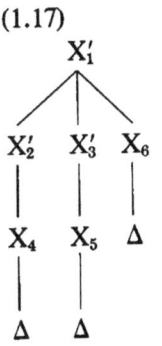

In (1.17) we can see that X'_2 is dominated by an X' (X'_1) and that X_6 is also dominated by X'_1. For the purposes of lexical insertion, though, we are interested only in the terminal nodes, Δ. A lexical item and its associated features replace the terminal node, Δ. Hence, lexical insertion can be viewed as a transformation that replaces these Δs with the lexical material. Included in the feature matrix of the lexical item is a specification for case that is later spelled out as *ga* (nominative), *ni* (dative), or *o* (accusative).[8]

Modularity in Syntax   14

(1.18)

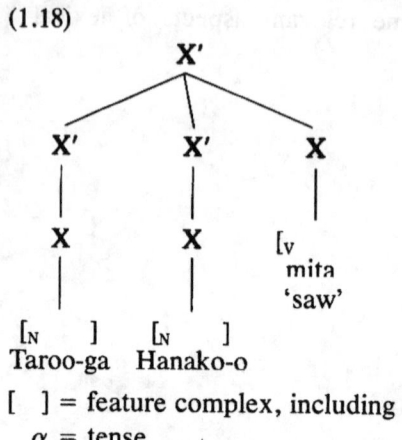

[ ] = feature complex, including (among others):
α = tense
β = person
γ = case, etc.

There is no way of controlling the lexical insertion to guarantee a particular configurational/lexical item linkup. The following result is entirely possible:

(1.19)

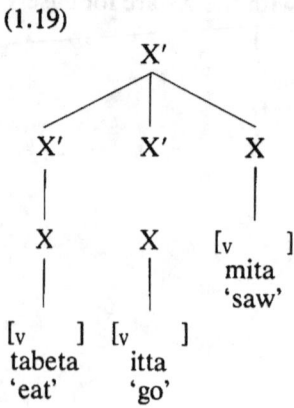

1.3.1.4 Node Labeling Williams (1981a) offers a feature percolation system for the level of the word. Suppose this notion of feature percolation can be extended up into the syntactic tree (that is, beyond X^0 or lexical level). The unspecified nodes are then given categorial content by the action of the percolating features.

Defining the Base   15

(1.20)

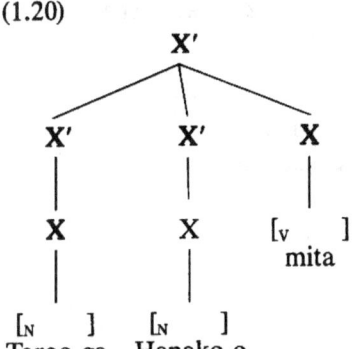

Feature percolation proceeds as follows: [∝ F] percolates up to X^{max}, where F = features of the lexical item. In the sentence *Taroo ga Hanako o mita* 'Taro saw Hanako', the features would climb up in the following manner:

(1.21)

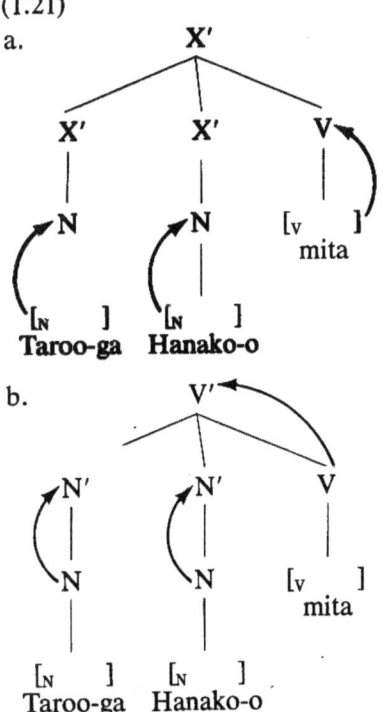

Notice that in Japanese S (X') is a projection of V in this theory.[9]

Another, more complex example would be (1.22), with structure (1.23).

(1.22)
Taroo wa   Hanako ga   katta   hon o   yonda.
Taro-topic Hanako-nom buy-past   book-acc   read-past
'Taro read the book that Hanako bought.'

(1.23)
a.

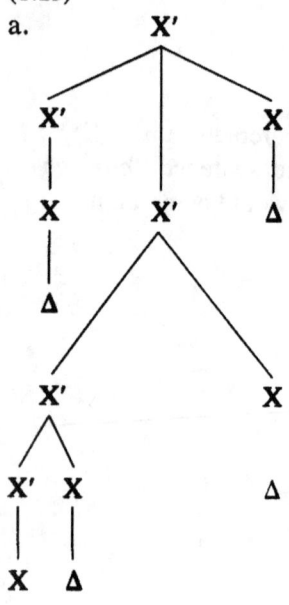

Defining the Base

b.

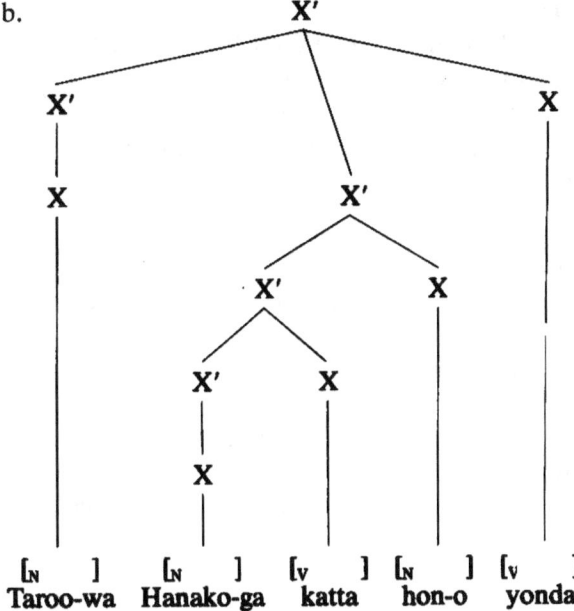

After feature climbing:

c.

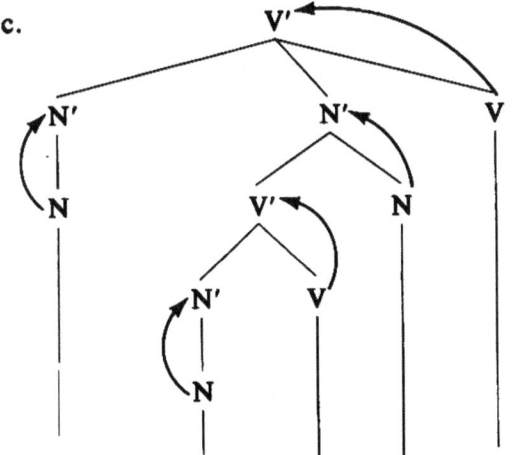

Taroo-wa **Hanako-ga** katta hon-o yonda

I have shown only instances of lexical items that are compatible with the structure in which they are embedded. Cases of incompatibility raise the question of overgeneration that is inherent in a modular theory. I will discuss this issue more fully in chapter 3.

1.3.2 English Phrase Structure

As I did for Japanese, I will claim that the rule for defining hierarchical structure in English specifies the location of the head with respect to its complements. The rule does not "project" categories. The following statements, from Stowell (1981, 87), are the rules and principles that will be adopted in this theory:

(1.24)
a. Every phrase is endocentric.
b. Specifiers appear at the X" level;[10] "subcategorized" complements appear within X'.
c. The head always appears adjacent to one of the boundaries of X'.
d. The head term is one bar-level [prime-level] lower than the immediately dominating phrasal node.
e. Only maximal projections may appear as nonhead terms within a phrase.

(1.25)
a. X" → (X") X'
b. X' → X X"*
c. X → Δ

Structure (1.26) is one that is defined by rule (1.25).

(1.26)
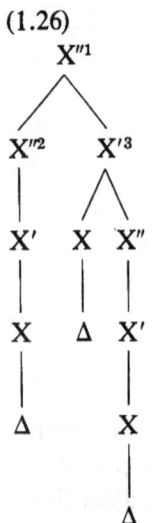

Lexical insertion involves replacing the Δs with lexical items.

Defining the Base

Rules (1.25a,b) have some noteworthy properties. First, they make [X", X"] (i.e., "subject") an optional constituent. Second, S turns out to be an instance of X", which is a projection of V, Modal, *have,* or *be.* The former point involves the "obligatoriness" of the subject, and the latter involves the question of whether S is a projection of V. The obligatory subject question is extensively discussed in chapter 4; the projection problem will be redefined there, as well. I now turn to investigating some of the consequences of the category-neutral theory.[11]

1.4 Ramifications of the Category-Neutral Theory

A theory of hierarchical structure that is defined independently of category immediately raises several fundamental questions. It is no longer possible, as in an *Aspects*-type model, to express categorial dependencies via the rewrite rules of the base. As noted before, Chomsky (1981b, 31–32) questions whether the PS rules are truly functioning as redundancy rules or not. Chomsky describes an instance of a redundancy rule (p. 32):

... if it [i.e., an item] has the property that it begins with three consonants, then it has the property that it begins with /s/. In such cases, the redundancy rules are effective in the sense that once the rule is stated that an item with property *P* has the property *P'*, then it is unnecessary to include the property *P'* in the entry of any lexical item with the property *P*.

But, as Chomsky points out, the rules of the categorial component do not have the effect of minimizing the amount of information needed in the lexicon. The category-neutral approach renders nondefinitive the following kind of substitution test for establishing the categorial status of an element. Take some mystery element, E. If it can be shown (it is usually argued) that E substitutes for, say, a verb V, then it follows that E is also a V, and categories affiliated with V by virtue of the PS rules can cooccur with E. This is sound only if it can be maintained that the PS rules are truly autonomous. That is, generalizations represented by the PS rules are independent generalizations that hold true of any lexical item given its categorial affiliation. It is well known that this kind of substitution test for determining category affiliation is problematic. For example, if we are trying to determine the category of *sleep,* we could run into the following problem: if we know that *read* is a verb in the sentence *Mary read the book,* then if *sleep* is a verb it should substitute for *read*, giving *Mary slept the book*. But since *Mary slept the book* is odd, we should conclude that *sleep* is *not* a verb. Obviously this is not the tack that has been taken. *Read* and *sleep* are both said to be verbs; the reason the test doesn't work is that they are different types of verbs, i.e., one is transitive and the other is intransitive. This difference is recorded in the lexicon.[12] Utilizing the lexicon in this way leads to the demise of the "PS rule alias redundancy rule" claim.

It appears, then, that the role of expressing categorial dependencies does not necessarily fall into the domain of the rewrite rules. Instead, the category-neutral theory will rely heavily on lexical information (i.e., predicate argument structures (PASs)), the case-assigning properties of verbs, and general principles of interpretation (i.e., "mapping" lexical structure and the syntactic string) to effect or simulate the expression of many dependencies formerly expressed via PS rules. In effect, since this theory strives to characterize other possible origins of dependencies, I am trying to avoid settling on PS rules as the relevant level of explanation. That is certainly not to say that there are no categorial generalizations to be made, only that the relationship between the rules that define the hierarchical structure and these generalizations is not an isomorphism. An even more radical claim would be that the hierarchical structure is epiphenominal. For now I will not go so far as to attempt to reduce the structure to, say, a set of functions.

Another consequence of the category-neutral theory is the above-mentioned overgeneration. Assuming that lexical insertion is simultaneous for all categories (i.e., verbs are not inserted before nouns or vice versa), then the only context is the terminal symbol, Δ, for which the lexical item substitutes. Obviously, a terminal string could end up consisting solely of nouns, or prepositions, etc. Such a state of affairs runs counter to the spirit of the earliest work in syntactic theory, where only "deep structures" or kernel strings that were associated with well-formed "surface" strings were generated by the base component. A reconceptualization of the grammar is required. The grammar to be developed here will be highly modular, much in the spirit of Harnish (1976), Chomsky (1981a,b, 1982), Hale (1980), Farmer (1980), and Jaeggli (1981). The underlying assumption will be that the grammar is composed of (autonomous) components each of which contributes a critique (interpretation) of a (given) string. It is only after these components have "interacted" (made their contribution) that the string can be judged as "well formed" or not.

1.5 Consequences for Japanese and English

Altering rather basic assumptions concerning the role of phrase structure rules forces a reexamination of many theoretical issues that have been defined within the bounds of a theory that embraces the alternative conception of the PS rules. We will now begin to consider the issues affected by the new approach, specifically with regard to Japanese and English. Section 1.5.1 outlines the consequences of the category-neutral theory of the base for Japanese; section 1.5.2 is concerned with pertinent issues in English morphology and syntax. Chapters 2 through 5 will be devoted to mapping out a theory of Japanese and English that embraces an "impoverished" PS system, while offering an alternative account of some old problems such as control, NP-movement, and anaphora, among others.

1.5.1 Japanese

The category-neutral theory of the base eliminates the need for a scrambling rule in Japanese; eliminating the scrambling rule results in not being able to define grammatical relations configurationally; and not defining grammatical relations configurationally obviates the need for a complex syntactic analysis of *tabesase*.

Many of the points to be brought up here have been discussed extensively before in Farmer (1980, 1981a,b) and in Hale (1980). Hale in fact noticed one of the first consequences of the category-neutral theory, which involves scrambling. In a simple Japanese sentence, the only phrase structure requirement seems to be that the "head" (e.g., the verb) must appear on the right; the other constituents can appear in any order to the left of the "head." Previous accounts, of which Kuno (1973) is representative, involve generating a basic, "preferred" order and then using a "stylistic" scrambling rule to produce all the alternative orders associated with the basic string. The literature makes frequent reference to "scrambling" rules, especially the Extended Standard Theory literature. The status of the rule has been challenged many times, for example by Whitman (1979) and Bach (1977). But then, at least for Japanese, there are reasons for having the scrambling rule *if* it is necessary to define grammatical relations configurationally, at the level of PS. A theory that does *not* incorporate a scrambling rule cannot identify "subject" as the "leftmost [NP, S]," for example; the leftmost [NP, S] may in fact turn out to be the direct object of the verb. Thus, a theory that crucially uses the syntactic configuration to identify "subject" or "direct object" must use a scrambling rule. Since we are not using a scrambling rule, we cannot identify grammatical relations configurationally; hence the reference to Japanese as a "nonconfigurational" language. This is not to say that Japanese does not have *any* "hierarchical" structure—only that this structure is not a guide to the function (i.e., grammatical function) of an N' constituent.

Another question arises, concerning the syntactic status of morphologically complex verbs like *tabe-sase* 'cause to eat'. Theories such as the one developed in Kuno (1973) have analyzed these verbs as having a complex syntactic structure at the level of representation where lexical insertion takes place.[13] This makes sense *if* grammatical relations are defined or identified configurationally, since it appears that the "subject" of the main verb continues to act like a subject even after the bound verbalizing morpheme *-sase* is attached. Under such an analysis, rules presumably sensitive to the notion "subject" (e.g., "reflexivization") must apply in a cyclic fashion and before the syntactic structure is collapsed. Scrambling follows all these procedures; that is, it is the last rule to apply. The following example is from Kuno (1973, 305):

(1.27)
a. Deep structure:
   John ga Mary ni [Mary ga *Mary* no uti   de hon   o yom] (s)ase-ta.
                              's house in book   read cause-ed
b. First cycle:
   Reflexivization
   John ga Mary ni [Mary ga *zibun* no uti de hon o yom] (s)ase-ta.
c. Second cycle:
   (i) Deletion of the embedded subject
   John ga Mary ni zibun no uti de hon o yom-(s)ase-ta.
   'John made Mary read a book in her own house.'
   (ii) Pure Passivization
   Mary ga John ni zibun no uti de hon o yom-(s)ase-rare-ta.
   'Mary was made by John to read a book in her own house.'

In a theory that has no scrambling rule, however, the following question arises: what is the relevant level of representation at which to identify "subject"? This involves answering a second question: at what level of representation is *tabe-sase* complex? There seems to be no utility in positing a complex syntactic level (something like deep structure or D-structure, for instance).[14] Hence, the motivation for treating

-*sase* as a higher verb that takes a sentential complement (*tabe* in this case) disappears. By this I do not mean that *tabesase* does not involve some kind of complex embedding; rather, I am saying that the relationship between the complex structure and the scrambled structure is not one of mapping if "mapping" is understood as transforming one level *into* another level. In Farmer (1980) I arrived at this conclusion via a rather different route. There I claimed that if word formation occurred prior to lexical insertion, then the syntactic structure of *tabesase* was "flattened out."[15] The flat structure of *tabesase* in Farmer (1980) was therefore a consequence of saying that morphologically complex verbs were formed before lexical insertion. Another consequence was that the "subject" of *tabe* could not be configurationally distinguished from its "object"; nor were the case particles of any aid. While the position taken in Farmer (1980) was reasonable, the conclusion that *tabesase* involves a "flat" syntactic structure need no longer depend solely on whether or not the assumption that word formation takes place prior to lexical insertion is correct.[16] What I have suggested here is that a complex syntactic structure for *tabesase* is unnecessary once there is no scrambling rule.

1.5.2 English

For English an immediate question arises concerning the status of "subject." Chomsky (1981b) addresses the issue of "obligatory subject," claiming that rule (1.28) (= Chomsky's (25)) is responsible for the subject's being necessary.

(1.28)
S → NP INFL VP

Chomsky's position is based on attributing the behavior of pleonastic elements to structural properties of configurations, the relevant configurations being defined by (1.28). In the case of infinitival complements and gerunds, the [NP, S] will be "phonologically null," but structurally present nonetheless.[17] This phonologically null subject may correspond to PRO or NP-trace. Much of the current research in Government-Binding theory is devoted to characterizing the status of "gaps," which correspond to one of three phonologically null entities: PRO, NP-trace, or WH-trace.[18] But what if (1.28) is not the basis for "obligatory" subject? In the category-neutral theory we could alternatively adopt the view that the position is obligatory but not specified for category, and that something must fill it.[19] This commits us to recognizing PRO as being a syntactic entity in the narrow sense discussed earlier; that is, in (1.29) the syntactic subject of *go* is PRO, or rather a phonologically null element that "is an" NP.

(1.29)
John wants PRO to go.

This is a plausible move to make; indeed, there is an entire tradition based on just this move (i.e., EST to GB theory). If we do not take such a position, however, a rather different picture emerges.[20]

1.6 Other Questions

One of the major questions that arises from the category-neutral theory of PS rules concerns the status of empty categories. To deal with this, we will begin to develop a theory that does not utilize empty categories that have intrinsic content and are present in the syntax in the sense discussed earlier. The next question is, what is the status of S-structure? S-structure in Chomsky (1981b) and in the work of others is a syntactic level of representation that contains phonologically null elements. What is the analogue of S-structure in the Modular Grammar theory? It turns out that "S-structure" is not a single level of representation but is at least the "sum" of two levels: the argument structure of the verb and a syntactic analysis of the surface string.[21]

The remainder of this book is devoted to developing a theory that does not utilize a scrambling rule and accounts for the distribution and interpretation of so-called PRO and NP-trace "gaps."

Chapter 2
Japanese Syntax: Prevailing and Alternative Analyses

The purpose of this chapter is twofold: first, to familiarize the reader with some of the major issues of Japanese syntax, putting these issues into theoretical perspective (sections 2.1 and 2.2); and second, to develop an alternative account of the syntax of morphologically complex verbs, case-marking arrays, the generation of dative noun phrases in the causative construction, and scrambling. Section 2.3 outlines these alternative assumptions, proposing various mechanisms and showing how the different levels of the grammar interact. It also offers a detailed analysis of the passive construction in Japanese. Discussion of the topic construction, *tough* sentences, indirect passives, and special case-marking arrays, as well as "reflexivization," is left for the more speculative chapter 3.

2.1 A Review of Major Issues in Japanese Syntax

2.1.1 The Syntax of Morphologically Complex Verbs
Japanese verbal morphology includes a class of bound verbalizing suffixes; among these are -(s)ase[1] (causative), -(r)are (passive), and -rare ~ -e (potential). The process of affixing these suffixes to verbal stems is quite productive.

Causative:
O causative[2]

(2.1)
a. Hanako ga[3]   hatarak-ta.[4]
           nom work-past
   'Hanako worked.'

b. Taroo ga   Hanako o   hatarak-ase-ta.
      nom   acc work-cause-past
   'Taro made Hanako work.'

Ni causative

(2.2)
Taroo ga   Hanako ni   hatarak-ase-ta.
      nom   dat work-cause-past
'Taro let Hanako work.'

Causative with a direct object

(2.3)
Hanako ga   hon o   yon-da.
       nom book-acc read-past
'Hanako read the book.'

(2.4)
Taroo ga   Hanako ni   hon o   yom-ase-ta.
      nom   dat book-acc read-cause-past
'Taro made/let Hanako read the book.'

Passive:
Direct passive[5]

(2.5)
Sensei wa   John o   sikar-ta.[6]
teacher-top   acc scold-past
'The teacher scolded John.'

(2.6)
John wa   sensei ni   sikar-are-ta.
     top teacher-dat scold-passive-past
'John was scolded by the teacher.'

Indirect passive[7]

(2.7)
Ame ga   hut-ta.
rain-nom fall-past
'The rain fell.'

(2.8)
John ga   ame ni hur-are-ta.
     nom rain-dat fall-passive-past
'(Lit.) John was fallen on by rain.'

(2.9)
Tuma ga sin-da.
wife-nom die-past
'The wife died.'

(2.10)
John ga   tuma ni sin-are-ta.
     nom wife-dat die-passive-past
'(Lit.) John was died on by his wife.' (or: 'John was adversely affected by his wife dying.')

(2.11)
Taroo ga   mesi ga[8] tak-e-ru.
      nom rice-nom cook-potential-nonpast
'Taro can cook rice.'

The theoretical characterization of these constructions involving complex verbs has been the focus of concern in Japanese linguistics for the past seventeen years. The "syntax" of the complex verbs is intimately connected with the particles: *ga, ni,* and *o*. Establishing just what the correlations and dependencies are between these verbs and the case particles has occupied those interested in Japanese syntax ever since Kuroda's dissertation, *Generative Grammatical Studies in the Japanese Language,* the first study of Japanese undertaken within a generative transformational framework.

2.1.2 The Case Particles

The three grammatical case particles in Japanese are *ga* (nominative case), *ni* (dative case), and *o* (accusative case).[9] A major effort of theoreticians has been to account for the distribution of these particles. One feature that complicates this issue is that there is not always a one-to-one correspondence between the grammatical relations (subject, direct object, and indirect object) and case (nominative, accusative, and dative) (see Shibatani (1977, 1978)). It has been assumed that the following are among the facts to be accounted for:

(i) Every sentence requires at least one nominative.[10]

(ii) No sentence/clause can have two accusative arguments.

(2.12)
*Taroo wa *Hanako o hon o* yom-ase-ta.
'Taro made Hanako read the book.'

(iii) Object of a stative verb is marked *ga* (Kuno (1973)).

(2.13)
Taroo wa nihongo   ga wakaru.
            Japanese   understand
                              [+stative]
'Taro understands Japanese.'

Object of derived statives can optionally be marked *ga*:

(2.14)
Taroo wa nihongo $\begin{Bmatrix} o \\ ga \end{Bmatrix}$ hanas-e-ru.
                                     speak-potential-nonpast
                                     [−stative, +stative]
'Taro can speak Japanese.'

(iv) Subject of some stative verbs can be marked *ni* when the object is marked *ga*:

(2.15)
a. Dare *ga* kore *ga* dekiru   ka?
   who   this   can   question particle
                       [+stative]
b. Dare *ni* kore *ga* dekiru ka?
   'Who can do this?'

(2.16)
a. Dare *ga* kono uta *ga* uta-e-ru   ka?
              this song sing-potential-nonpast question particle
                            [+stative]
   'Who can sing this song?'
b. Dare *ni* kono uta *ga* uta-e-ru ka?
c. *Dare *ni* kono uta *o* uta-e-ru ka?
d. Dare *ga* kono uta *o* uta-e-ru ka?

The above sentences illustrate an interaction between the complex verbs and the case particles. In order to understand the role that certain noun phrase arguments play in sentences like those above, certain diagnostics have been developed. One of these involves "reflexivization."

2.1.3 *Zibun*

Unlike English, where the antecedent of the reflexive pronoun *himself* may be a subject or an object (*John$_i$ showed Bill$_j$ a picture of himself$_{i,j}$*), *zibun* (often romanized as *jibun*) requires that its antecedent be a subject.[11] The antecedent must also command *zibun*, though it does not have to be a clausemate.

(2.17)
a. John$_i$ ga Bill$_j$ ni zibun$_{i,j*}$ no koto o hanasita.
        nom   dat self   's matter-acc talked
   'John talked to Bill about self's matter.'

b. John$_i$ ga Bill$_j$ ni zibun$_{i,j*}$ no syasin o miseta.
        nom   dat self   's picture-acc showed
   'John showed Bill a picture of self.'

The indices *i* and *j* indicate that only *John* in (2.17a,b) may be the antecedent of *zibun*. One might think that the requirement for the antecedent is that it be marked "nominative." However, the situation is more complicated. The following example is taken from Shibatani (1978, 56):

(2.18)
Taroo$_i$ ga Hanako$_j$ ga zibun$_{i,j*}$ no guruupu de itiban suki da.
'Taro$_i$ likes Hanako$_j$ the best in self's$_{i,j*}$ group.'

The second noun phrase, though marked with the nominative case particle, cannot be an antecedent for *zibun*. Note, however, the following ambiguity (example from Kuno (1973, 294)) (indices added):

(2.19)
John$_i$ ga Mary$_j$ ni zibun$_{i,j}$ no uti de hon o   yom-(s)ase-ta.
        nom   dat self   's house-at books-acc read-cause-past
'John made Mary read books in self's house.'

Here not only *John* but also *Mary* can be the antecedent for *zibun*, even though *Mary* is marked with the dative case.

It was noticed independently by Kuno and Noriko McCawley that the various passive constructions offer different antecedent possibilities; that is, direct passive sentences with *zibun* are unambiguous, whereas indirect passives are usually ambiguous. (In these and following examples from Kuno's work, the word-for-word glosses are mine, as are the indices.)

Indirect passives (examples from Kuno (1973, 303–304))

(2.20)
a. John$_i$ wa Mary$_j$ ni   zibun$_{i,j}$ no kazoku no hanasi bakari
         top   dat self   's family 's talk   only
   s-(r)are-ta.
   do-passive-past
   'John was affected by Mary's talking only about (lit.) self's family.'

b. John$_i$ wa Mary$_j$ ni   zibun$_{i,j}$ no koto o   zimans-(r)are-ta.
         top   dat self   's matter-acc boast-passive-past
   'John suffered from Mary's bragging about (lit.) self's matter.'

Direct passives (examples from Kuno (1973, 307))

(2.21)
a. Mary$_i$ wa John$_j$ ni *zibun*$_{i,j*}$ no uti de   koros-(r)are-ta.
         top   dat self   's house-in kill-passive-past
   'Mary$_i$ was killed by John$_j$ in *her* own [= self's$_{i,j*}$] house.'

b. Mary$_i$ wa John$_j$ ni *zibun*$_{i,j*}$ no uti de   hon o
         top   dat self   's house-in book-acc
   yom-(s)ase-rare-ta.
   read-cause-passive-past
   'Mary$_i$ was made by John$_j$ to read the book in *her* own [= self's$_{i,j*}$] house.'

In both (2.20a) and (2.20b) either *John* or *Mary* may be the antecedent for *zibun*, whereas in (2.21a) and (2.21b) only *Mary* is a potential antecedent.

2.1.4 Dative Noun Phrases and the Causative Construction

Thus far we have seen the close interaction of a number of phenomena (i.e., complex verbs interacting with case particle distribution and *zibun*). Next consider the generation of dative noun phrases in the causative construction. Notice the following sentences with varying numbers of "embeddings":[12]

Intransitive

(2.22)
a. Hanako ga   isya ni/o   ko-sase-ta.
         nom doctor-dat/acc come-cause-past
   'Hanako let/made the doctor come.'[13]

b. ?Taroo ga Hanako ni isya ni/o ko-sase-sase-ta.
   'Taro let (make) Hanako make/let the doctor come.'

Japanese Syntax

c. *Yooko ga Taroo ni Hanako ni isya ni/o ko-sase-sase-sase-ta.
   'Yoko let (make) Taro let (make) Hanako let/make the doctor come.'

Transitive

(2.23)
a. ??**Taroo ga Hanako ni isya ni** kodomo o koros-ase-sase-ta.
                                    child   kill
   'Taro made (let) Hanako make (let) the doctor kill the child.'

b. *Yooko ga Taroo ni Hanako ni isya ni kodomo o koros-ase-sase-sase-ta.
   'Yoko made (let) Taro make (let) Hanako make (let) the doctor kill the child.'

Transitive with dative object

(2.24)
a. ?Taroo ga   isya ni   Hanako ni   kusuri o   age-sase-ta.
        nom   dat   dat medicine-acc give-cause-past
   'Taro made (let) the doctor give Hanako the medicine.'

b. *Taroo ga isya ni Yooko ni Hanako ni kusuri o age-sase-sase-ta.
   'Taro made (let) the doctor make (let) Yoko give the medicine to Hanako.'

The productive nature of the bound suffix -*sase*, whether its productiveness is characterized via multiplicity of syntactic embedding or through productive word formation, raises certain important questions concerning the role of the phrase structure component in such a case as this. Several observations can be made regarding the above sentences, the foremost of which is that the judgments in these sentences indicate that the "ungrammaticality" of (2.24b) cannot be due to the number of -*sase*s, since (2.22b), which also has two -*sase*s, is not nearly so deviant as (2.24b). We return to this question in section 2.2.3.

2.1.5 Scrambling

The final issue to be described here is the well-known scrambling property of Japanese. A few examples will suffice to illustrate this phenomenon, though just what constitutes an instance of "scrambling" and what is actually due to some other property of the grammar is still very much debated (Kuno and Tonoike (1980)).

(2.25)
a. Mary ga okasi o taberu.
   nom cake-acc eat-past
   'Mary eats cake.'
b. Okasi o Mary ga taberu.

(2.26)
a. John ga Mary ni okasi o tabe-sase-ta.
   'John made (let) Mary eat the cake.'
b. Mary ni John ga okasi o tabe-sase-ta.
c. Okasi o Mary ni John ga tabe-sase-ta.
d. Mary ni okasi o John ga tabe-sase-ta.

In short, many of the possible permutations are grammatical, the one clear constraint being that the verb must always remain final.

(2.27)
a. *Mary ga taberu okasi o.
b. *Okasi o taberu Mary ga.

For a discussion of how scrambling is to be constrained, see Kuno and Tonoike (1980), as well as Hale (1980).

2.2 Prevailing Analyses

This section will outline some of the accounts and explanations that have been proposed for the phenomena described above. Most of the problems discussed in section 2.1 were discovered and their properties explored by linguists such as Inoue, Kuroda, Shibatani, Kuno, and Harada. They share a number of very basic assumptions. One fairly consistent assumption is that the morphologically complex verbs (causative, passive, etc.) involve syntactically complex structures, the bound verbalizing morpheme being a matrix verb that requires a sentential complement. Proposing this type of structure is a reflex of a set of more basic assumptions: (1) the syntax corresponds closely to the semantic representation, (2) syntactic transformations such as Equi NP Deletion and Predicate Raising map deep structures onto surface structures, and (3) word formation is postsyntactic. Another fairly consistent assumption is that case marking necessarily indicates some specific underlying syntactic configuration (though see Tonoike (1979) for a notable exception).

2.2.1 The Case Particles *ga, ni,* and *o*

The most widely accepted accounts of the grammatical case particles in Japanese are based on proposals made by Kuno (1973) and Kuroda (1965, 1978). Kuno and Kuroda agree that the particles *ga* and *o* are distinct from other particles in that they are not generated in the base but are assigned to a noun phrase via case-marking transformations. They differ in the following interesting way: Kuno uses context-sensitive case-marking transformations, the context being defined not only by syntactic position but also by reference to a lexical feature (i.e., stativity); Kuroda, on the other hand, uses a much simplified case-assignment rule, limiting overgeneration by an autonomous filtering component consisting of a set of stipulated "canonical sentence patterns." The mechanisms employed by these two different approaches possibly reflect different intuitions about how case marking interacts with the rest of the grammar. I will try to draw out this difference after the following brief summary of the two positions.

2.2.1.1 Kuno's Analysis of Case Marking Kuno questions the validity of Martin's (1962, 44) statement that the "particle *ga* shows the subject" in sentences like the following:

(2.28)
a. Eiga ga   suki desu.
   movies-nom like copula
   'I like movies.'
b. Watakusi wa eigo ga   hanas-e-ru.
   I-top   English-nom speak-can-nonpast
   'I can speak English.'
c. Watakusi wa okane ga   hosii.
   I-top   money-nom want
   'I want money.'
d. Watakusi wa Mary ga   suki   da.
   I-top   nom fond-of copula
   'I like Mary.'

Kuno demonstrates that these *ga*-marked NPs do not have the same cluster of properties associated with "true" subjects. In addition, sentences represented by (2.28a–d) do not behave like the so-called double subject sentences. Kuno compares the following pairs of sentences (1973, 80–81):

(2.29)
a. Bunmeikoku ga   dansei no heikin-zyumyoo ga   mizikai.
   civilized countries-nom male 's average-life span-nom short-is
   'It is the civilized countries that males' average life span is short in.'
b. φ Dansei no heikin-zyumyoo ga mizikai.
   'It is males' average life span that is short.'

(2.30)
a. Watakusi ga eiga ga   suki   desu.
   I-nom   movie-nom fond-of copula
   'I like movies.'
b. φ Eiga ga suki desu.
   '(I am, he is, etc.) fond of movies.'

Deletion of an initial *ga* phrase from (2.29a) yields a nonelliptical sentence; by contrast, deletion of the initial subject in (2.30a) gives the elliptical sentence (2.30b).[14] Thus, Kuno concludes (1973, 81) that there are cases where *ga* is used to mark direct objects "of all transitive adjectives and nominal adjectives . . . and of a certain class of transitive verbs."

Kuno relates the special case marking observed in (2.28) to the feature [stative] present in the predicate. He offers the following cyclic case-marking transformations (1973, 330).

(2.31)
a. *Indirect Object Marking*
   Attach *ni* to the second of the three unmarked NPs (noun phrases), that is, the NPs that do not yet have a particle.
b. *Subject Marking*
   Attach *ga* to the subject NP.
c. *Object Marking*
   Attach *o* to the first nonsubject unmarked NP to the left of the main verb if it is [−stative], and *ga* if it is [+stative].

The following illustrative derivations are taken from Kuno (1973, 330).

(2.32)
a. Deep structure: [John]$_{NP}$ [Mary]$_{NP}$ [okane]$_{NP}$ [yatta]$_V$.
                                                          [−stative]
   'John gave money to Mary.'
b. Indirect Object
   Marking: [John]$_{NP}$ [Mary]$_{NP}$ *ni* [okane]$_{NP}$ [yatta]$_V$.

Japanese Syntax

c. Subject Marking: [John]$_{NP}$ *ga* [Mary]$_{NP}$ ni [okane]$_{NP}$ [yatta]$_V$.
[−stative]
d. Object Marking: [John]$_{NP}$ ga [Mary]$_{NP}$ ni [okane]$_{NP}$ *o* [yatta]$_V$.

(2.33)
a. Deep structure: [John]$_{NP}$ [Mary]$_{NP}$ [suki da]$_V$.
[+stative]
 'John likes Mary.'
b. Subject Marking: [John]$_{NP}$ *ga* [Mary]$_{NP}$ [suki da]$_V$.
[+stative]
c. Object Marking: [John]$_{NP}$ ga [Mary]$_{NP}$ *ga* [suki da]$_V$.

These case-marking rules do not account for all surface case arrays. For example, (2.15b) represents the class of sentences in which the subject is marked dative. To account for this class, Kuno (1973, 88) proposes a rule converting *ga* to *ni*.

2.2.1.2 Kuroda's Analysis of Case Marking Kuroda's approach toward case marking differs conceptually from Kuno's in a very interesting way. Kuroda's aim is to (i) account for the *ni/o* causative variants and (ii) give a unified account of the *ni* argument that appears in the adversity passive, the *ni* causative, and the potential. Kuroda's conception of the grammar necessarily allows massive overgeneration. His system involves the following mechanisms:

(2.34)
a. Case marking (1978, 34): mark the first unmarked noun phrase with *ga*, and mark any other unmarked noun phrase or phrases with *o*.
b. Two deletion rules, Counter Equi NP Deletion (Harada (1973)) and ordinary Equi, which apply as free variants.
c. Canonical sentence patterns [which apply cyclically] (1978, 35):
    I Transitive sentence pattern: NP *ga* NP *o*
    II Ergative sentence pattern: NP *ni* NP *ga*
    III Intransitive sentence pattern: NP *ga*
d. Subject *ni*-Raising, "which makes the embedded subject a clausemate of a matrix and assigns it the particle *ni*" (p. 30). This process is bound with predicate raising.

e. Since the subject *ni*-raising rule yields a sentence that does not "contain a *ga* phrase," Kuroda allows the *ga* case-marking rule to mark the accusative-marked NP from the previous cycle with *ga*. That is, "For the purpose of case marking, a noun phrase is, by definition, considered 'unmarked' even if the particle *o* has already been assigned to it prior to the cycle in question" (1978, 34).

Kuroda proposes that Counter Equi and normal Equi apply in free variation. That is, he does not impose an extrinsic ordering relation between these two deletion rules. His system therefore overgenerates and consequently needs the filtering device (2.34c). The interaction of these components can be observed in the following derivations (from Kuroda (1978, 33)):

(2.35)

	[Taroo	[Taroo hatarak] eru]
Straight Equi:		φ
Predicate Raising:	Taroo	hatarak-eru
Case Marking:	Taroo ga	
	Taroo ga hatarak-eru.	
	'Taro can work.'	

(2.36)

	[Taroo [Taroo mesi tak] eru]
Case Marking:	Taroo ga mesi o
Counter Equi:	φ
Subject *Ni*-Raising:	Taroo ni mesi o tak-eru
Case Marking $o \to ga$ (see (2.34e)):	mesi ga
	Taroo ni mesi ga takeru.
	'Taro can cook rice.'

If Straight Equi is applied to (2.36) instead of Counter Equi, the derivation would look like (2.37):

(2.37)

	[Taroo [Taroo mesi tak] eru]
Straight Equi:	φ
Case Marking:	mesi o
Predicate Raising:	tak-eru
Case Marking:	Taroo ga

Taroo ga mesi o takeru.
'Taro can cook rice.'

Where does the overgeneration come in? A look at the causative construction reveals this possibility (example from Kuroda (1978, 37)):

(2.38)

	[Taroo Hanako [Hanako mesi tak] saseta]
Cycle I	
Case:	Hanako ga mesi o
Cycle II	
Straight Equi:	φ
Case Marking:	Taroo ga Hanako o mesi o
Predicate Raising:	takaseta

*Taroo ga Hanako o mesi o takaseta.

But now the sentence is subject to the sentence pattern filters. None of the patterns sanctions this sentence; therefore, it is ruled out.

The ergative pattern allows for the case arrays associated with stative predicates. An example is (2.39), which is derived from (2.40) (both from Kuroda (1978, 36)).

(2.39)
Taroo ni (wa) kane ga aru.

(2.40)
Taroo ni kane aru.

Kuroda does not seem to have an account of the NP *ga* NP *ga* arrays. His approach is nonetheless intriguing, since it depends on the interaction of various autonomous components to define the set of grammatical sentences. Also, his version of case marking seems to differ crucially from Kuno's in that since his account generates the double accusative (NP *o* NP *o*) sentences, it is conceivable that under his analysis there could be a language exactly like Japanese, except for not having the case array filters. The double-*o* sentences would then be good in this language.

2.2.2 Passive and *Zibun*

Recall from section 2.1.3 that the antecedent of *zibun* must be "some sort of subject." The prevailing opinion is that the antecedent's subjectness must be characterized syntactically. Coupling this assumption with the observed ambiguity of sentences (2.20a,b) (Kuno's (31a,b)) versus the clear unambiguity of (2.21a,b) (Kuno's (21a), (33)) results in various analyses of the indirect/direct passive construction. The two alternatives discussed here are popularly referred to as the *uniform* and the *nonuniform* analyses. These differing positions are represented by Kuno (nonuniform) and Howard/Niyekawa-Howard (uniform).

I should first mention that all parties assume a reflexivization transformation; that is, a noun phrase is changed to *zibun* under identity with another NP that commands it.

2.2.2.1 The Nonuniform Hypothesis This hypothesis argues that direct passives are derived from a simple sentence. Kuno cites the following example, along with its underlying structure (1978, 256):

(2.41)
Hanako ga   sensei ni   sikar-are-ta.
         nom teacher-dat scold-passive-past
'Hanako was scolded by the teacher.'

(2.42)
Underlying structure

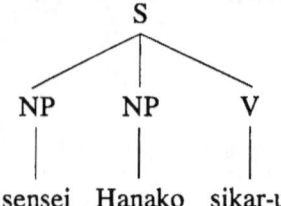

sensei Hanako sikar-u

The adversity or indirect passive is derived from a complex source (examples from Kuno (1978, 257)).

(2.43)
Hanako ga   sensei ni   musuko o   sikar-are-ta.
         nom teacher-dat son-acc   scold-passive-past
'Hanako was adversely affected by the teacher's scolding her son.'

(2.44)
Underlying structure

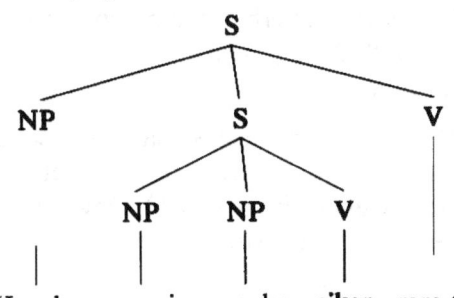

Hanako sensei musuko **sikar** rare-ta

This analysis is based on the assumption that the reflexivization rule applies cyclically and follows passivization (example from Kuno (1978, 257)).

(2.45)
a. Taroo$_i$ ga Hanako$_j$ o zibun$_{i,j*}$ no ie de sikat-ta.
   'Taro scolded Hanako in self's (Taro's) house.'
b. Hanako$_i$ ga/wa Taroo$_j$ ni zibun$_{i,j*}$ no ie de sikar-are-ta.
   'Hanako was scolded by Taro in self's (Hanako's) house.'

Since the adversity passive has a complex source, there are two cycles. Therefore, reflexivization has two opportunities to apply in the derivation.

(2.46)
Hanako sensei (trigger) musuko sensei.

zibun

no ie de sikar-are-ta.

(2.47)
Hanako (trigger) sensei musuko Hanako.

zibun

no ie de sikare-ta.

Thus we see that the ambiguity/nonambiguity of the anaphor/antecedent relationship is correlated with the complexity of the syntactic structure.

2.2.2.2 The Uniform Hypothesis The uniform hypothesis also assumes that the indirect passives involve embedding (see (2.44)). In addition, Howard and Niyekawa-Howard (1976) assume the following:

(2.48)
a. Case-marking transformations (cf. Kuno (1973)).
b. Predicate raising (adjoin the embedded verb to the matrix verb).
c. Node deletion (in accordance with Ross (1969)).
d. Reflexivization applies cyclically.

This hypothesis differs from the nonuniform analysis in that it posits a complex underlying source for both the indirect *and* the direct passive. In order to account for the nonambiguity of (2.45b), Howard and Niyekawa-Howard propose the following constraint:

(2.49)
Reflexive Coreference Constraint (RCC)[15]
Two instances of the reflexive pronoun *zibun* commanded by the same pair of possible antecedents must be coreferential. If they are not, the sentence is marked as ungrammatical.

The use of this constraint relies on the following two assumptions (taken from Kuno (1978, 262)):

(2.50)
a. Embedded Object Deletion must apply after reflexivization and the Reflexive Coreference Constraint (RCC) must apply after reflexivization, but before Embedded Object Deletion.
b. Reflexivization of the embedded object is obligatory.

The following is the derivation of (2.45b) under the uniform hypothesis (not detailing case marking or predicate raising):

(2.51)
Hanako$_i$ ga Taroo$_j$ ni zibun$_{i,j*}$ no ie de sikar-are-ta.

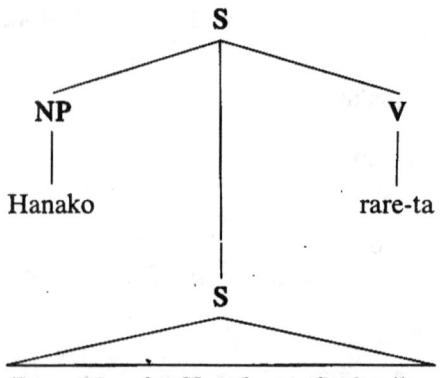

Cycle I
Reflexivization: Taroo Hanako$_i$ zibun$_i$ no ie de sikar

Cycle II
Reflexivization: Hanako$_i$ Taroo zibun$_i$ o zibun$_i$ no ie de sikar-rare-ta

Embedded
Object Deletion: Hanako$_i$ ga Taroo ni ϕ zibun$_i$ no ie de sikar-rare-ta

With coreference between *Taroo* and *zibun*, (2.45b) has the following derivation:

(2.52)

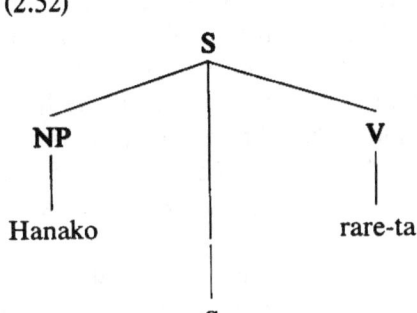

Taroo Hanako Taroo no ie de sikar

Cycle I
Reflexivization: Taroo$_i$ Hanako zibun$_i$ no ie de sikar

Cycle II
Reflexivization: Hanako$_j$ Taroo$_i$ zibun$_j$ zibun$_i$ no ie de sikar-rare-ta

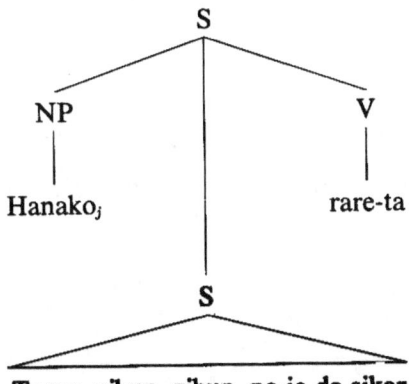

Taroo$_i$ zibun$_j$·zibun$_i$ no ie de sikar

The above derivation would ultimately generate the possibility indicated in (2.53) if something like the RCC were not invoked at some point:

(2.53)
Hanako ga Taroo$_i$ ni zibun$_i$ no ie de sikar-rare-ta.

The prediction would be that (2.53) is ambiguous. But Howard and Niyekawa-Howard rule out (2.53) by imposing the RCC on the derivation. (2.53) is a case where the two instances of *zibun* are not coreferential; therefore, the derivation is rejected. The ordering dependency among the reflexivization rule, Embedded Object Deletion, and the RCC was mentioned above. Reflexivization of the embedded object is obligatory because unless there are two instances of *zibun*, the RCC cannot be used to reject the derivation. Thus, the introduction of the RCC, coupled with ordering and obligatoriness of the application of rules, is a reflex of the attempt to minimize the number of possible underlying structures.

The last two issues to be discussed are the generation of dative noun phrases in the causative construction and scrambling. I will draw on these phenomena to shed more light on the theoretical picture outlined above.

2.2.3 The Causative Construction and Its Arguments

In section 2.1.4, several examples were given illustrating the productive nature of the causative suffix *-sase*. Since in the theory represented by Kuno, Kuroda, and Howard the suffix *-sase* is actually a verb that requires a sentential complement, it is theoretically possible to generate the following sentence:

(2.54)
Yooko ga Taroo ni Hanako ni isya ni/o ko-sase-sase-sase-ta.
'Yoko made (let) Taro make (let) Hanako make/let the doctor come.'

Structures that start out like (2.55) end up like (2.56) after predicate raising:

Japanese Syntax   43

(2.55)
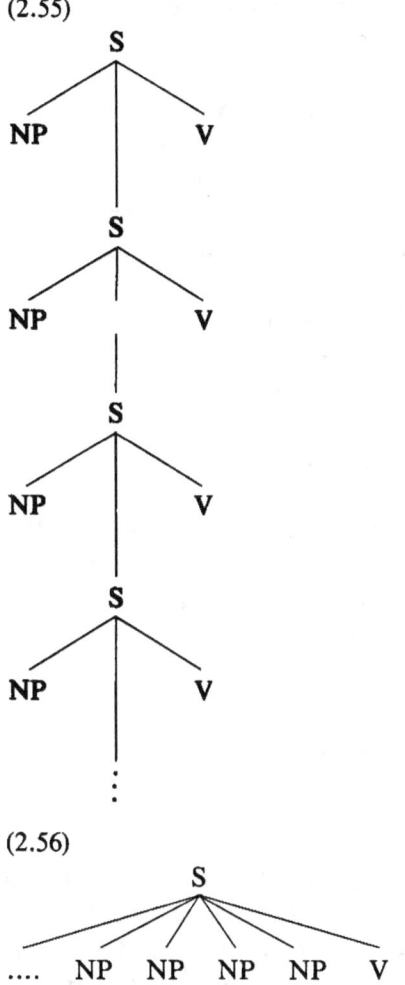

(2.56)

Implicit in this theory is the claim that the phrase structure component cannot in fact play any kind of role in delimiting the number of arguments a verb (at least a derived verb) may have, and I agree with this claim explicitly.

2.2.4 Scrambling
Section 2.1.5 gives some examples of scrambling. The one constraint that seems to be agreed upon is that the verb must be the rightmost constituent in its clause. There has been less general agreement about the various other constraints on scrambling. Tonoike (1980) argues that

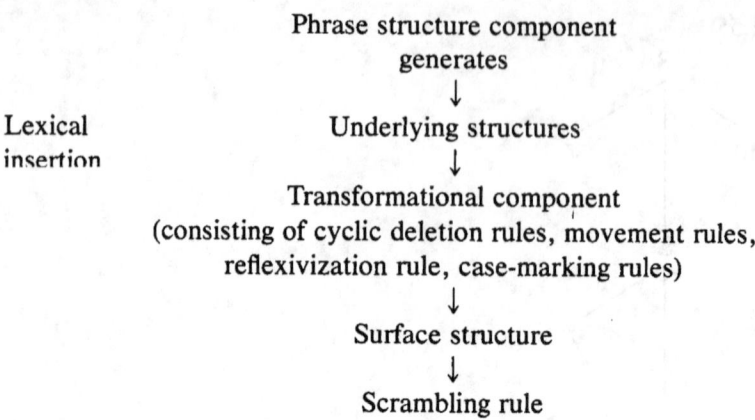

Figure 2.1
The *Aspects* model for a grammar of Japanese

only constituents within the same clause may permute, whereas Kuno claims that, in fact, the domain of scrambling is not limited to the clause. Instead, Kuno imposes a "cross over" constraint to account for the impossibility of scrambling in (2.57):

(2.57)
a. Taroo ga   sakana ga   suki   da.
         nom fish   nom fond-of copula
    'Taro likes fish.'
b. *Sakana ga Taroo ga suki da.

Tonoike claims that *Taroo* and *sakana* in (2.57) are not clausemates. Rather than venturing into this particular controversy here, I refer the reader to the Kuno/Tonoike exchanges (1980). One general property of the grammar that can be extracted is that a Kuno-, Kuroda-, Howard-type theory suggests that scrambling necessarily follows all transformations (case marking, predicate raising, etc.).

In concluding this section, I summarize the basic theoretical assumptions discussed here by reference to the descriptive model shown in figure 2.1.

The transformational component consists of many types of rules (deletion rules, movement rules, etc.) whose proper interaction is mediated by the imposition of strict ordering relations. This extrinsic ordering is necessary since all these rules operate within the same domain, namely, the syntactic domain.

Within this model of grammar the tendency is to distinguish rule types within the syntactic domain. On the one hand, Kuno (1973) opts for sensitizing transformations so that they, in concert with nonuniform structures, will never overgenerate; on the other hand, Kuroda and Howard allow some overgeneration in order to gain generality. Kuroda proposes to allow the equi-NP deletion transformations to apply as free variants, relying on the "canonical sentence patterns" to filter out the deviant sentences. Howard and Niyekawa-Howard (1976) propose to unify the structure of the various passives, resorting to the RCC to reject potentially deviant sentences. The various attempts to simplify areas of the grammar have resulted in introducing principles of a type to be distinguished from transformations (i.e., filters and constraints), thus giving more texture to the part of the grammar that involves mapping "deep structure" to "surface structure."

This concludes the review of various major issues in Japanese. In the remainder of this chapter and in chapter 3 I will address some of these same issues from a slightly different point of view. In some respects, my approach is similar to Kuroda's and Howard's; that is, parts of the grammar are allowed to overgenerate. I do not, however, call on filters to rule out sentences. Instead, I rely on the interaction of autonomous components to achieve the result of a filter. In other respects this theory is not unlike Kuno's in that it employs case-linking rules that appear to be similar to Kuno's case-marking rules. But the overall theory I will be developing differs from those of previous works. The differences are rooted in the attempt to deduce some of the effects of various phenomena, such as passivization, from independent properties of the grammar.

2.3 An Alternative: Predicate Argument Structures, Linking, and Evaluation

In section 2.3.1 I will outline a theory that differs in some crucial respects from previous theories of Japanese syntax. In section 2.3.2 I will bring this theory to bear on the direct passive, causatives, and the case particles associated with those constructions.[16]

2.3.1 The Case Arrays
The cases that I will examine here are the grammatical cases: *ga*, *ni*, and *o* (I will not discuss the genitive, *no*). (2.58) lists the case arrays to be accounted for (the order used here reflects the "preferred" word order):[17]

(2.58)
a. N'-ga
b. N'-ga N'-o
c. N'-ga N'-ni
d. N'-ga N'-ni N'-o
e. N'-ga N'-ni N'-ni
f. **N'-ga N'-ni N'-ni* N'-o**

The case arrays correspond to the following types of sentences:

(2.59)
N'-ga
Mary ga aruita.   (intransitive)
'Mary walked.'

(2.60)
N'-ga N'-o
a. Mary ga okasi o tabeta.   (transitive–simple verb)
   'Mary ate the cake.'
b. Mary ga nihongo o hanaseru.   (potential–derived verb)
   'Mary can understand Japanese.'
c. Taroo ga Mary o arukaseta.   (*o* causative–derived verb)
   'Taro made Mary walk.'

(2.61)
N'-ga N'-ni
a. Taroo ga Mary ni au.   (transitive–simple verb)
   'Taro meets Mary.'
b. Taroo ga otooto ni sinareta.   (indirect passive–derived verb)
   'Taro's brother died on him.'
c. Taroo ga sensei ni sikarareta.   (direct passive–derived verb)
   'Taro was scolded by the teacher.'

(2.62)
N'-ga N'-ni N'-o
Taroo ga Mary ni hon o ageta.   (ditransitive–simple verb)
'Taro gave Mary the book.'

(2.63)
N'-ga N'-ni N'-ni
a. Inu ga Mary ni John ni agerareta.   (direct passive with dative)
   'The dog was given to Mary by John.'

b. John ga Mary ni Bill ni awaseta. (causative of 'meet')
   'John made/let Mary meet Bill.'
c. John ga Mary ni Bill ni arukasesaseta. (double causative)
   'John made/let Mary let Bill walk.'

(2.64)
N'-ga N'-ni N'-ni N'-o
a. Taroo ga Mary ni John ni sono koinu o agerarete shimatta. (indirect passive with accusative)
   'Taro was adversely affected by Mary's having given the dog to John.'
b. John ga Taroo ni Mary ni okasi o tabesaserareta. (passive/causative)
   'John was adversely affected by Taro's making Mary eat cake.'

2.3.2 Predicate Argument Structures

Each verb has associated with it a *predicate argument structure* (PAS)[18] that supplies information regarding its argument requirements.[19] The following are the PASs for *aruk* 'walk', *tabe* 'eat', and *age* 'give':

(2.65)
a. (___ aruk)   intransitive
b. (___ ___ tabe)   transitive
c. (___ ___ ___ age)   ditransitive

(2.65) illustrates three types of PASs: intransitive, transitive, and ditransitive. An intransitive predicate has only one argument slot, a transitive predicate has two, and a ditransitive predicate has three. Each of these predicates has an argument slot that will be called the *subject slot*.[20]

The bound verbalizing morphemes (causative *-sase*, passive *-rare*, etc.) also have PASs:

(2.66)
a. (___ (___) sase)   causative
b. ((___) rare)   passive

In the case of (2.66a,b), the position indicated by (___) is to be filled by the PAS of another predicate:

Modularity in Syntax 48

(2.67)
a. (___ (___ aruk) sase)
b. (___ (___ ___ tabe) sase)
c. (___ (___ ___ ___ age) sase)

2.3.3 The Role of the Case-linking Rules

The purpose of the case-linking rules (which are to be viewed as operating only after word formation) is to assign a *case-linking register* to each argument in the PAS of a verb. A case-linking register is either a __GA__, a __NI__, or an __O__:

(2.68)
(___ aruk) 'walk'
GA case-linking rule: (__GA__ aruk)

A completely specified PAS (one whose argument slots are specified for case particles) is then utilized for the purpose of *evaluation*. Evaluation is a process that mediates between the syntax and the PAS. Its purpose is to associate an argument position with an overt N′ that is a sister to the verb. The N′-*ga* in (2.69a) evaluates the GA argument position in (__GA__ aruk). This evaluation is indicated by the use of indices $i, j, k,$ etc. (The indexing employed in these examples is simply a convenient notation and should not be confused with other current uses of indexing; that is, these are not "referential" indices.)

(2.69)

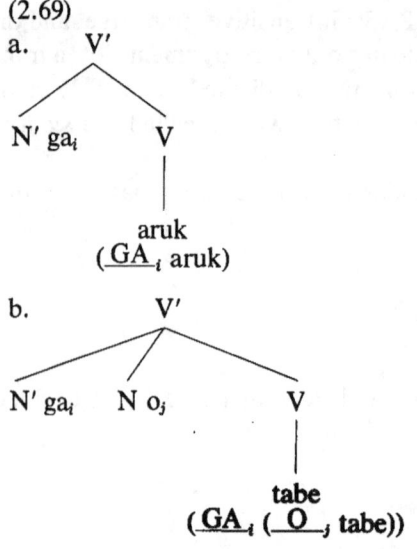

Japanese Syntax 49

c.
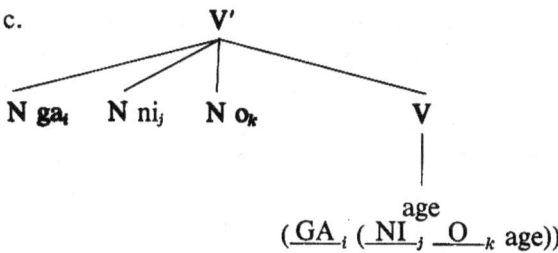

$(\underline{GA}_i \ (\underline{NI}_j \ \underline{O}_k \ age))$

Notice that the case-marked noun phrase can be in any position to the left of the verb (i.e., leftmost N', rightmost N', etc.) and that the argument slots do not have to be evaluated in any particular order; that is, the GA-marked argument can be associated with an overt N' before the O-marked argument, and so on. The procedure can be viewed as moving from left to right; it can take any "scrambled" version and produce the same indexing. This, it turns out, is quite different from the evaluation procedure to be developed for English, which must, in the Modular Grammar theory, associate the object argument slot first.

The evaluation procedure contributes to the filtering effect of the interpretive component that we are relying on to handle the "overgeneration" inherent in a system that does not employ the PS rules to express categorial dependencies. Take the following example:

(2.70)
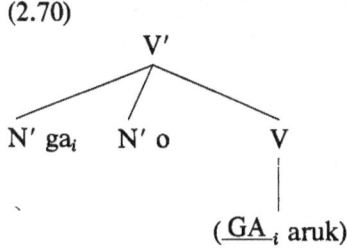

$(\underline{GA}_i \ aruk)$

The evaluation procedure assigns an index, i, to the overt N'-ga and to the $\underline{GA}$ argument. The N'-o phrase is not associated with an argument position; therefore, unless it can pick up a locative interpretation, the sentence will be anomalous.[21] Note that regardless of whether a theory akin to that of Kuroda (1965, 1981) or that of Farmer (1980) is chosen (that is, no matter how one resolves the question of when word formation takes place with respect to lexical insertion), that theory must in any event be able to account for the possible case arrays of section 2.3.1. The linking rules as they are developed here are not intended to favor either hypothesis. One major difference between the approach adopted in developing these rules and previous accounts of

Japanese case particles is that here the cycle is not used for some case particles (GA and O). The linking rules do not recognize the brackets of the inner predicate argument structure. This means that in (2.67a) the PAS (___ (___ aruk) ase) is interpreted as (___ ___ arukase) for the purposes of linking. Such an approach raises questions. For example, certain "residue" case markings whose explanation requires the equivalent of the cycle will be discussed in section 2.3.5.

2.3.4 The Regular Case-Linking Rule

Of the arrays in (2.58), we will first discuss the cases in (2.59a), (2.60a), and (2.62); that is, only arrays involving simple, nonderived verbs will be accounted for. The following rule will properly assign a linking register to the positions in the PASs of the verbs in these sentences ((___ aruk), (___ ___ tabe), and (___ ___ ___ age)).

(2.71)
Regular Case Linking
a. Link leftmost argument slot: __GA__
b. Link rightmost argument slot: __O__
c. Elsewhere link: __NI__

The subparts of the rule are extrinsically ordered with respect to one another: (a) must apply before (b) and (b) must apply before (c).

Example (2.72) illustrates all three parts of Regular Case Linking being used:

(2.72)

Regular Case Linking:
GA: (___ ___ ___ age)
     (__GA__ ___ ___ age)
O: (__GA__ ___ __O__ age)
NI: (__GA__ __NI__ __O__ age)

2.3.5 Semantic Linking

Regular Case Linking as presented in this chapter is considered to apply postcyclically. Noncyclic application of this rule entails claiming that there are no effects of the application of a rule on an earlier cycle. There are examples that cast doubt on the assertion that no "linking rules" have any residual effects:

(2.73)
a. John wa Mary ni au.
   'John meets Mary.'

b. Bill wa John ni Mary *ni* awaseta (a -(w)- ase - ta)
                                        meet   cause past
    'Bill made/let John meet Mary.'
c. John wa Mary ni ikaseta.
    'John let Mary come.'
d. Bill wa John ni Mary *ni* ikasesaseta.
    'Bill made/let John let Mary go.'

These examples involve the embedding of a PAS that contains a *DATIVE*[22] argument slot. The marking of this argument can be traced to *au*. Regular Case Linking alone cannot account for the case arrays in (2.73a,b) and (2.73c,d). Concerning *au*, let us consider viewing the dative argument as in some way involving inherent, or semantic, case. Semantic case in this instance is distinct from the grammatical cases: case is semantic when a verb specifies a *particular* case particle for a *particular* argument position. It may be that *ni* in (2.73a,b) is not the dative case, but instead one of the semantic case particles. Among these semantic particles are *kara* 'from', *e* 'to', *de* 'with'. *Ni* does occur as a location particle:

(2.74)
Mary wa Tokyo *ni* itta.
'Mary went to Tokyo.'

The question is: is the *ni* in (2.73a,b) an instance of grammatical linking or some other type of linking? Other semantic particles exhibit the same behavior as the *ni* in (2.73a,b) and (2.73c,d); that is, they need not change when embedded. The verb *okur* 'send' optionally links the leftmost argument slot (*kara*) semantically:

(2.75)
a. Taroo *kara* Hanako ni tegami o okutta.
    'Taro sent Hanako a letter.'
b. Hanako wa Taroo *kara* tegami o okurareta. (passive)
    'Hanako was sent a letter from Taro.'
c. Taroo *kara* Hanako ni tegami o okuritagatte ita. (desiderative)
    'Taro wanted to send a letter to Hanako.'
d. Hanako wa Taroo *kara* tegami o okuraretagatte ita. (passive/desiderative)
    'Hanako wanted to be sent a letter from Taro.'

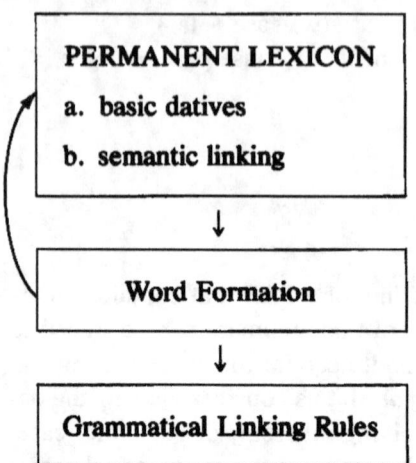

Figure 2.2
Case-linking rules and the lexicon in Modular Grammar theory

The point of these examples is to show that overlap occurs: that is, sometimes semantic cases can be "called upon" to mark an argument position of a verb. This is an idiosyncratic property of that verb (called *semantic linking* in Farmer (1980); the term *linking* itself is due to Dick Carter). If a verb (optionally) links a semantic case particle, that case will show up even when further embeddings take place (a "residue" effect). If *ni* sometimes were an instance of this type of linking, its "anomalous" behavior would be accounted for. It would, in fact, not be anomalous at all; instead, its behavior would accord with that of the other semantic case particles.

Given these parallelisms between the *ni* in examples (2.73a–d) and other semantic particles, Ken Hale has suggested that the lexicon has the organization shown in figure 2.2.

A morpheme (i.e., *tabe, aw, okur*) may trigger a particular kind of "linking." In the case of *aw*, the second argument slot is obligatorily marked NI. The morpheme *okur* optionally marks the leftmost argument KARA, whereas the morpheme *tabe* has no such option. Figure 2.3 illustrates the interaction of these components:

Japanese Syntax

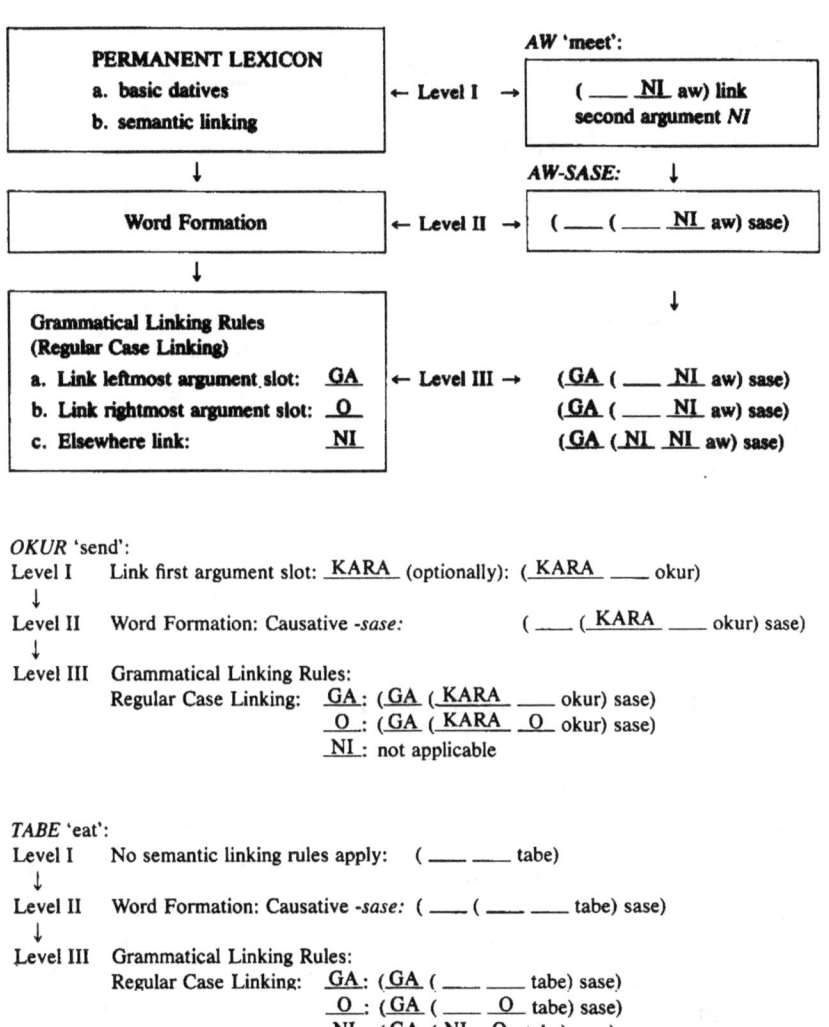

Figure 2.3
Semantic and grammatical case linking

KO 'come':
Level I   No semantic linking rules apply: (___ ko)
  ↓
Level II   Word Formation: *ni* causative: (___ (___ ko) sase)

Level I   Link second argument slot: _NI_: (___ (_NI_ ko) sase)
  ↓
Level III Grammatical Linking Rules:
           Regular Case Linking: _GA_: (_GA_ (_NI_ ko) sase)
                                   _O_ : not applicable
                                   _NI_: not applicable

Figure 2.4
NI Linking (semantic): Causative

The indirect passive as well has the residue *ni:*

(2.76)
Taroo wa Hanako *ni* sinareta.
'Taro was adversely affected by Hanako's having died.'

A rule of NI Linking applies, as it stands now, before Regular Case Linking. Following Hale's suggestion, the above ordering relation will be expressed by way of relegating NI Linking to the domain of the "permanent lexicon." Figure 2.4 gives an account of the *ni* causative. For the indirect passive, the GA-marked N' can be associated with an argument slot of the predicate (Farmer (1980)), as figure 2.5 shows. This construction is given a slightly different analysis in chapter 3.

Thus, the grammar is organized as shown in figure 2.6. By placing the rule of NI Linking in the permanent lexicon, we are in effect recognizing that there are some "cyclic" rules.

Japanese Syntax   55

Indirect passive
SIN 'die':
Level I   No semantic linking rules apply: (___ sin)
↓
Level II   Word Formation: indirect passive: (___ (___ sin) are)

Level I   Link second argument slot: __NI__ :   (___ (__NI__ sin) are)
↓
Level III Grammatical Linking Rules:
           Regular Case Linking: __GA__ : (__GA__ (__NI__ sin) are)
                                   __O__ : not applicable
                                   __NI__ : not applicable

Figure 2.5
NI Linking (semantic): Indirect passive

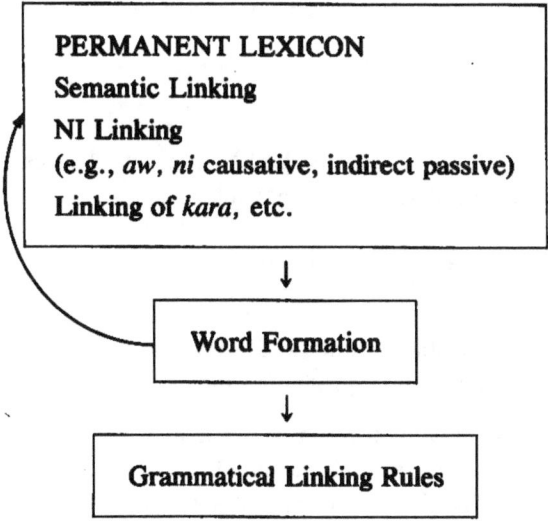

Figure 2.6
Case-linking rules and the lexicon in MG theory

2.3.6 Cyclic vs. Noncyclic Analyses

Since the grammatical case-linking rules operate after all word formation is completed, we are, for the purposes of grammatical linking, abandoning the cycle. I will discuss the pros and cons of such a move here by comparing Kuno's cyclic approach to case marking with the linear approach of the theory developed here. As mentioned earlier, Kuroda's account of the *ni* and *o* causatives reflects an intuition that differs from Kuno's regarding the interaction of case marking with other transformations in the grammar. Although both employ cyclic case-marking rules, the output of Kuno's cyclic case-marking rules is always a possible case-marking array, whereas Kuroda allows the system to generate the sequence *NP-*o* NP-*o*, which is then ruled out by a filter. Like Kuno, I have not relied on any explicit filter to rule out impossible case arrays. Unlike Kuno, however, I have developed case-linking rules that apply noncyclically. I repeat Kuno's (1973, 330) case-marking transformations, which were briefly discussed in section 2.2.1.

(2.77)
a. *Indirect Object Marking*
   Attach *ni* to the second of three unmarked NPs (noun phrases), that is, the NPs that do not yet have a particle.
b. *Subject Marking*
   Attach *ga* to the subject NP.
c. *Object Marking*
   Attach *o* to the first nonsubject unmarked NP to the left of the main verb if it is [−stative], and *ga* if it is [+stative].

These transformations account for the same arrays as the regular case-linking rules and the stative rule of Farmer (1980). The case arrays in the *ni* causatives and indirect passives are accounted for by the above rules and a special Agentive-*ni* Attachment rule. In sentences involving a potential (i.e., a derived stative), the direct object can be either *ga* or *o*. Kuno adopts the following strategy (1973, 334–335, 337):

Let us assume that NP's that are followed by *ga* or *o* are *unmarked*. Since *nihongo o* is unmarked by definition, and since it is the first unmarked NP to the left of *re* [+stative], *ga* is attached to it by Object Marking . . . Object Marking by *ga* is optional when the object is already followed by *o*. Thus . . . since *nihongo* is already followed by *o*, the transformation does not have to apply . . . [However,] Object Marking with *o* is obligatory.

The cyclic case-marking rules and the above condition on their application act in concert with deletion and raising rules to provide the case arrays discussed in section 2.3.1.

The Passive rule performs three tasks: (i) adds *-rare* to the verb, (ii) switches order of NPs, and (iii) adds the particle *ni* to *John* in the following example. (Notice that the passive is a third source for *ni*.) Example (2.79) demonstrates Kuno's reason for ordering Indirect Object Marking before Pure Passive Formation:

(2.78)
[NP John] [NP Mary] [NP kunsyoo] atae-ta.
　　　　　　　　　　　medal　　give-past
'John gave Mary a medal.'

(2.79)
a. Pure Passive　　　kunsyoo John ni (yotte) Mary
　　　　　　　　　　　medal　　　　　by
　 Formation:　　　　atae-rare-ta
　　　　　　　　　　　give-passive-past
b. Subject Marking:　kunsyoo *ga* John ni (yotte) Mary atae-rare-ta
c. Object Marking:　 *Kunsyoo ga John ni (yotte) Mary *o* atae-rare-ta.

This is therefore the ordering we will assume:

(2.80)
a. Indirect　　　　　John Mary *ni* kunsyoo atae-ta
　 Object Marking:　　　　　　to　medal　give-past
b. Pure Passive　　　kunsyoo John ni (yotte) Mary ni atae-rare-ta
　 Formation:　　　　　　　　　　by　　　　　　　give-passive
c. Subject Marking: Kunsyoo *ga* John ni (yotte) Mary ni atae-rare-ta.
d. Object Marking:　(does not apply)

This extrinsic ordering is necessary because of (i) viewing the Passive rule as involving NP movement and (ii) viewing case marking as sensitive to the relative order of NPs in the syntactic tree.

The following list, quoted from Kuno (1973, 349–350), summarizes the transformations discussed in this last section:

(2.81)
a. *Agentive*-Ni *Attachment:*
Mark the subject of the constituent clause with *ni.*
b. *Equi-NP Deletion:*
Delete the subject of the constituent clause under identity with the object (or the subject, depending upon individual verbs) of the matrix sentence.
c. *Aux Deletion:*
Delete the tense auxiliary of the constituent clause that is not dominated by the NP node.
d. *Verb Raising:*
Attach the tenseless verb of the constituent clause to the left of the matrix verb. (Note: The VP node and the S node of the constituent clauses are deleted by the tree-pruning convention.)
e. *Indirect Object Marking:*
Attach *ni* to the second of three unmarked NPs. (Note: An NP is unmarked if it is not followed by any particle or if it is followed only by *o* or *ga.*)
f. *Pure Passive Formation:*
Place the direct object or dative object NP in subject position, and place the original subject NP after it with *ni (yotte)* attached.
g. *Subject Marking:*
Attach *ga* to the subject NP.
h. *Object Marking:*
If the matrix verb is [−stative], attach *o* to the first unmarked nonsubject NP to the left of the verb. If the matrix verb is [+stative], attach *ga* to the first unmarked nonsubject NP to the left of the verb. In the latter case, the transformation is optional if the object is already followed by *o*.
i. Ga/Ni *Conversion:*
Attach *ni* to the first NP-*ga* of the *NP-ga-NP-ga Verbal* construction.
j. Ga/O *Deletion:*
Delete *ga* and *o* if they are followed by some other particle.

With these preliminaries, we are now able to summarize and compare the two approaches to case marking.

2.3.6.1 Theory of Cyclic Case Marking

The assumptions inherent in this system are:

1. Deep structure reflects semantic distinctions (cf. *ni* versus *o* causative: NP-*ga* NP-*ni* NP-*o* can come from different deep structures).
2. Rules (i.e., transformations) map deep structures onto surface structures.
3. Transformations may: (i) case-mark NPs (Agentive-*Ni* Attachment, Indirect Object Marking, Pure Passive Formation, Subject Marking, Object Marking, *Ga/Ni* Conversion), (ii) delete elements (Equi-NP Deletion, Aux Deletion, *Ga/O* deletion), (iii) move elements (Verb Raising, Pure Passive Formation), and (iv) substitute a lexical item (e.g., *zibun* for *John*).
4. The above transformations apply cyclically.

The ramifications of the above assumptions are:

1. Because the case-marking transformations apply cyclically, case particles must be allowed to stack up on a noun phrase in order to derive such sentences as (2.82), (2.83):

(2.82)
Mary wa nihongo *ga* hanaseru.
'Mary can speak Japanese.'

(2.83)
Mary wa hon *o* yomitagaru.
'Mary wants to read.'

This follows from Kuno's formulation of Object Marking, along with the assumptions it requires (cited below example (2.77)).

2. The *Ga/O* Deletion transformation is a consequence of cyclic case marking coupled with the assumption in (1). This transformation pares the number of particles on an NP down to one.
3. Another result is that an NP can be marked with *ni* in three different ways: (i) Agentive-*Ni* Attachment (employed in *ni* causatives and the indirect passive), (ii) Indirect Object Marking, (iii) Pure Passive Formation.
4. Though not mentioned in the summary of transformations, the rule of Reflexivization must follow Pure Passive Formation.
5. The grammatical case-marking rules—Indirect Object Marking, Subject Marking, and Object Marking—do not apply in a block but are extrinsically ordered with respect to other rules—specifically, Pure Passive Formation.

6. Because Object Marking follows Pure Passive Formation, Indirect Object Marking must precede Passive. One immediate consequence is that Passive, which permutes either a "direct object" or "dative NP" with a subject NP, can front (subjectivize) NPs marked with *ni*. Subject Marking will mark subject NPs (defined configurationally as leftmost NP dominated by S). This gives rise to an NP marked NP *ni ga*. Recall that the particle deletion rule (*Ga/O* Deletion) deletes only *ga* or *o*. (2.84) is ungrammatical:

(2.84)
*Mary ni ga John ni kunsyoo o ataerareta.
'Mary was awarded the medal by John.'

In the cyclic case-marking theory of Kuno (1973), a single rule can refer to both grammatical and relational terms. Recall that Pure Passive Formation refers both to "direct object" and to "dative object." The rule could have been written to refer only to configurational information—that is, by referring to the indirect object as "the second of three unmarked NPs" and to the direct object as the "first unmarked nonsubject NP to the left of the verb"—so the criticism does not involve any inability to express in a consistent way the target NP. Rather, the point is that reference to grammatical and relational terms is interchangeable in Kuno's system. The question becomes: is there a principled way to choose the appropriate notion to be used when characterizing a particular phenomenon?

2.3.6.2 Theory of Noncyclic Grammatical Case Linking The assumptions inherent in this system are:

1. Deep structure does not play a role in distinguishing the *ni* and *o* causatives.

2. The phrase structure component does not express verb-argument dependencies (recall the PS rule $X' \rightarrow X'^* X$ and the discussion in section 2.2.3).

3. Each verb is associated with a predicate argument structure.

4. Grammatical case linking takes place after word formation.

5. Semantic linking occurs before Regular Case Linking.

6. V + *sase* is formed *before* lexical insertion.

The ramifications of these assumptions are:

Assumption (2) requires that insertion be context free. This type of insertion yields a scrambling effect (Hale (1980) and Farmer (1980)). Taken together, these assumptions also result in overgeneration, which

Japanese Syntax   61

then must be accounted for in part by a system of evaluation. Another consequence is that grammatical relations cannot be defined configurationally.

2.3.6.3 The Theories Compared The two theories have a number of properties in common. For example, Kuno's Agentive-*Ni* Attachment transformation is utilized by the *ni* causative and indirect passive, which are the same two cases that trigger the NI Linking rule of the permanent lexicon. This transformation is ordered very early; in fact, it is the first transformation. The extrinsic ordering of the cyclic theory thus parallels the ordering imposed by the organization of the autonomous components of the noncyclic theory.

Although the cyclic theory involves complex syntactic structures at some level (i.e., at deep structure), the surface structure is a simplex one. The change in structure is effected by verb raising and tree-pruning, the purpose of verb raising being to recognize the lexical integrity of such complex verbs as *tabe-sase-ta*. The noncyclic approach characterizes this process in a word formation component that is independent of the syntax.

The two theories also differ in the types of rules they offer. The word formation hypothesis assumed in Farmer (1980) and here does not rely on Equi-NP Deletion, Aux Deletion, *Ga/Ni* Conversion, or *Ga/O* Deletion. Notice that the majority of those transformations are deletion rules. The need for them is related to the proliferation of lexical and case information associated with the interaction of complex syntactic structures and cyclic case-marking rules. The most significant of these deletion rules is *Ga/O* Deletion. The effect of the cyclic case-marking rules followed by *Ga/O* Deletion parallels the effect of applying Regular Case Linking "postcyclically."

Another discrepancy between the cyclic and noncyclic theories stems from the assumption that deep phrase structure configuration reflects semantic differences. Recall that Kuno (1973, 1978) makes a distinction at deep structure between the *ni* and the *o* causative. Let us assume that there is a single *-sase* that subcategorizes as follows: [NP NP S ___] and [NP S ___]. The first NP is the subject NP, the second NP is the controller of the subject of the sister S.[23] These two structures are supposed to account for the semantic difference between the *ni* and the *o* causative. Many authors have pointed out that it is not obvious which structure corresponds to which causative. Kuroda (1978) suggests that both are derived from the following structure:[24]

(2.85)

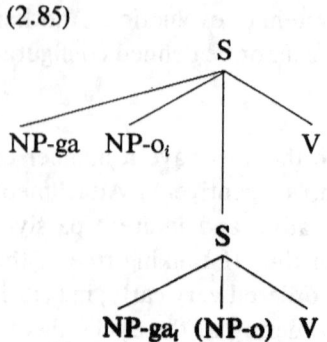

The *o* causative is derived via Equi-NP Deletion; the *ni* causative is derived via a rule called Counter Equi. Counter Equi deletes the matrix object (accusatively marked NP). This rule is then followed by a rule of "Subject *Ni* Raising." But if the *ni* and *o* causatives have different meanings, then, given such an analysis, the assumption that deep structure reflects the semantic differences of these surface strings is thrown into question.

One of the two major differences between a theory of grammar such as the one proposed by Kuno (1973, 1978, 1980) and the theory outlined here is that the former posits only one rule type (the transformations of Kuno's works), whereas the latter apportions rule types to autonomous components of the grammar. The other greatest difference between them is in the way extrinsic ordering is used. Kuno's theory must use extrinsic ordering to a much greater extent than the theory proposed here. For example, in Kuno's theory the extrinsic ordering of Indirect Object Marking with Passive and Direct Object Marking is necessary because of the way Passive is viewed (i.e., as involving NP movement). In the modular theory I am proposing, ordering is at least partly a derivative of the organization of the components.

At the empirical level the two theories make different predictions concerning passive causative sentences. Kuno's theory predicts that (2.86a,b) are both acceptable. The modular theory predicts that only (2.86b) is not ill formed. Judgments are not perfectly clear, but the consistent response among speakers who can get these passive causative sentences (they are not possible for all speakers) is that (2.86b) is much preferred to (2.86a). (2.86a) is considered very marginal at best.

(2.86)
a. ??Mary wa Taroo ni Ziroo ni homeraresaseta.
b. Mary wa Taroo o Ziroo ni homeraresaseta.
 'Mary made Taro be praised by Ziro.'

The discussion so far has focused on the case particles. The next section will extend the critique to include passive. We will see how some of the effects of the two passives—dative and direct passives—can be attributed to independently necessary properties of the grammar.

2.3.7 Passive

In this section we will develop an analysis of passive in Japanese, relying heavily on case linking to achieve our ends. First a discussion of the notion "subject" in Japanese is in order, which will lead to motivating a diacritic feature 'S' that will figure in our account of passive.

Shibatani (1978, 52) quotes Akira Mikami (1972, 48) as having said, "I have never encountered any satisfactory definition or explanation as to what 'subject' refers to in Japanese grammar." Mikami dismissed the use of the term *subject* for Japanese since nominatively marked NPs exhibit no special primacy over other case-marked NPs. That is, there is no subject-verb agreement in Japanese. As Shibatani notes (1978), Mikami's dismissal of the notion "subject" is based on assuming a direct correlation between the grammatical relation, *subject*, and the grammatical case, *nominative*. Many authors (among them Kuroda, Shibatani, Kuno, Inoue, and Kitagawa) have discussed this relationship. Reference to "subject" has been made by way of labeling the NP that triggers reflexivization "the subject."

It has often been noticed that a one-to-one correspondence does not exist between nominative case-marked NPs and NPs that can serve as antecedent for *zibun*.

(2.87)
a. Taroo ga$_i$ Hanako ga$_j$ zibun$_{i,j*}$ no guruupu de itiban suki da.
 'Taro likes Hanako the best in self's (Taro's) group.'
b. Taroo ga$_i$ Hanako o$_j$ zibun$_{i,j}$ no ie e ikas(as)eta.
 'Taro made Hanako go to self's$_{i,j}$ house.'

In (2.87a) a nominative (*Hanako ga*) cannot serve as antecedent for *zibun*. However, an accusative NP (*Hanako o*) in (2.87b) *can* serve as antecedent for *zibun*.

If a structural or configurational definition of "subject" is appealed to, then the possible antecedents in (2.87a,b) can be identified as the "leftmost NP," given the configurations in (2.88):

(2.88)
a. [Taroo ga$_i$ Hanako ga$_j$ zibun$_{i,j}$· no guruupu de itiban suki da]
b. [Taroo ga$_i$ [Hanako o$_j$ zibun$_{i,j}$ no ie e ik] ase]

The clause is the domain for defining "leftmost NP." Thus, (2.88a) contains only one such NP, whereas (2.88b) contains two, since it has two clauses (one embedded in the other).

Since it has most often been assumed that reflexivization is a syntactic phenomenon and that the bound verbalizing morphemes *-sase, -rare,* and *-are~-e* are "higher" verbs, the observation that embedded sentences yield antecedent ambiguities has led to the use of a cyclic rule of reflexivization. Although at first it appears adequate to appeal to structural configuration in attempting to define "subject," this turns out to be an overgeneralization. (2.89) illustrates the fact that not all "leftmost NPs" can be antecedents.

(2.89)
a. [Ziroo wa$_i$ [Hanako o$_j$ zibun$_{i,j}$ no ie e ik] ase]
   'Ziro made Hanako go to self's house.'
b. Hanako$_j$ wa Ziroo$_i$ ni zibun$_{i^*,j}$ no ie e ikaserareta.
   'Hanako was made by Ziro to go to self's (Hanako's) house.'

This problem was discussed in section 2.2. If the nonuniform hypothesis of Kuno (1973, 1978) is assumed, then extrinsic rule ordering must be imposed. Reflexivization *must* follow Passive. On the other hand, if the uniform hypothesis is assumed, then there are two cycles and hence two leftmost NPs. The nonambiguity of (2.89b) must be accounted for by a condition on antecedent relationships among sequences of *zibun*. This condition interacts in a crucial way with other rules in the derivation. That is, it is extrinsically ordered with respect to Object Deletion (section 2.2.2.2). The proposal to be outlined here again relies heavily on the concept that the grammar is composed of levels or dimensions of autonomous components. The task of accounting for the phenomenon of, say, "passivization" is viewed as a process of properly apportioning various aspects of the passive to the various levels of the grammar.[25] This view is incompatible in spirit with a theory that attributes all the effects of the passive to a single rule. For example, recall Kuno's (1973, 350) description of passivization:

Pure Passive Formation:
Place the direct object or dative object NP in subject position, and place the original subject NP after it with *ni (yotte)* attached.

This rule is presumably accompanied by the attachment of *-rare* to the verb stem. Instead, I will construct a system whose subparts operate independently of each other. These subparts are "ordered"; that is, the "output" of one component is the "input" to another. It is not until *after* these components have interacted that the "antecedent" of *zibun* can be identified. This system claims, therefore, that a possible reason for the confusion over and indeed the complexity of the *zibun* phenomenon is the apparent dependency on a multidimensional definition of "subject." Thus, reliance on any particular dimension—i.e., structural position or case—leads to only partly accurate results. In what follows a proposal will be made concerning the interaction of these dimensions.

We can now try to identify the possible subjects in several types of constructions. "Subject" refers to the NP that "triggers" Subject Honorification (Harada (1976)) and the rule of reflexivization (i.e., the NP that can act as antecedent for *zibun*). Following a suggestion by Ken Hale, I will use '*S*' as a diacritic to stand for "subject." At this point, for purposes of exposition, I will adopt a rule that assigns the diacritic '*S*'. Later, this "rule" will be replaced by a general principle that identifies "subjects."

Note the following simple sentence:

(2.90)
Taroo ga okasi o tabeta.
'Taro ate the cake.'

The "subject" can be described superficially either as the nominatively marked NP or as the leftmost NP. In any case, the "subject" NP is identifiable. Since we have seen that nominative case particle is inadequate for picking out the subject, the only other option is to refer to argument position. (2.91) gives the argument structure for *tabe* 'eat':

(2.91)
(___ ___ tabe)

We can adopt the following rule that relates '*S*' to "leftmost" argument position in PASs:

(2.92)
'S' Assignment
Assign the diacritic 'S' to the leftmost argument position in a predicate argument structure.

Example: (____ ____ tabe)
           S

'S' Assignment applies to a new PAS (i.e., derived argument structure) at the time of its formation.

(2.93)
(____ (____ ____ tabe) sase)
  S   S

Hale (personal communication) has noticed that adopting such a rule suggests a reformulation of Regular Case Linking:

(2.94)
Regular Case Linking
a. Link leftmost 'S' argument slot: GA
b. Link rightmost argument slot: O
c. Elsewhere link: NI

Chomsky (personal communication) suggests a modification to the Passive rule proposed in Farmer (1980, 131–132), which had two parts: (i) remove leftmost 'S' and (ii) reassign 'S' to another argument position. Chomsky's suggestion amounts to retaining only (i). Passive (-*rare*) stipulates that the leftmost 'S' cannot be a "subject." In the case of simple predicates, the effect is to render the PAS "subjectless":

(2.95)
a. (____ ____ tabe)
     S

b. ((____ ____ tabe) rare)
     ϕ

If we assume that there is a general condition against "subjectless" PASs, then (2.95b) must be changed, by reapplication of 'S' Assignment. If we combine (2.92) with the subject-removing effects of Passive, the principle of 'S' Assignment is stated as follows:

(2.96)
'S' Assignment (Revised)
Assign 'S' to the leftmost argument. If this argument cannot be a subject for some reason, then assign 'S' to any other argument. (All

PASs—that is, both innermost and outermost PASs—are subject to the principle.)

We must claim that Passive removes the leftmost argument slot from the domain of application of (2.96). That is, Passive does more than erase a diacritic. If this were not the case, then (2.96) would apply and reassign the diacritic to the position from which 'S' had just been deleted. Below, this blocking will be indicated by ϕ. After Passive, (2.95b) would be susceptible to 'S' Assignment.

(2.97)

$$((\underset{\phi}{\underline{}} \ \underline{} \ tabe) \ rare)$$

'S' Assignment (2.96): $((\underset{\phi}{\underline{}} \ \underset{S}{\underline{}} \ tabe) \ rare)$

Rule (2.96) is written so as to account for both the so-called dative passive and the so-called direct passive.

(2.98)

a. $(\underline{} \ \underline{} \ \underline{} \ atae)$

'S' Assignment (2.96): b. $(\underset{S}{\underline{}} \ \underline{} \ \underline{} \ atae)$

Passive: c. $((\underset{\phi}{\underline{}} \ \underline{} \ \underline{} \ atae) \ rare)$

'S' Assignment (2.96): d. $((\underset{\phi}{\underline{}} \ \underset{S}{\underline{}} \ \underline{} \ atae) \ rare)$ (dative passive)

or

e. $((\underset{\phi}{\underline{}} \ \underline{} \ \underset{S}{\underline{}} \ atae) \ rare)$ (direct passive)

(2.98d,e) correspond to (2.99b,c), respectively (taken from Kuno (1980, 103)):

(2.99)
a. Yoshida-syusyoo ga Tanaka-tuusandaizin ni kunsyoo o ataeta.
  'Prime Minister Yoshida awarded a medal to Minister Tanaka.'
b. Tanaka-tuusandaizin ga Yoshida-syusyoo ni kunsyoo o ataerareta.
  'Minister Tanaka was awarded a medal by Prime Minister Yoshida.'
c. Kunsyoo ga Yoshida-syusyoo ni Tanaka-tuusandaizin ni ataerareta.
  'The medal was awarded to Minister Tanaka by Prime Minister Yoshida.'

Modularity in Syntax   68

We will now see how this account of the passive handles two well-known problems concerning the impossibility of "subjectivizing" certain object NPs (cf. Kuno (1978, 1980)). These problems arise in (2.100c,f). (Hasegawa (1981) also discusses these examples.)

(2.100)
a. Taroo wa Hanako ni sono hon o kawaseta.
   'Taro made Hanako buy that book.'
b. Hanako wa Taroo ni sono hon o kawasaserareta. (kawaserareta)
   'Hanako was made by Taro to buy that book.'
c. *Sono hon wa Taroo ni Hanako ni kawasaserareta. (kawaserareta)
d. Taroo wa Hanako ni Ziroo o zibun no ie e ika(sa)sesaseta.
   'Taro made/let Hanako make Ziro go to self's house.'
e. Hanako wa Taroo ni Ziroo o zibun no ie e ikasesaserareta.
   'Hanako was made/let by Taro to make Ziro go to self's house.'
f. *Ziroo wa Taroo ni Hanako ni zibun no ie e ikasesaserareta.

Kuno has proposed the following global constraint to rule out (2.100c,f) (restated in Kuno (1978)):

(2.101)
Passive cannot subjectivize an NP that used to be a constituent of a sentence embedded in the sentence to which the rule applies.

Sono hon o in (2.100) meets the condition in (2.101); therefore, it cannot be subjectivized:

(2.102)

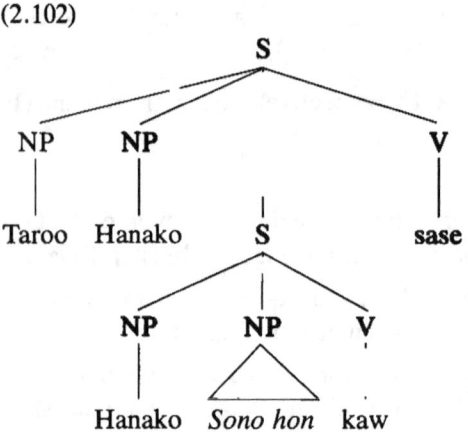

Japanese Syntax

In contrast, the modular theory proposed here can account very straightforwardly for the ungrammaticality of (2.100c,f). It can be shown that condition (2.101) is unnecessary, given a theory of the interaction of Passive with the principle of 'S' Assignment and embedding of predicate argument structures. The above phenomenon can be properly characterized only if a distinction can be made between simple 3-place predicates and derived 3-place predicates:

(2.103)
Taroo wa Hanako ni sono syoo o ataeta.
                             that prize
'Taro awarded that prize to Hanako.'

(2.104)
Taroo wa Hanako ni sono hon o yomaseta.
'Taro made Hanako read that book.'

Sono syoo o in (2.103) can be subjectivized—marked *ga*—whereas *hon o* in (2.104) cannot be. The PASs of the verbs in (2.103) and (2.104) are (2.105) and (2.106), respectively.

(2.105)
(___ ___ ___ atae)

(2.106)
(___ (___ ___ yom) ase)

After 'S' Assignment, these representations are:

(2.107)
(___ ___ ___ atae)
  S

(2.108)
(___ (___ ___ yom) ase)
  S   S

If the passive -*rare* is attached to these PASs, (2.109) and (2.110) result:

(2.109)
((___ ___ ___ atae) rare)
   φ

(2.110)
((___ (___ ___ yom) ase) rare)
   φ   S

The contrast between these two argument structures is clear. (2.109) contains no 'S', but (2.110) does. This contrast is crucial since it interacts with 'S' Assignment (2.96). Recall that this principle is *based* on the assumption that every PAS must have an 'S'. Thus, given that (2.109) has no 'S', (2.96) must apply to it:

(2.111)

$$((\underset{\phi}{\underline{}} \ \underline{} \ \underline{} \ \text{atae}) \ \text{rare})$$

'S' Assignment (2.96): $((\underset{\phi}{\underline{}} \ \underset{S}{\underline{}} \ \underline{} \ \text{atae}) \ \text{rare})$

or

$((\underset{\phi}{\underline{}} \ \underline{} \ \underset{S}{\underline{}} \ \text{atae}) \ \text{rare})$

The PAS in (2.110) already has an 'S'; therefore, (2.96) will not apply. (2.112) becomes an *impossible* PAS:

(2.112)
$((\underset{\phi}{\underline{}} \ (\underset{(S)}{\underline{}} \ \underset{S}{\underline{}} \ \text{yom}) \ \text{ase}) \ \text{rare})$

This account obviates any necessity for a global condition, like (2.101), on Passive.

Let us return to (2.110) and (2.111) and apply Regular Case Linking:

(2.113)

$((\underline{} \ \underset{S}{\underline{}} \ \underline{} \ \text{atae}) \ \text{rare})$

Regular Case Linking: GA: $((\underline{} \ \underset{S}{\underline{\text{GA}}} \ \underline{} \ \text{atae}) \ \text{rare})$

O: $((\underline{} \ \underset{S}{\underline{\text{GA}}} \ \underline{\text{O}} \ \text{atae}) \ \text{rare})$

NI: $((\underline{\text{NI}} \ \underset{S}{\underline{\text{GA}}} \ \underline{\text{O}} \ \text{atae}) \ \text{rare})$

or

Regular Case Linking: GA: $((\underline{} \ \underline{} \ \underset{S}{\underline{\text{GA}}} \ \text{atae}) \ \text{rare})$

O: (not applicable)
NI: $((\underline{\text{NI}} \ \underline{\text{NI}} \ \underset{S}{\underline{\text{GA}}} \ \text{atae}, \ \text{rare})$

Japanese Syntax

(2.114)

$$((\underline{}_{\phi} (\underline{}_{S}\underline{} \text{ yom) ase) rare})$$

Regular Case Linking: GA: $((\underline{}_{\phi} (\underline{\text{GA}}_{S} \underline{} \text{ yom) ase) rare})$

O: $((\underline{}_{\phi} (\underline{\text{GA}}_{S} \underline{\text{O}} \text{ yom) ase) rare})$

NI: $((\underline{\text{NI}}_{\phi} (\underline{\text{GA}}_{S} \underline{\text{O}} \text{ yom) ase) rare})$

The rightmost argument slot in (2.114) will not receive GA because it will not be assigned the 'S' diacritic; and it will not receive the 'S' diacritic because the PAS already has one.

2.4 Summary and Conclusions

I have been assuming a lexicon that has roughly the following properties: Items, whether words or stems, are listed in the lexicon.[26] Each item is associated with a category (though I will not be concerned here with the inventory of categories), a "definition" (what the item means), a phonological representation, and in some cases an argument structure. These argument structures associate, for example, a verb with argument slots. The verb *tabe* 'eat' has two argument slots.[27] These argument slots are subject to numerous rules, principles, and conditions. Idiosyncratic properties are stated at this level of representation. For example, the verb *okur* 'send' has the idiosyncratic property that the "subject" can be marked or associated with the particle *kara* instead of the usual nominative case particle *ga*; this is the semantic linking discussed in section 2.3.5. Argument slots can also be associated with particles via the grammatical case-linking rules. These rules simply state which arguments are associated with the accusative particle *o*, the dative particle *ni*, or the nominative particle *ga*. These case particles aid in evaluation, which is a process of associating overt NPs with argument positions. In Japanese, I claim, this process relies on (i) case particles and (ii) the sisterhood relation. An entity must be in construction with a verb and marked with a particular kind of particle in order to be construed as being associated with an argument slot of that verb. Evaluation will be discussed at greater length in chapter 3.

I have also assumed that there is a rule that defines the relationship between the head and its complements. For Japanese this rule must capture the fact that in a given domain the complements of the head are to the left. For example, the complements of a verb are always to the left, the head of a relative clause is to the right, etc. To state this condition, I have adopted the rule $X' \rightarrow X'^* X$ (1.13), where X stands for a preterminal node that is not specified for category. This preterminal node is then rewritten to give a terminal node Δ. Lexical insertion then can be viewed as a transformation that replaces these Δs with lexical material (an approach to lexical insertion first suggested in Chomsky (1965)). The categorial features of the lexical item then "climb up" the tree, filling in the X nodes with categorial content. The only context for inserting a lexical item is Δ. Anything can be inserted underneath these Δs; order plays no role. Two immediate consequences emerge: grammatical relations cannot be defined configurationally, and no scrambling rule is needed.[28] (Actually, one more assumption underlies these results: that there is no transformation Move α which relates D-structures to S-structures in Japanese. Given this assumption, coupled with the "scrambling" property of Japanese, it is not possible to define grammatical relations configurationally.) Since the grammar needs no scrambling rule, I have gone so far as to assume that it needs no syntactic transformations, that is, no rule defined over phrase markers that moves or deletes these entities.

Another question arises, involving the status of the entity known as PRO in the Extended Standard and Government-Binding theories. This entity is presumably a phonologically null lexical item that carries such features as person and number and holds a phrase marker position in the "tree." The modular theory proposed here could also make use of this entity, but I choose not to adopt it for reasons that will become clear in chapters 4 and 5. This theory, then, will include no phonologically null item that is a syntactic entity holding a phrase marker position.[29] What has been identified as PRO is, in this theory, actually an *unevaluated argument,* that is, an argument slot of a predicate that is not associated with an overt, phonologically nonnull entity.[30] Under this conception, PRO does not have any intrinsic features independent from those associated with the argument slot of the predicate.

Farmer (1980) and Miyagawa (1980) have argued that complex Japanese verbs such as the derived causative are formed in the lexicon before lexical insertion. As I have noted, this runs counter to most early transformational studies of Japanese (for example, Kuno (1973), Kuroda (1965), Tonoike (1979)). Farmer's and Miyagawa's arguments were based primarily on the assumption that all words are formed prior to lexical insertion (that is, if a complex verb can be shown to consti-

Japanese Syntax

tute a single word, then it must be inserted into the syntax already derived). Here I would like to propose another type of argument that does not rely on this assumption. The argument is highly theory-dependent and does not work under other assumptions. The two crucial assumptions here are that there are no syntactic movement rules—that is, no rules that change the order of constituents at the PS level of representation—and that evaluation in Japanese only involves sisters to the head. The following data play an important role in the argument:[31]

(2.115)
Simple Verb:
a. Taroo ga Hanako ni sono hon o ageta.
b. Taroo ga sono hon o Hanako ni ageta.
c. Sono hon o Taroo ga Hanako ni ageta.
  'Taro gave that book to Hanako.'

(2.116)
Complex Verb:
a. Taroo ga Hanako ni kodomo o sikaraseta.
b. Taroo ga kodomo o Hanako ni sikaraseta.
c. Kodomo o Taroo ga Hanako ni sikaraseta.
  'Taro made Hanako scold the child.'

Notice that the N' constituents associated with the complex causative verb may "scramble," just like the N' constituents of a simple predicate. If the complex verb is actually an instance of two syntactic verbs, one having one N' constituent and one sentential complement and the other having only N' constituents, then the two possible structures for (2.116c) would be (2.117a,b):

(2.117)
a.

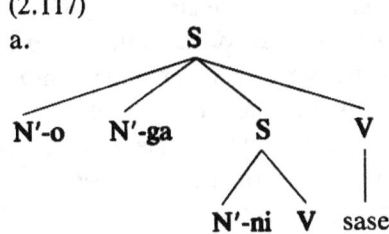

b.
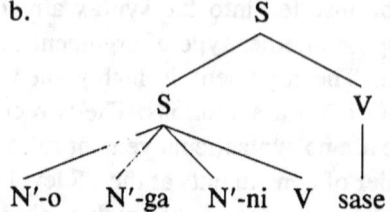

To accommodate the ordering relation exhibited in these examples, either the N'-*o* must be placed in the matrix S or the N'-*ga* in the embedded S. But notice that there is now a problem for evaluation. Either the N'-*o* is not a sister to its verb (2.117a) or the N'-*ga* is not a sister to its verb (2.117b). Neither structure expresses the dependency between N'-*ga* and -*sase,* and between N'-*o* and V. Notice also that the structure would have to be collapsed in order for evaluation to work as we assume it does. This solution—collapsing the structure—is the one we will adopt. A bi-clausal analysis of V + -*sase* seems to be incompatible with a theory that does not use any syntactic movement rules. Consequently, the generalizations that were stated over a syntactic level of representation that involved this type of embedding must be reconsidered. I will attempt to state some of these generalizations over lexical structure and some over syntactic structures. In one basic respect the modular theory presented here is not unlike previous, standard theory accounts in that the lexical structure imposes its will on the syntax, so to speak. However, from Standard to Government-Binding theory, the relationship between the lexicon and the syntax has had the character "work from the bottom up and don't look back." That is, all the relevant information from the lexicon is "projected" into the syntax, so that both lexical and syntactic information are composed at a single level of representation. Lexical items are inserted at D(eep)-structure, which represents the logical or basic relations of predicates and their arguments; transformations (such as Move α) then map this level onto S(urface)-structures. S-structures are then mapped onto another, interpretive level, logical form (LF). Throughout this derivation, after lexical insertion, the lexical structure of a predicate is not accessed independently, since all lexical information has been "projected" into the phrase marker level of representation. The modular theory proposed here turns this picture on its side, no longer employing derivations. The connection between the lexicon and syntax does not involve projecting all the lexical information into the syntax (syntax in the narrow sense discussed earlier in chapter 1, note 14). The syntactic level of representation is one domain and the lexical structure represents another. Rules, principles, and generalizations can be stated over these domains independently. The task, then, is to take a string, give it a syntactic analysis using the vocabulary "is an X," where X stands for a phrase (e.g., "is a noun phrase"), and then to interpret the various syntactic constituents by way of accessing the lexical structures of predicates as one part of this process.

Chapter 3
Extending the Modular Theory: Japanese

In this chapter I will return to the questions raised earlier, discussing the import of the modular approach for other constructions and problems in Japanese. Specifically, I will consider another type of case array, touch on the anaphora question, and extend the account of evaluation to include the topic construction, *tough* sentences, and indirect passives.

For the purposes of this investigation, I have assumed a particular type of interaction between lexical and syntactic structures—that is, I have assumed that derivational word formation takes place before lexical insertion. Naturally, such an assumption involves dealing with other phenomena that touch on this issue tangentially, such as the PS component, "cylic" subject, and case marking, to mention a few. With regard to the PS component, the question of interest has involved the problem of expressing certain dependencies. Briefly, should the PS rules delimit the number of arguments any (derived) verb can take? As for the notion "cyclic" subject, Kuno and others have demonstrated that Japanese has a special NP that seems to be identifiable only if some notion of the syntactic cycle is adopted. Given the assumptions made here, this "cycle" *cannot* be expressed syntactically. A third important issue involves case marking. It has been shown (Lekach (1978)) that the case arrays of causatives are not unlike those of simple sentences with morphologically simple verbs. In short, for the purposes of case marking, the structure must be simplex, but for the purposes of reflexivization the structure must be complex. In this chapter my purpose is—as it was in chapter 2—to resolve (or partially resolve) such issues.

Modular Theory: Japanese

3.1 The Investigation

3.1.1 The Phrase Structure Component

The theory of the PS component outlined in chapter 1 envisions it as being composed of two independent dimensions: a structural and a categorial dimension. (See Hale (1980) for the origin of this idea.) The proposal for Japanese amounts to removing the categorial dimension from the PS rules, leaving only the structural dimension. The PS rules project nodes unspecified for category. These rules specify only structure; that is, they stipulate where the head is in relation to its sisters and the depth of the structure.

(3.1)
a. $X' \rightarrow X'^* \, X$
b. $X \rightarrow \Delta$

Since rule (3.1b) provides only the terminal node Δ, lexical insertion must, by necessity, be context free. After lexical insertion the categorially unspecified X node is converted to specify the features of the lexical item it dominates. The X' node, in turn, acquires the features of its head, by virtue of percolation (see section 1.3.1).

3.1.2 Developing an Account of Case

In chapter 2 I proposed and developed a theory of semantic and grammatical case linking. For Japanese this theory utilizes predicate argument structures (PASs), over which case assignment is defined. (See Ostler (1979) for the original application of this idea to Japanese.) Derived causatives involve the embedding of one PAS in another:

(3.2)

____, ____ sase
$\updownarrow$

____ (____, ____ V) sase

These PASs can become quite complex; that is, they involve multiple embeddings. I have claimed in chapter 2 that the grammatical case-linking rules do not directly interact with this embedding process. Instead, the rule of Regular Case Linking does its work *after* word formation—after the building of complex PASs. I also suggested that a principle of 'S' Assignment operates at the level of the PAS. These three phenomena, PAS embedding, 'S' Assignment, and grammatical case linking, interact indirectly. The output of the case-linking rule is in part a function of the configuration of embeddings and subject diacritics in the maximal PAS.

3.1.3 Defining the Domain of "Subject"

The 'S' Assignment principle was stipulated in chapter 2 in response to the need for identifying the arguments that can be antecedents for *zibun* and trigger Subject Honorification. The domain for the application of this principle is the PAS. Section 3.2 will detail the argument representations where 'S' is identified. These argument structures are associated with numerous types of verbs, such as simple verbs, verbs that take sentential complements, and bound verbalizing elements.

3.2 Results of PS Rules and Case Linking

The theory of phrase structure rules developed in chapters 1 and 2, coupled with the theory of case linking developed in chapter 2, offers several new accounts of some old problems.

3.2.1 Scrambling

Scrambling now follows from the interaction of the PS rules, which project nodes unspecified for category, and context-free lexical insertion. The domain of this effect also follows. That is, there appears to be no scrambling outside of the clause because an N' can evaluate an argument position of a given verb only if the N' is a *sister* to that verb. In short, the theory *does not need* either a rule of scrambling or a condition constraining it.

3.2.2 Nonsubjectivizability of Some Direct Objects

In chapter 2, we concluded that the "nonsubjectivizability" of *sono hon o* in (3.3) was in fact attributable to the interaction of the embedding of PASs with 'S' Assignment and grammatical case assignment. Recall the following types of sentences, (2.99a–c) and (2.100a–c):

(3.3)
a. Taroo wa Hanako ni sono hon o kawaseta.
    'Taro made Hanako buy that book.'
b. Hanako wa Taroo ni sono hon o kawasaserareta.
    'Hanako was made by Taro to buy that book.'

c. *Sono hon wa Taroo ni Hanako ni kawasaserareta.
   (The book was by Taro made Hanako to buy.)

(3.4)
a. Yoshida-syusyoo ga Tanaka-tuusandaizin ni kunsyoo o ataeta.
   'Prime Minister Yoshida awarded a medal to Minister Tanaka.'
b. Tanaka-tuusandaizin ga Yoshida-syusyoo ni kunsyoo o ataerareta.
   'Minister Tanaka was awarded a medal by Prime Minister Yoshida.'
c. Kunsyoo ga Yoshida-syusyoo ni (yotte) Tanaka-tuusandaizin ni ataerareta.
   'A medal was awarded to Minister Tanaka by Prime Minister Yoshida.'

The PASs for (3.3a) and (3.4a) are (3.5a) and (3.5b), respectively:

(3.5)
a. (___ (___ ___ kaw) ase)
     S   S
b. (___ ___ ___ atae)
     S

The Passive rule amounts to saying that the leftmost argument cannot be a "subject":

(3.6)
a. ((___ (___ ___ kaw) ase) rare)
      φ   S
b. ((___ ___ ___ atae) rare)
      φ

The principle for assigning "subject" to a PAS is triggered only in (3.6b):

(3.7)
((___ ___ ___ atae) rare)
   φ $\vee$
       S

It is not triggered in (3.6a), because the PAS of *kaw* already contains a subject. Thus, the rightmost argument slot in (3.6a), which corresponds to *hon o*, will never be subjectivizable. Note that we need neither a constraint on the Passive rule of word formation, nor a global condition such as the one proposed by Kuno (see section 2.3.7).

3.3 Another Case-marking Problem

In this section we will look at several constructions and case arrays that we have not yet discussed. We have so far examined two types of linking: semantic case linking and grammatical case linking. The semantic case-linking rules, which some verbs employ to link an argument slot with a case particle other than a grammatical one, apply in the permanent lexicon. The grammatical case-linking rules, on the other hand, apply after all word formation is completed. The following is a list of the linking rules discussed in this work:

Semantic case-linking rules:
KARA Linking: link leftmost argument slot: __KARA__
Example: (__KARA__, ___, ___ okur)
                        send

NI Linking: link second argument slot: __NI__
Examples: (___ (__NI__ ko)   sase)   (*ni* causative)
                come

         (___ __NI__ aw)   (simple verb 'meet')
            meet

NI Linking: link leftmost argument slot: __NI__
Example: ((__NI__ sin) are)   (indirect passive)
           die

Grammatical case-linking rules:
Regular Case Linking
a. Link leftmost 'S' argument slot: __GA__
b. Link rightmost argument slot: __O__
c. Elsewhere link: __NI__

We will modify Regular Case Linking to handle examples like (3.8):[1]

(3.8)
Bill wa John o Mary ni   soodan s-ase-ta.
    top   acc   dat consult do-cause-past
'Bill made John consult Mary.'

The predicate *soodan sase* 'cause to consult' poses certain problems for our account of case arrays. The PAS associated with (3.8) would be something like (3.9):

Modular Theory: Japanese

(3.9)
(__ (__ __ soodan s-) ase)
  S   S

Because of sentences like (3.10), we know that *soodan suru*, like *au* 'meet', assigns NI to the object argument slot.

(3.10)
John wa Mary ni soodan suru.
     top   dat
'John consulted (with) Mary.'

This means that in (3.9) *soodan s-* assigns NI to the object argument slot, yielding (3.11) after semantic linking and before grammatical case linking.

(3.11)
(__ (__ NI soodan s-) ase)
  S   S

As it stands now, the second 'S' would be assigned NI rather than O. To handle such examples, Ueda (1981, 110) suggests

A possible solution to this problem is to stipulate the autonomy of the two components of case linking rules, i.e., the semantic linking rules and the regular rule, to the effect that the latter does not count the argument position linked by the former.

That is, Regular Case Linking would identify the "rightmost" argument position as being the rightmost *unmarked* argument position. If a semantic linking rule has marked the rightmost argument, then that argument is no longer counted as the "rightmost" argument position for the purposes of Regular Case Linking.[2] With this proviso, the output of the subrules of Regular Case Linking would be:

(3.12)
(GA (O NI soodan s-) ase)
  S   S

The above PAS is used for the purposes of evaluation.[3]

3.4 A Modular Account of Related Constructions

In this section I will characterize the syntax of the topic construction, *tough* sentences; and indirect passives in such a way as to reveal a structural property that all three constructions share—namely, that after Direct Evaluation a constituent remains that has not been associated with an argument slot. To do this, I will introduce (i) a syntactic coindexing device called *Predication* (following Williams (1980))[4] and (ii) a procedure called *Indirect Evaluation*, which follows *Direct Evaluation* in the evaluation process. The net result of Predication and Indirect Evaluation is that in the topic construction and in *tough* sentences, Indirect Evaluation may coindex an N'-*ga/wa* with any unevaluated argument slot. In the indirect passive and sometimes in the topic construction the X'-*ga/wa* is not linked to an argument slot. Each of these constructions needs further comment. My account of these constructions is not by any means complete (for example, I do not offer an account of the role of pragmatics, nor do I have an account of why V-*rare* is often associated with an "adversity" interpretation). I claim simply that a certain structural relationship seems to exist between X'-*ga/wa* expressions and predicates, a relationship that I have tried to state in very general terms via indexing.

3.4.1 Predication and Indirect Evaluation
Here I will introduce some new mechanisms, enriching the theory so that it can embrace the topic construction, *tough* sentences, and indirect passives. I adopt, for Japanese, the following coindexing procedure.

(3.13)
Predication
Coindex X'-*ga/wa* with V.

This is a purely syntactic gesture that indexes an *un*indexed X'-*ga/wa* with the head V.

Indirect Evaluation involves taking an index from the head V and assigning it to any unevaluated argument slot of the PAS of that verb. I will assume that Predication and Indirect Evaluation follow Direct Evaluation, though this is not crucial.

3.4.2 The Data
We will be concerned with the following data for the three constructions under consideration.

Topic Construction:[5]

(3.14)
Naomi wa udon o tabe-ta.
   top noodle-acc eat-past
'Naomi ate udon noodles.'

(3.15)
Taroo wa Hanako ga iede-si-ta.
   top   nom leave home-do-past
'As for Taro, Hanako ran away from home.'

(3.16)
Bunmeikoku wa dansei no heikin zyumyoo ga naga-i.
civilized-nation-top man 's average life-span-nom long-pres
'Civilized countries, their male population's average life span is long.'

(3.17)
Hana wa sakura ga i-i.
flower-top cherry-nom good-pres
'As for flowers, cherry blossoms are best.'

Tough Sentences:[6]

(3.18)
a. Gakusei-tati ga kono hon o yom-u.
   student-pl-nom this book-acc read-pres
   'Students read this book.'

b. Kono hon ga (gakusei-tati ni totte) yomi-yasu-i.
   this book-nom student-pl   read-easy-pres
   'This book is easy (for the students) to read.'

(3.19)
a. John ga kono tosyokan kara hon o nusum-u.
      nom this library-from book-acc steal-pres
   'John steals books from this library.'

b. Kono tosyokan (kara) ga hon o nusumi-niku.
   this library-(from)-nom book-acc steal-hard-pres
   'This library is hard to steal books from.'

(3.20)
a. Kim ga   asahayaku   benkyoosu-ru.
   Kim-nom early in the morning   study-pres
   'Kim studies early in the morning.'
b. Asahayaku ga   (suzusi-i node)   benkyoosi-yasu-i.
   early in the morning-nom cool-pres because study-easy-pres
   'It is easy/easier to study early in the morning, because it is cool.'

Indirect Passives:[7]

(3.21)
Taroo wa kodomo ni sin-are-ta.
     top child-dat   die-passive-past
'Taro was adversely affected by his child's dying.

(3.22)
Taroo wa Hanako ni   tokei o   kowas-are-ta.
     top   dat watch-acc break-passive-past
'Taro had his watch broken by Hanako.'

(3.23)
Kanzya wa kangohu ni kanbu o   huk-are-ta.
patient-top nurse-dat diseased part-acc wipe-passive-past
'The patient had a nurse wipe the affected part.'

(3.24)
Kodomo wa sensei ni   yasasiku atama o   nade-rare-ta.
child-top   teacher-dat gently   head-acc pat-passive-past
'The child had the teacher pat his head gently.'

(3.25)
Taroo wa Hanako ni   piano o   hik-are-ta.
     top   dat piano-acc play-passive-past
'Hanako played the piano and Taro was affected.'

3.4.3 The Account

Throughout this analysis I will be incorporating aspects of Kitagawa's (1982) account of topic constructions, for the general purpose of linking overt N's with argument slots.[8] For example, an argument designated (via Regular Case Linking) to take an O-marked N' would be coindexed with an overt N'-*o* by means of Direct Evaluation. If, however, an N' is marked N'-*wa*, no such matchup can be made on the basis of case marking. Any leftover N's must be incorporated somehow.[9] This

Modular Theory: Japanese

is where Predication and Indirect Evaluation come into play. First Predication coindexes X'-ga/wa with V; then Indirect Evaluation optionally assigns the index on the verb to some unevaluated argument slot of the PAS. I will illustrate this process with (3.14) (repeated here):

(3.14)
Naomi wa udon o tabeta.
'Naomi ate udon noodles.'

The constituent structure would be (3.26):

(3.26)
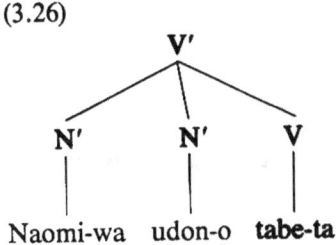

The PAS of *tabe* is (_GA_ _O_ tabe). This, of course, is the representation after the grammatical case-linking rules have operated. Direct Evaluation associates *udon o* with the O argument slot of *tabe*.

(3.27)
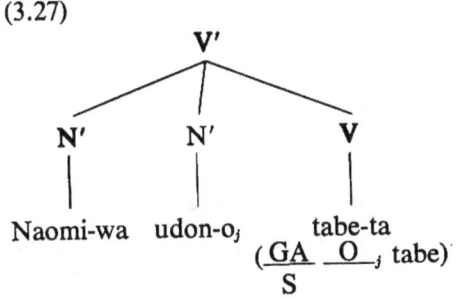

Naomi wa is left over. Predication coindexes *Naomi wa* with the V *tabeta*. Indirect Evaluation now applies. The PAS may take the N'-*wa* index appearing on the verb and assign it to the unevaluated GA argument slot. All overt N's are now associated with argument slots, thanks to Direct and Indirect Evaluation.

Example (3.15) is of a different sort, in that the X'-*wa* ends up not being construed as associated with an argument slot.

(3.15)
Taroo wa Hanako ga   iede-si-ta.
       top   nom leave home-do-past
'As for Taro, Hanako ran away from home.'

The constituent structure for (3.15) would be (3.28):

(3.28)

```
            V'
          / |  \
        N'  N'   V
        |   |    |
     Taroo-wa Hanako-ga iede-si-ta
```

After Direct Evaluation, only *Hanako ga* is associated with an argument slot:

(3.29)

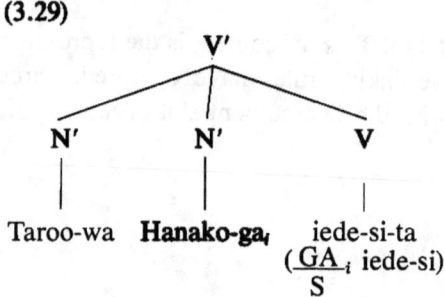

Predication now coindexes *Taroo wa* with the V *iede-si-ta*. There are no unevaluated argument slots in the PAS, so Indirect Evaluation, which is optional, does not take place. (3.30) now has the following indices:

(3.30)

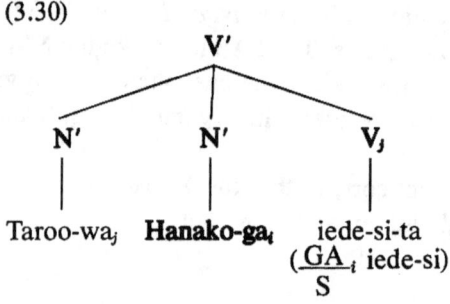

The next task is to assess whether or not the string is odd in any pragmatic sense. Crucially, I am assuming that an inferential system, in the sense of Bach and Harnish (1979) and Harnish (1983),[10] plays an important role from here on. Recall from the introduction that the language system as conceived here utilizes pragmatics that is modular in the sense that the structure of an expression, which is defined by the grammar (narrowly construed), plays a crucial role in determining its literal and direct interpretation; in other words, principles delimiting the literal and direct interpretation of an expression form a part of the language system. The linguistic object, which is defined by the grammar, is in part composed of a syntactic string, the PAS, and the array of indices (i.e., the output of Direct Evaluation, Predication, and Indirect Evaluation). In (3.30) the linguistic object designates that *Taroo wa* is coindexed with the V *iede-si-ta,* but not with an argument position. I suggest that such a situation requires that a pragmatic inference of the following sort be made:

(3.31)
Pragmatic Inference
Given X'-wa_i and V_i, if the speaker is speaking literally and directly, then the PAS of V_i is somehow "relevant" to X'-wa.

As the literature on Japanese richly attests, the possibilities for being "relevant" are enormous. For example, (3.17) (*Hana wa sakura ga i-i*) illustrates that the connection can be that of generic to specific, where N'-*wa* is generic and *sakura ga* is specific. The N'-*wa* and the object (in the nonlinguistic sense) that satisfies an argument position in the PAS are connected via this generic/specific property. Another kind of connection can involve kinship relations. Kitagawa's example (3.15) (*Taroo wa Hanako ga iede-si-ta* 'As for Taro, Hanako ran away from home') can be accounted for in this way. Unlike Kitagawa's proposal, the version of indexing adopted here does not coindex *Taroo wa* with *Hanako ga*. Instead, the pragmatic inference is made that some "connection" must exist between N'-*wa* and the predicate, and one possibility is that the referent of N'-*wa* is related to one of the objects that satisfies an argument position, that is, an object in the world. If Taro is married to Hanako, that would certainly be a sufficient "intrinsic connection" (see Akmajian and Kitagawa (1976) for a discussion of this kind of connection).

Now consider Kitagawa's example (25) (= 3.16)).

(3.16)
Bunmeikoku wa   dansei no heikin zyumyoo ga naga-i.
civilized-nation-top man   's average life-span-nom long-pres
'Civilized countries, their male population's average life span is long.'

Kitagawa coindexes *bunmeikoku wa* 'civilized nation' with *dansei* 'man', saying that "the referent of the target NP is understood, in some relevant sense, to belong to the Topic NP referent . . ." (p. 187). Indeed, there must be some "relevant" connection in order for the sentence not to be pragmatically odd (recall the Pragmatic Inference rule (3.31)). The only sense in which my analysis differs from Kitagawa's involves the claim that there must be a target NP. The question now is whether this connection always involves the referent of some NP-argument. Kitagawa's answer is affirmative: there must be some NP that can be identified as the target NP for Topic Binding. This is not uncontroversial. Kuno (1973, 253), for one, argues that ". . . it is not possible to derive all themes (topics) from nonthematic sentences." From what I have outlined so far, it does not necessarily follow that there must be a target to connect the N'-*wa* and the predicate. The judgments needed to resolve this question are no doubt extremely subtle, and I leave its resolution to those competent to make them.

To sum up: I am not attempting to list all the possible ways an N'-*wa* can be pragmatically related to its predicate (since this could only be done by native speakers of Japanese, if at all). In terms of the linguistic object, what was needed was a way of distinguishing between X'-*was* that end up being coindexed with an argument slot of a predicate and X'-*was* that are simply coindexed with the verb—a distinction I have characterized with indices. In effect, I have broken Kitagawa's Topic Binding rule into two parts. First, when the referent of an X'-*wa* satisfies an argument slot, Predication and Indirect Evaluation take place. Second, any X'-*wa* that is merely coindexed with the V falls under the Pragmatic Inference rule (3.31); this rule requires that a connection be made between X'-*was* and the predicate, connections involving such notions as kinship relations, which in turn involve beliefs and knowledge of the world. A breakdown at this second stage—in other words, failure to make a relevant connection—yields not an "ungrammatical" sentence but a pragmatic oddity.

Let us now consider *tough* sentences.[11] It appears that when *yasu-i* 'easy' or *niku-i* 'difficult' attaches to a verb, *ga* can be attached to any constituent. The question that arises is, What is the status of the *ga-*

marked phrase? As we have seen in chapter 2, *ga* often marks the subject argument slot, though this need not be the case. The traditional tests for "subjecthood" fail in the *yasu-i/niku-i* examples. That is, in such sentences X'-*ga* cannot necessarily be an antecedent for *zibun* 'self' and does not trigger Subject Honorification. A fair generalization concerning this construction is that any element—adverbial, P', N', etc.—can be marked *ga*. The X'-*ga* does not have to be an argument of the verb. I am claiming that this property of X'-*ga* parallels what was found in the topic and X'-*wa* constructions.

I will assume, as does Tomoda (1982), that -*yasu* is attached to a verb via word formation in the lexicon. For example, -*yasu* can attach to the verb *yom*, yielding *yomiyasu*. The argument structure is not changed; that is, no arguments are added or deleted.

(3.32)
($\underline{\quad\quad} \underline{\quad\quad}$ yom)
 S

(3.33)
(($\underline{\quad\quad} \underline{\quad\quad}$ yom) yasu)
  S

Next, -*yasu* triggers a rule of *NI* Case Linking (a version of which can be found in Tomoda (1982)).

(3.34)
NI Linking
Link leftmost argument slot: $\underline{\text{NI}}$

This linking rule can be viewed as operating like the other semantic linking rules discussed in chapter 2. It applies before Regular Case Linking. Its output is shown in (3.35).

(3.35)
(($\underline{\text{NI}}$ $\underline{\quad\quad}$ yom) yasu)
   S

This PAS is now subject to Regular Case Linking (2.94). Since the leftmost 'S' argument slot of *yomiyasu-* is already marked, it cannot be marked GA by part (a) of Regular Case Linking. Part (b) marks the rightmost argument slot O, and part (c) (Elsewhere link: $\underline{\text{NI}}$) is inapplicable. All argument slots of the PAS are now specified for case:

(3.36)
(($\underline{\text{NI}}$ $\underline{\text{O}}$ yom) yasu)
   S

This is the PAS that will undergo evaluation. We will now see how (3.18b) is interpreted using the PAS in (3.36).

(3.18)
b. Gakusei-tati ni (totte) kono hon ga   yomi-yasu-i.
    student-pl-dat   this book-nom read-easy-pres
   'This book is easy for the students to read.'

The structure associated with (3.18b) is (3.37):

(3.37)

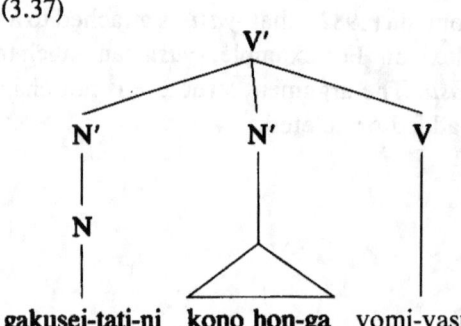

After Direct Evaluation, only *gakusei-tati ni* is associated with an argument slot, since it is the only N' that has a corresponding identically case-marked argument slot in the PAS. The structure following Direct Evaluation is (3.38).

(3.38)

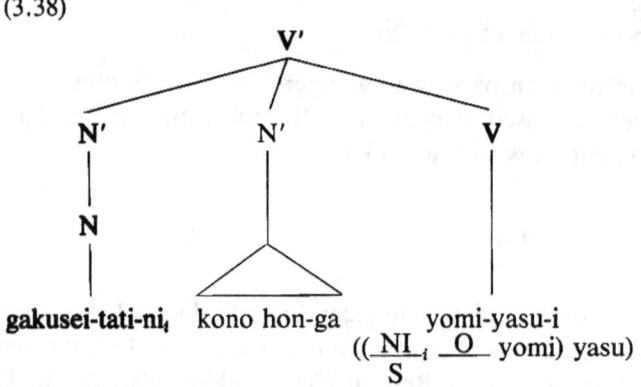

Kono hon ga, on the other hand, is not associated with an argument slot, since there is no available argument specified for GA. Predication now applies, to "coindex X'-*ga/wa* with V":

Modular Theory: Japanese

(3.39)

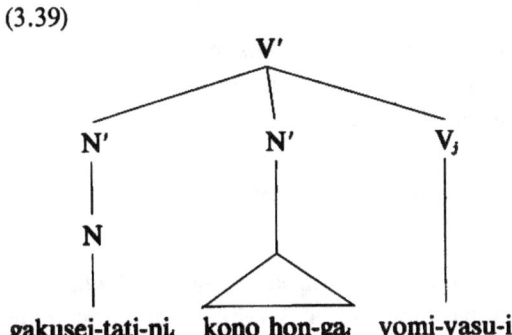

gakusei-tati-ni$_i$ kono hon-ga$_j$ yomi-yasu-i

The predicate V-*yasu* triggers Indirect Evaluation under the following condition:

(3.40)
Indirect Evaluation of an X'-ga
Given an X'-*ga* whose index is assigned to V, the index may be used for any unevaluated argument slot.
(Note: Any predicate may use X'-*wa* for the purposes of Indirect Evaluation.)

(3.41)

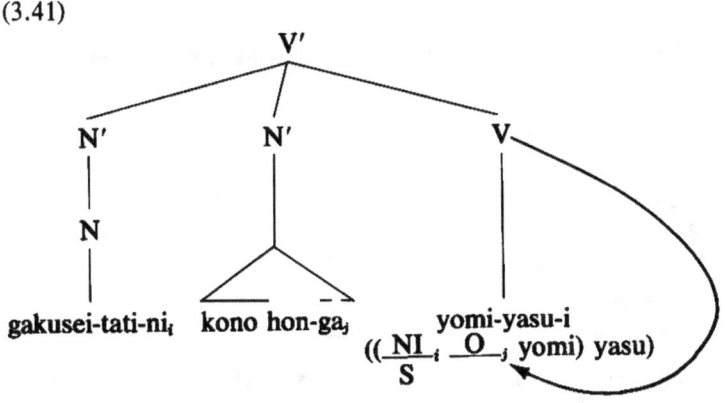

The next example raises the question of how to handle the evaluation of postpositional phrases.

(3.19)
a. John ga   kono tosyokan kara hon o   nusum-u.
       nom   this library-from book-acc steal-pres
   'John steals books from this library.'

b. Kono tosyokan (kara) ga hon o   nusumi-niku-i.
   this library-(from)-nom book-acc steal-hard-pres
   'This library is hard to steal books from.'

How the postposition phrase in (3.19a) is directly evaluated will determine just how Indirect Evaluation works in (3.19b). After Direct Evaluation, (3.19b) would have the structure (3.42):

(3.42)

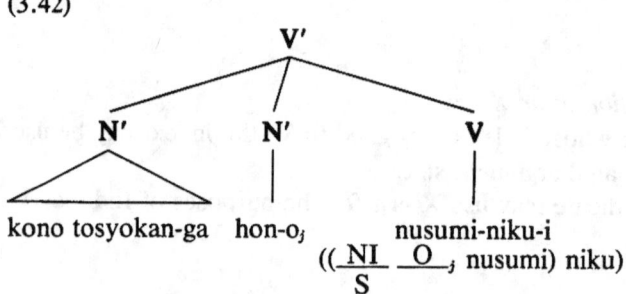

Next Predication coindexes *kono tosyokan ga* with the V *nusumi-niku-i*.

(3.43)

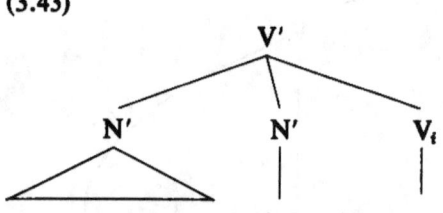

kono tosyokan-ga$_i$ hon-o$_j$ nusumi-niku-i

Indirect Evaluation *optionally* uses the index on the V *nusumi-niku-i*. If this index is associated with the NI argument slot, then the sentence receives the interpretation, roughly, that 'it is difficult for this library to steal books'. This raises questions concerning "overgeneration" and "nonliterality" to which I return in section 3.6. In order to receive the interpretation associated with the translation in (3.19b), *kono tosyokan ga$_i$* must be construed with the PP *kara*. Tentatively, I propose that when a PAS is accessed, an array of PPs associated with the PAS is also accessed and that these PPs may be targeted for the purposes of Indirect Evaluation. (See Kitagawa (1982) for a different approach to these questions.) I will represent this as shown in (3.44):

(3.44)

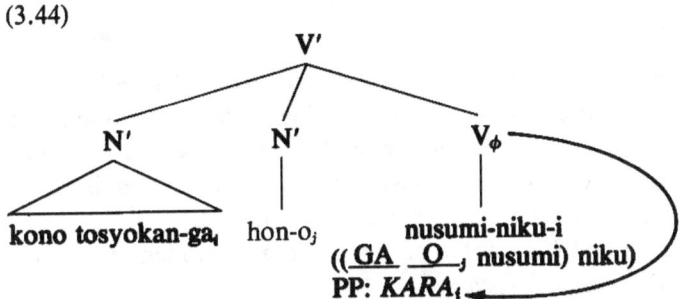

In (3.44) the GA argument slot is unevaluated and is interpreted as "arbitrary," that is, 'this library is hard *for one* to steal books from'.

Example (3.20b) illustrates that time adverbials may also appear marked with *ga*.

(3.20)
a. Kim ga   asahayaku   benkyoosu-ru.
   Kim-nom early in the morning   study-pres
   'Kim studies early in the morning.'
b. Asahayaku ga   (suzusi-i node)   benkyoosi-yasu-i.
   early in the morning-nom cool-pres because study-easy-pres
   'It is easy/easier to study early in the morning, because it is cool.'

After Direct Evaluation, Predication, and (vacuously) Indirect Evaluation have applied, none of the argument slots of the V *benkyoosi-yasu-i* has been indexed, and *asahayaku ga* has been coindexed with the V. The Pragmatic Inference rule (3.31) now applies, basically calling for the inference to be made that the predicate is somehow relevant to *asahayaku* 'early in the morning'.[12]

Finally, let us consider indirect passives. Section 2.2.2 reviewed two accounts of the indirect versus the direct passive, the uniform hypothesis (Howard and Niyekawa-Howard) and the nonuniform hypothesis (Kuno). Both hypotheses claim that the indirect passive involves embedding, *-rare* being viewed as a matrix verb that has its own subject. The motivation behind this kind of representation is to handle the ambiguity in (2.20b) (repeated here).

(3.45)
John$_i$ wa Mary$_j$ ni zibun$_{i,j}$ no koto o zimans-(r)are-ta.
　　　 top　　　 dat　 self　 's　 matter-acc boast-passive-past
'John suffered from Mary's bragging about (lit.) self's matter.'

Zibun can be interpreted as anaphorically related to either *John* or *Mary*. This is of course based on the widely accepted assumption that there is a "subjecthood" requirement for the antecedent of *zibun*. That is, if the antecedent of *zibun* must be a subject and if *John* is a potential antecedent, then *John* must be a subject; and since *John* occurs when -*rare* is attached (i.e., there seems to be a dependency there), *John* must be the subject of -*rare*.

Though the level of representation differed, this complex structure for indirect passives was used in Farmer (1980). I assumed there that when -*rare* was attached, an argument was added as well (the example is from p. 89):

(3.46)
(___ (___) rare)

The (___) stands for the PAS of the verb to which -*rare* is attached. In Farmer (1980) the leftmost argument—i.e., the subject of -*rare*—received nominative case, and the second argument received dative case. However, Oehrle and Nishio (1981) suggest that this approach to the construction is wrong. Indeed, they state (p. 170) that

the basic difference between the "direct" passive and the "indirect" passive is that in the former the referent of the passive subject is directly involved in the represented state-of-affairs, whereas in the latter, since the subject NP plays no role in the argument structure of the verb from which *V-(r)are* is derived, this need not be the case.

I will leave the *zibun*-antecedent question for the moment, intending to return to it later. In the meantime, I propose a speculative answer to Oehrle and Nishio's question (pp. 163–164), "How is the noun phrase whose referent is taken to be adversely affected integrated compositionally with the structure of the rest of the sentence?"

Turning to example (3.21), I will assume that after word formation the PAS of *sinare* is as follows:

(3.47)
(($\underset{S}{\_\_\_}$ sin) are)

Modular Theory: Japanese

The morpheme *-are* assigns NI to the subject argument slot, as in (3.48a); this is an instance of semantic linking.[13] The syntactic string associated with (3.21) would be (3.48b).

(3.48)
a. ((NI sin) are)
       S

b.

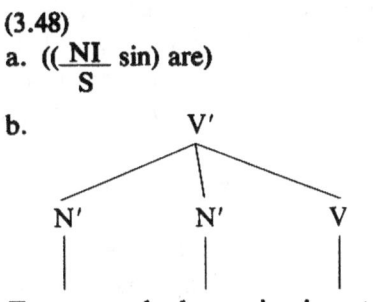

Taroo-wa kodomo-ni sinareta

After Direct Evaluation, *kodomo ni* is coindexed with the NI-marked argument slot.

(3.49)

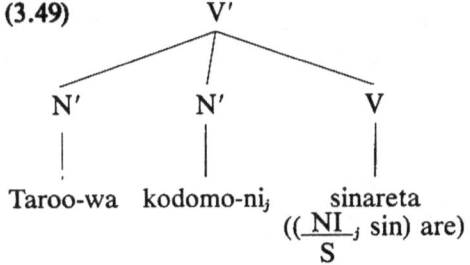

Taroo-wa kodomo-ni$_j$ sinareta
                   ((NI_j sin) are)
                      S

Next, Predication coindexes *Taroo wa* and the V *sinareta*. There is no argument slot that *Taroo wa* can be associated with. This situation is quite similar to what was found in the *tough* sentences and other topic constructions. Next the Pragmatic Inference rule (3.31) states that the predicate, *sinareta*, is somehow "relevant" to *Taroo wa*. Oehrle and Nishio (1981) discuss the adversity construction, noting that two elements (which they call *x* (in this case *Taroo wa*) and *y* (*kodomo ni*)) must be somehow related. They say (p. 165),

> Consider a situation in which *x* stands in some relation R to *y*, which we shall denote by writing "xRy", and some event E occurs in which *y* undergoes a change of state of some kind, which we shall denote by, $y \xrightarrow{E} y'$, a consequence of this change of state is that *x* no longer stands in relation to *y*, but rather to *y'* as in $xRy \xrightarrow{E} xRy'$.

The situation they are describing involves saying that the predicate is somehow relevant to *x* (or *Taroo wa*), with an elaboration on the consequences of this relationship. Predication sets up the following relation: the predicate is relevant to X'-*wa*/*ga*. In the adversity construction, just as in the *tough* construction, there is an elaboration on this relationship. Clearly, it must be determined just how X'-*wa* can be related to the predicate, in all the constructions we have been discussing. Establishing the relationship involves knowledge of the world and not linguistic knowledge. Linguistic information can involve an elaboration on the relation, i.e., coindexing. For example, the *tough* construction involves a morpheme such as -*yasu* 'easy', which contributes to the interpretation of the X'-*ga*, for example, *That X'-ga/wa is easy for y* . . .

The indirect passive construction raises the same question that we encountered with respect to the topic construction, namely, must there be a single argument in the PAS that alone is relevant to X'-*ga/wa*? Recall Kitagawa's claim that the topic construction must contain a particular argument that links to the topic-*wa*. However, Oehrle and Nishio (1981, 175) notice, for indirect passives at least, that ". . . it is not clear that we can find an expression in the sentence whose referent stands in such a relation to the subject." Their statement refers to examples like (3.50) and (3.51) (= their (41) and (42)).

(3.50)
Taroo wa ame ga hur-are-ta.
      top rain-nom fall-passive-past
'Taro had it rain on him.'

(3.51)
Taroo wa Hanako ni piano o hik-are-ta. (= (3.25))
      top   dat piano-acc play-passive-past
'Hanako played the piano and Taro suffered.'

It is not at all clear that any single N' in the sentence is alone relevant to *Taroo wa*. Each example mentioned earlier in this section demonstrates a slightly different relationship. In (3.22) the referent of *Taroo wa* is the owner of the watch, *tokei o*, which was broken, so the relationship is one of ownership. In (3.23) the relationship is that the object being wiped by the nurse is a body part of the referent of *kanzya wa* 'patient'. Example (3.24) also involves a body part. (3.51) could possibly involve a number of situations, as Oehrle and Nishio point out (p. 171):

(i) In a competition, Hanako got to play instead of Taro and thus Taro was jealous of his competitor; (ii) Taro had his delicate piano ruined because Hanako played it; (iii) Taro experienced great pain in hearing the noises Hanako produced at the piano.

Situations (i) and (iii) involve something more than simply *Taroo wa* as being in relation to *piano o* or *Hanako ni*.

Looking back over this discussion of topic constructions, *tough* sentences, and indirect passives, we can see a common thread that runs through them. Every case involves applying the Predication rule (3.13), that is, coindexing an X'-*ga/wa* with the head V. These X'-*ga/wa*s are in a sense "extra NPs." That is, after Direct Evaluation there are X's left over. Indirect Evaluation is employed to link these "extra NPs" with unevaluated argument slots. The Pragmatic Inference rule (3.31) applies when Indirect Evaluation has not. We have seen cases in which an extra X'-*wa* coindexed with V has been subject to the Pragmatic Inference rule, but not instances of X'-*ga*. The theory being developed here, then, predicts that we should find X'-*ga*s that are coindexed with V and never coindexed with an argument slot. It is to such cases that I now turn.

3.4.4 An Analogue to Move α

What seems to be emerging here is the Japanese analogue to Move α. The "movement" metaphor in Japanese is extended to cases where an X' is associated with an argument slot via Predication and Indirect Evaluation. That is, the particle attached to the X' is not the same as the one associated with the argument slot the X' is linked to. In some instances this looks like particle "changing," for example, deleting *o* and adding *ga*. It is not surprising that Japanese should use the case particles rather than position to juxtapose the entire predicate with some entity, since it is the case particles and not position that are relevant for evaluation. For English, in chapter 4, I will use a Predication rule that does something different: it coindexes according to position and not case. Unlike previous analyses, the analysis of *tough* sentences that I have given does not involve changing grammatical relations (cf. Saito (1981)). Notice that the indexing relation is set up regardless of the form of the verb. That is, X'-*ga/wa* is coindexed with the verb without first analyzing the morphological composition of the verb. This procedure is generalized to handle not only topic sentences but also *tough* sentences and indirect passives. The considerable generality of this procedure implies that there should be sentences that have an "extra" X'-*ga* but no -*yasu* or -*niku* suffixed to the verb. In fact such sentences do exist, and they are well known: namely, examples that are often referred to as involving *multiple subjects*. The following sentences are from Kuno (1973, 67, 69)):

(3.52)
a. Kono class wa dansei ga yoku dekiru.
   this   male   well are-able
   'Speaking of this class, the boys do well.'
   (*dansei ga:* exhaustive listing and neutral description)

   b. Kono class ga dansei ga yoku dekiru.
      'It is this class that the boys do well in.'
      (*dansei ga:* neutral description)

(3.53)
a. Nihon wa dansei ga tanmei   desu.
   Japan   male   short-life-span are
   'Speaking of Japan, men have a short life span.'
   (*dansei ga:* exhaustive listing and neutral description)

   b. Nihon ga dansei ga tanmei desu.
      'It is Japan that men have a short life span in.'
      (*dansei ga:* neutral description)

(3.54)
a. John no otoosan ga sinda.
       's father   died
   (i) 'John's father died.'
   (ii) 'It is John's father that has died.'

   b. John ga otoosan ga sinda.
      'It is John whose father died.'

(3.55)
a. Yama   no ki ga kirei desu.
   mountain 's trees pretty are
   (i) 'It is trees in the mountains that are pretty.'
   (ii) '(Look!) The trees in the mountains are pretty.'

   b. Yama ga ki ga kirei desu.
      (i) 'It is the mountains that trees are pretty in.'
      (ii) '(Look!) The mountains—their trees are pretty.'

To handle these sentences and the topic construction, Kuno proposes a set of ordered rules: *Subjectivization, Marking for Exhaustive Listing,* and *Thematization*. I quote his formulation of these rules from (1973, 71) (square brackets are his):

(3.56)
a. *Subjectivization* (tentative formulation) [optional]: Change the sentence-initial NP-*no* to NP-*ga*, and make it the new subject of the sentence.
b. *Marking for Exhaustive Listing* [obligatory for the matrix sentence]:
If the predicate of a sentence represents a state or a habitual/generic action, and if the sentence-initial NP-*ga* does not contain a numeral or quantifier, mark that NP-*ga* as [+exhaustive listing].
c. *Thematization* [optional]:
Add *wa* to an NP + *particle,* and prepose the NP + *particle* + *wa* to the beginning of the sentence.

Multiple subjects, in the present theory, would simply be a case of extra N'-*ga*s that are coindexed with the head V. Such an account would avoid the well-known problems connected with deriving all cases of multiple subjects from an underlying N'-*no* N'-*ga* (cf. Nishio (1982)).

I have not attempted to account for all the subtleties connected with the interpretation of *tough* sentences,[14] the topic construction, indirect passives, and multiple subjects. Rather, I have tried to explore the possibility that, given a modular view, these constructions might all involve some common procedure(s). In the past, attempts were made to relate constructions via derivations, one sentence type being derived from another sentence type. Here I am saying that different sentence types may involve some of the same procedures, but not that one sentence is derived from another.

3.5 Anaphora

I now return to the anaphoric interpretation of *zibun* 'self', specifically, and to anaphora in general. This section is intentionally programmatic. I will outline what I see as a plausible course of investigation, an investigation that can only be carried out in detail by a native speaker. In chapter 5 I will work out a similar program for English, carrying the analysis further than I can here for Japanese. In section 3.5.1 I briefly review previous accounts of *zibun* and then present an alternative approach. In section 3.5.2 I discuss the cases of *null-anaphora*, reviewing previous accounts and once again offering an alternative approach.

3.5.1 Zibun

The earliest accounts of *zibun* (references to which are found in chapter 2) involved a reflexivization transformation that was regulated by a subject-antecedent condition; that is, the antecedent had to be a subject in order to trigger the rule. Such an approach to the anaphoric interpretation of *zibun* went the way of the "pronominalization" transformation of English (on the latter case, see chapter 5). That is, the reflexivization rule was abandoned in favor of a *zibun* interpretation rule, of which Inoue (1976) gives one version.[15] The *zibun* interpretation rule which is defined over a syntactic level of representation (i.e., surface structure), is sensitive to various conditions. Below are several of these conditions, which are taken from Inoue (1976, 118) (examples (3.60) and (3.61) are also from Inoue (1976, 163)):

I. The antecedent must be [+human].

(3.57)
Taroo$_i$ wa zibun$_i$ no gareezi no hoo e hasiridasita.
                  garage of   towards start to run
'Taro started to run towards his (self's) garage.'

(3.58)
a. *Kuruma$_i$ wa zibun$_i$ no gareezi no hoo e hasiridasita.
   'The car started to run towards self's garage.'

b. Kuruma wa gareezi no hoo e hasiridasita.
   'The car started to run towards the garage.'

II. The antecedent must be a S(ubject).

(3.59)
a. Taroo$_i$ wa kodomo o zibun$_i$ no kutu de butta.
              child   shoe with hit
   'Taro hit the child with self's shoe.'

b. *Taroo wa kodomo$_j$ o zibun$_j$. no kutu de butta.

III. The antecedent and the reflexive do not have to be clausemates.

(3.60)
Taroo$_i$ ga Hanako ni zibun$_i$ ga Amerika e it-ta koto o
              to   to go-past that
hanas-anakat-ta.
tell-neg-past
'Taro did not tell Hanako that he had been to the States.'

IV. Zibun *cannot command the phrase which contains the antecedent.*

(3.61)
*Taroo$_i$ ga kai-ta hon ga zibun$_i$ o yorokob-ase-ta.
            write-past book   pleased-cause-past
*'The book Taro wrote pleased himself.'

The condition that the antecedent must be [+human] raises an interesting question: how is such a condition incorporated? Inoue (1976) includes the condition in the rule that is defined over syntactic structure. Example (3.58) is starred because *kuruma* 'car' is not [+human], and *zibun* therefore cannot be construed as anaphorically related to *kuruma*. But this seems to predict that if a speaker were using *kuruma* in this example to refer to a person (say, a car fanatic) then the speaker, when speaking nonliterally, would be using an ungrammatical sentence. However, this is counterintuitive. The following example illustrates that these concerns are justified:

(3.62)
"The atmosphere, as always, is casual. The woman who has as her bailiwick *Planes and Trains* is describing how a Washington hostess organizes the dinner parties for which she is universally famous.

'. . . You'll distribute the list in-house,' [says another character], 'to the section chiefs, who will start to run down the confirmations.'

'Sounds simple enough,' says *Planes and Trains*."

Robert Littel, the Debriefing, pp. 65, 67

Literally *Planes and Trains* can't say anything, but a contextually appropriate inference can be made that *Planes and Trains* is being used to refer to the woman whose "bailiwick" is *Planes and Trains*. We can conclude, then, that (3.58) is not "ungrammatical." However, if (3.58) is being used *literally*, it would appear to involve a semantic oddity: if *kuruma* 'car' is the antecedent for *zibun*, and the antecedent of *zibun* must be [+human], then this *entails* that *kuruma* is [+human]. Since one of the entailments of "is a car" is plausibly [−human], the semantic oddity results.[16]

The second condition, that the antecedent must be a S(ubject), appears to hold generally. However, there are cases where a "nonsubject" can be an antecedent and other cases where the matrix subject cannot be the antecedent.[17] (The following examples are from Inoue (1976, 132, 134, 148).)

I. *"Demoted" Subject can be an antecedent.*

(3.63)
a. Oyazi$_i$ wa boku$_j$ ni zibun$_{i,j}$ no kuruma o araw-ase-ta.
   Dad   I   self's   car   wash-cause-past
   'Dad$_i$ made me$_j$ wash self's$_{i,j}$ car.'

b. Boku$_j$ wa oyazi$_i$ ni zibun$_{j(i)}$ no kuruma o araw-ase-rare-ta.
   'I$_j$ was made to wash self's$_{j(i)}$ car by Dad$_i$.'

II. *Matrix Subjects that cannot be antecedents.*

(3.64)
*John$_i$ wa, Mary ga zibun$_i$ ni ai   ni kita   toki moo
                     self   with meet to come-past when already
sinde imasita.
dead be-past
'John, when Mary came to see him, was already dead.'

(3.65)
*John$_i$ wa Mary ga zibun$_i$ o miru toki wa itu mo kaoiro ga
                    self   see when   always complexion
warui soo da.
bad   I hear
'I hear that John looks pale whenever Mary sees him.'

(3.66)
*John$_i$ wa zibun$_i$ ga sinda toki, issen mo motte imasen desita yo.
            self   died when a penny have not   did
'John didn't have a penny when he died.'

(3.67)
*John$_i$ wa zibun$_i$ ga yopparatta toki dake, watasi ni yasasiku
            self   drunk-is   when only I   to kindly
narimasu.
become
'John becomes tender to me only when he gets drunk.'

The approach I am advocating might at first appear to be counterintuitive. I propose keeping the subject-antecedent condition as a *sufficient* condition, using the 'S' diacritic to identify these subjects. This is weaker than saying that it is a necessary condition. The remaining questions to be answered are (i) what other conditions are sufficient and (ii) under what conditions are sufficient conditions, like the subject-antecedent condition, overridden? My claim is that any satisfactory answer to these questions would involve a modular account; that is, there are generalizations to be stated at the lexical and the syntactic levels of representation. The lexical level (the PAS) is important for identifying the subject, whereas the syntactic level is important for stating condition IV, the command condition. The fact that the antecedent of *zibun* must be [+human] (or apparently some "higher" animal like *inu* 'dog') does not, for example, govern any mechanisms defined over the syntactic level of representation, though it certainly does play a role in forcing the antecedent to be construed as [+human]. And it may very well be that pragmatic inferences can appear to "override" semantic, lexical, or syntactic principles and conditions. Successfully characterizing *zibun* within this general framework is not a trivial task. I am suggesting that intuitions concerning possible antecedents of *zibun* in any given instance are a collection of facts, principles, and conditions relevant to different levels of representation. That is, there is no rule defined over a *single* level of representation that will succeed in capturing these intuitions. Furthermore, we cannot have access to the nature of these intuitions—intuitions that "x is a syntactic fact," "y is a lexical fact," etc. With this general picture in mind, let us turn to the question of null-anaphora.

3.5.2 Null-Anaphora

It is crucial to note at the outset that I have not been assuming the existence of a syntactic entity PRO.[18] This is significant because Oshima (1979) suggests that accounting for cases of disjoint reference requires a rule stated over a syntactic structure that includes the entity PRO, subjecting this PRO, like other NPs, to a Disjoint Reference rule.[19] The proposal offered in Farmer (1980) involved utilizing a version of Oshima's Disjoint Reference rule that was defined over the PAS. The proposal amounted to saying that arguments of a predicate are disjoint. Washio (1981, 129) has challenged this claim.

[Farmer (1980)] . . . says that the missing object in (185) *Taroo-ga mi-ta*, lit: 'Taro saw.' cannot refer to *Taroo*[20] and that the rule of Disjoint Reference applies to specify that *O*-marked argument cannot refer to *GA*-marked argument.

However, this analysis is not tenable simply because (186) is unacceptable as an independent sentence.[21]

(186) *Taroo-ga mita.
'Taro saw.'

This may be acceptable only as an answer to such questions as

(187) Dare ga Ziroo o mitaka?
'Who saw Jiro?'

But in that case, (186) is also acceptable as an answer to (188).

(188) Dare ga zibun o mitaka?
'Who saw himself?'

Here, the missing NP in (186) corresponds to *zibun* and therefore must refer to *Taroo* . . .

My explanation of the above examples illustrates clearly what I mean by a modular account of anaphora. Washio's example (186) involves a predicate with two argument slots. These argument slots, I claimed in Farmer (1980), are subject to a Disjoint Reference rule stating basically that the arguments that satisfy them are to be construed as disjoint. However, by pointing out that (186) can be an acceptable answer to (188), Washio demonstrates that this condition can be overridden by a contextually appropriate inference. Such examples can be found in English. For instance, it is claimed that the pronoun in (3.68) is disjoint in reference from *Tom*.

(3.68)
He likes Tom.

However, an appropriate context can override this disjointness property:

(3.69)
a. Question: Does Tom like anyone?
b. Answer: Well, he likes Tom.

There is no doubt that *he* and *Tom* can be used to refer to the same individual. However, I do not conclude from this that there is no principle of disjointness. In fact, I find it a virtue of the theory that the two cases are treated differently, receiving both a disjoint (3.68) and a coreferential (3.69) interpretation. In chapter 5 I will return to the anaphora question. For English, I spell out the difference between (intended) speaker reference and linguistically triggered referential presumptions, a distinction that is important in handling the kinds of points brought out by linguists such as Washio for Japanese and Evans (1980) for English.

3.6 Overgeneration

Overgeneration appears to be endemic to the modular theory. For example, since Direct Evaluation, Predication, and Indirect Evaluation do not examine the semantic properties of the X'-ga/wa (i.e., whether or not the N'-wa "is animate"), it is entirely possible that the following sentence would be sanctioned:

(3.70)
Kono hon wa Hanako o mita.
'This book saw Hanako.'

As mentioned earlier, however, I do not want to rule out the possibility that words can be used nonliterally. I am relying on the characterization of "oddities" to be the result of ". . . the interplay of independently motivated levels each of which *by itself* would make false predictions about the nonoddity of the examples in its domain" (Harnish (1982, 10)). Harnish continues, ". . . 'overgeneration' is to be *expected* in a modular theory, because each module must be as *general* as possible, with other modules acting as constraints . . ." With this in mind, I close this chapter with a general picture of the organization of the grammar as described so far (figure 3.1), and then turn to consider English in chapters 4 and 5.

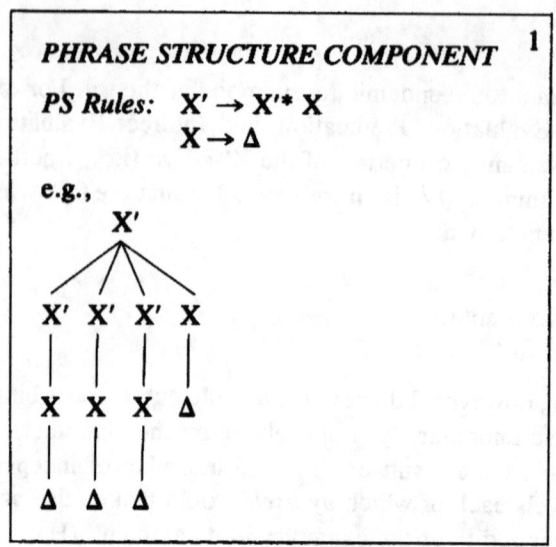

Provides syntactic structures

Lexical insertion
and feature climbing

(any order;
i.e., Scrambling)

Example:

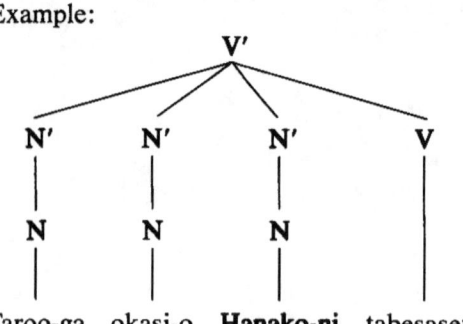

Taroo-ga okasi-o **Hanako-ni** tabesaseta

Figure 3.1
A tentative model of the language system (Japanese)

Modular Theory: Japanese   107

```
┌─────────────────────────────────────────────────┬──────────────────┐
│  LEXICAL COMPONENT                              │               2  │
│                                                 │  PRINCIPLES:     │
│   ┌─────────────────────────────────────┐       │  a. 'S' Assignment│
│   │  PERMANENT LEXICON                  │       │     Principle    │
│   │  Contains:                          │       │                  │
│   │  a. List of nondecomposable items   │       │                  │
│   │  b. Lexical entries (e.g., PASs)    │       │                  │
│   │  c. Device of semantic linking      │       │                  │
│   │     (e.g., kara, ni)                │       │                  │
│   └─────────────────────────────────────┘       │                  │
│                     ↓                           │                  │
│   ┌─────────────────────────────────────┐       │                  │
│   │  Principles of WORD FORMATION       │       │                  │
│   │  and operations on PASs             │       │                  │
│   └─────────────────────────────────────┘       │                  │
│                     ↓                           │                  │
│   ┌─────────────────────────────────────┐       │                  │
│   │  REGULAR CASE LINKING RULES         │       │                  │
│   │  e.g., ( GA , NI , O )              │       │                  │
│   │  e.g., ( GA ( NI   O  tabe) sase)   │       │                  │
│   │         S    S                      │       │                  │
│   └─────────────────────────────────────┘       │                  │
└─────────────────────────────────────────────────┴──────────────────┘
```

Provides PAS (P1.
Predicate Argument Principle)

Example: $(\underset{S}{GA}_i (\underset{S}{NI}_j \ O_k \ tabe) \ sase)$

Figure 3.1
(continued)

Modularity in Syntax 108

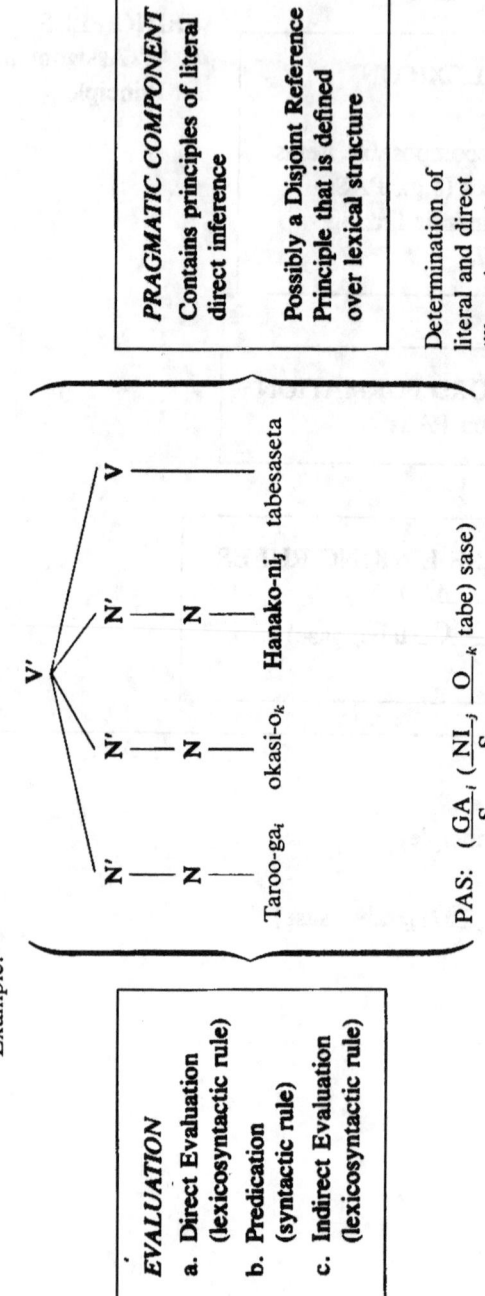

Figure 3.1
(continued)

Chapter 4
Extending the Modular Theory: English

In this chapter I will explore the consequences for English of the category-neutral theory of the base. My approach to English will be similar to the approach I have taken to Japanese. That is, I will assume that lexical insertion is context free, involving only replacing the terminal node Δ, and that the rules that define hierarchical structure do only that and nothing more. For my analysis of English I draw heavily from Chomsky (1981b) and Williams (1980) for many insights. One goal will be to account for the occurrence of the subject in English: the occurrence/nonoccurrence of an overt (phonologically realized) subject will be accounted for by case theory and evaluation.[1] Another goal is to develop an account of control phenomena without positing a syntactic entity PRO.[2] Both tasks are formidable, since I will not be relying on the phrase structure rules to designate subject as obligatory. The result will be a proposal concerning the nature of the interaction of the syntactic and lexical components. The nature of the rules mediating between the syntax and the lexicon will necessarily be different in some respects from those found in Japanese, due in part to the "configurational/nonconfigurational" distinction drawn between English and Japanese.[3]

4.1 Aspects and Components of the Grammar

I will be assuming that syntactic position plays an important role in English. Following Chomsky and others, I will define "subject" as [NP, S], object as [NP, VP], etc. I am also assuming that grammatical relations in English are syntactically encoded, contrary to the situation in Japanese. Recall that in Japanese, case particles are the crucial elements for associating overt N's with argument positions in the PAS. In English, a "configurational" language, structural position plays an important role in the vocabulary of the rules that mediate between the syntax and the lexical structure.

4.1.1 Evaluation: Syntactic and Lexical Sanctioning

In this section a distinction will be more fully developed for English between syntactic and lexical sanctioning. By *sanction* I mean that some element allows or permits a syntactic entity to occur. Syntactic sanctioning is carried out by way of case assignment, whereas lexical sanctioning requires affiliation with an argument slot and is executed by way of evaluation. Furthermore, NPs must be syntactically sanctioned in order to be lexically sanctioned,[4] and all syntactic or overt elements that are not pleonastic elements must be lexically sanctioned. That is, an NP that is either a denoting expression or a variable-binding NP (an NP containing a variable binder) must be both lexically and syntactically sanctioned. I will assume for the time being, following Chomsky (1981b), that something in INFL assigns nominative case to the subject,[5] the verb assigns accusative case to the object, and prepositions assign oblique case to their objects. The case assigner is the *governor* (Chomsky's (1981b) term), and the governor c-commands the element to which it assigns case:

(4.1)
John loves Mary.[6]

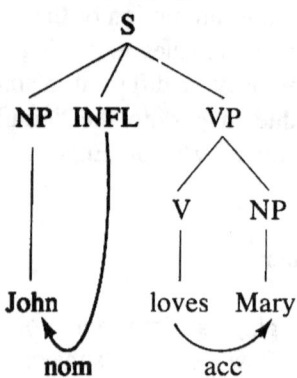

Both *John* and *Mary* are syntactically sanctioned; that is, both have case. We must turn to the lexical entry of the verb *love* in order to associate *John* and *Mary* with argument slots; this again involves the process of evaluation (coindexing an overt NP with an argument posi-

Modular Theory: English

tion in a PAS). The rules that mediate between the syntactic string and lexical structure to carry out the evaluation are called *lexicosyntactic rules*. These rules, which involve assigning an index to an argument slot, thus identifying it with an overt element, are either *direct* or *indirect*. Direct Evaluation involves the c-command domain of the constituent in question, as for Japanese. In the case of the verb, for example, its complements are directly evaluated. Indirect Evaluation involves taking an index (assigned via a rule of Predication)[7] from a projection of the constituent in question (say, the verb) and associating that index with an *unevaluated argument slot* (any argument slot that has no index after Direct Evaluation). After both Direct and Indirect Evaluation have applied, the representation of (4.1) will include the following information:

(4.2)

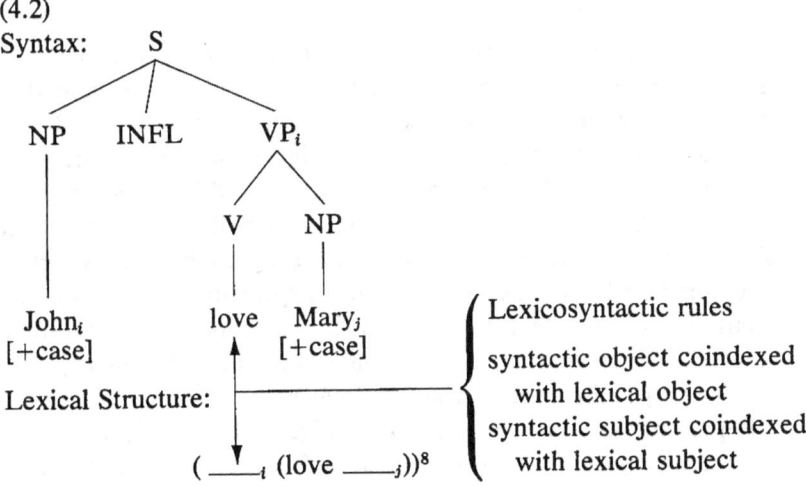

The indices on the [NP, S] and the VP are assigned by the above-mentioned general rule of Predication, to be discussed in more detail later. Thus, *Mary* has been directly evaluated and *John* has been indirectly evaluated. The interpretation of (4.1) has been successfully completed; that is, all overt NPs have been associated with an argument slot. What would happen if (for example) *John* did not have case? *John* would not be "visible" for the purposes of evaluation; it would therefore not be associated with an argument slot and as a result would not be lexically sanctioned.[9] In Chomsky (1981b) this would constitute a violation of the θ-Criterion.[10]

4.1.2 Case versus θ-Roles: The θ-Criterion and Projection Principle Revisited

We will be pursuing the notion that certain elements in the syntax (case assigners) provide the first step toward sanctioning an overt, phonologically realized NP (or entity) (an idea borrowed from Chomsky (1981a,b)). θ-roles, one could say, are argument slots in a PAS, nothing more. "Arguments" in a PAS *only* "show up" (i.e., are reflected) in the syntactic domain if they are sanctioned by case. This is, of course, incompatible with the θ-Criterion (4.3) (Chomsky (1981b, 36)) *if* by using the term "argument" one is referring to an NP, i.e., a syntactic entity in the traditional sense.

(4.3)
Each argument bears one and only one θ-role, and each θ-role is assigned to one and only one argument.

But if "argument" is taken to mean argument *slot* (in the sense of note 2), then the θ-Criterion is not incompatible with the modular theory being articulated here, but irrelevant to it, since this theory does not use the notion of θ-role. It does not assign θ-roles to argument slots. However, one is led to believe that Chomsky (1981b) uses "argument" in the former sense when he states (p. 35) that NPs like "... *the man, John, he* are assigned θ-roles, that is, are assigned the status of terms in a thematic relation. Let us call such expressions 'arguments' ..." Thus, it does seem that the proposal made here is at variance with any analogue of the θ-Criterion in Modular Grammar (MG) theory.[11]

Chomsky's Projection Principle (1981b, 29) roughly dictates that "Representations at each syntactic level (i.e., LF, and D- and S-structure) are projected from the lexicon, in that they observe the subcategorization properties of lexical items.[12]

Both of these principles appear to require that all three syntactic levels reveal or reflect all the argument slots of the predicate. The position taken here is weaker. The syntax corresponds *in part* to the lexical structure. That is, where case is assigned, an "argument" of a predicate can "surface." If there is no syntactic sanctioning, then the argument is not expressible at the syntactic level.

In some cases syntactic and lexical sanctioning overlap; when this happens, an "argument" of a predicate is phonetically realized (see example (4.2)). In other cases the two systems do not overlap. For example, the pleonastic element *it* receives case but is not associated with an argument slot. *It* is a syntactic entity that carries case. I am assuming that case assigners must be able to assign their case; hence, pleonastic elements exist to accommodate this requirement. On the other hand, when no syntactic sanctioning is available, the argument slot is not evaluated; that is, when no corresponding overt element is found in the syntactic string, no index is assigned to the argument slot. Unevaluated argument positions will end up being the MG theory analogue to the PRO and the NP-trace of GB theory.[13] Chapter 5 is devoted to accounting for the properties associated with these two phonologically null elements by way of binding unevaluated argument slots.

4.1.3 Obligatory Subject Redefined

One important aspect of GB theory (circa 1980–1981) that will not be adopted here is the phrase structure rule (4.4):

(4.4)
S → NP INFL VP

Chomsky (1981b) and others have argued cogently for the necessity of this particular PS rule, which entails that every sentence must have a subject, i.e., [NP, S]. Supporters of (4.4) argue that a grammar that assumes only (4.4) is simpler than a grammar that incorporates the PS rule (4.5) (see Chomsky (1981b, 25, (24))):

(4.5)
$$S \rightarrow \begin{cases} \text{(NP) to VP} \\ \text{NP Tense VP} \end{cases}$$

(4.5) involves a disjunction that in part expresses the dependency between [NP, S] and tense. In GB theory this dependency is captured not by the PS component but by case and θ-theory. An alternative to (4.4) is also discussed in Chomsky (1981b, 25–26, (27)) (bars changed to primes):

(4.6)
a. VP′ → COMP VP_1
b. S′ → COMP S
c. S → NP VP_1 when COMP = *for;* S → NP VP_2 otherwise
d. VP_1 is *to*-VP and VP_2 is Tense-VP

Assuming that PS rules express categorial and structural dependencies, the arguments for (4.4) versus (4.5) and (4.6) are at least threefold. First, according to Chomsky (1981b, 25), (4.6) is a ". . . considerably clumsier system of rules . . ." Second, with rules (4.5) and (4.6) subcategorization frames must be complicated; that is, some verbs will take VP′ complements and some will take S′ complements.[14] By contrast, rule (4.4) will allow subcategorization to be quite simple, not distinguishing between VP′ and S′ complements. Third, Chomsky adduces an argument involving the pleonastic elements *it* and *there*. Chomsky gives the following examples (1981b, 26, (28i,ii,v)):

(4.7)
a. *There* is a good reason for his refusal.
b. I believe *there* to be a good reason for his refusal.
c. I believe *it* to be clear who won.

It and *there* must appear; the sentences are ungrammatical if they are absent. These elements occur because [NP, S] is an obligatory position as defined by rule (4.4). (4.5), on the other hand, does not capture the obligatoriness of [NP, S]. Chomsky argues (pp. 26–27) that

Obligatory insertion of the NP α follows from the fact that the constructions illustrated [in (4.7)] require subjects for some structural reason; call it the principle P. Clearly, P does not derive from θ-theory; the italicized elements [*it* and *there*] bear no θ-roles. Nor does P derive from considerations of subcategorization. Verbs do not subcategorize for subjects, which may be freely missing when P is inapplicable . . . The principle P, plainly, is the structural requirement that certain configurations—infinitivals and gerunds—must have subjects; i.e., the principle P is simply the rule [(4.4)].

These, then, are some of the arguments for adopting (4.4), one of the major consequences of which is PRO. For example, in (4.8) *to win* is part of a sentential complement.

(4.8)
John wants to win.

The S-structure would be something like (4.9):

(4.9)
John wants [$_{S'}$[$_S$ PRO to win]]

PRO in GB theory is a phonologically null element that occupies a structural position. In this case it is the subject of *win*. Since PRO can't occur just anywhere, accounting for and predicting its distribution via θ-theory and government has led to considerable research.[15]

To summarize, while (4.4) simplifies the PS rules and subcategorization and provides a structural position for pleonastic elements, thus giving them a raison d'être, it also necessitates positing phonologically null syntactic entities (i.e., PRO) in order to keep "obligatory subject" a syntactic generalization. The alternative proposed here is guided by the intuition that if a principled alternative to PS rules can be found that captures a dependency, then it should be explored and its ramifications sought out.

Returning to the motivation for rule (4.4), I would like to address each of the three arguments in turn. The first argument is directed against a theory that enriches the system of PS rules rather than attempting to further simplify it. The second argument, which involves subcategorization, is a potential criticism of the theory being developed here. This is because subcategorization is independent of how the syntactic structure is defined. I will not be assuming, contra GB theory, that only sentential complements are subcategorized for. Indeed, it may well be that a *to* complement or a *that* complement may be associated with an argument slot of a predicate.[16] The third argument is perhaps the most cogent one in favor of (4.4). I will assume that *it* and *there* are present in order to carry case and not simply because of an obligatory structural position as defined by (4.4). The pleonastic elements always have case. If they were simply placeholders, this would suggest that there should be an entity that has neither a θ-role nor case and merely holds a structural position. Such an entity would be something like trace of *it*. However, in my view the status of this entity is dubious.[17] I will assume, then, contrary to (4.4), that the role of the PS rules is simply to define hierarchical structure and not to designate [NP, S] as obligatory. This means that there will be complements that lack overt subjects (e.g., *John wants* [$_x$ *to go*])[18] and overt subjects that are not associated with an argument slot but carry case (e.g., It *seems John wants to go*). There is, therefore, no syntactic entity PRO or NP-trace. Without these entities in the syntax, we must rethink how control and NP-movement are to be characterized.[19]

4.1.4 Generalized Control

I am assuming that not all the lexical information associated with a verb is projected into the syntax. That is, since only syntactically sanctioned items occur in the syntax and there can be no syntactic PRO, we must posit a series of lexicosyntactic rules that mediate between lexical structure and syntactic structure in order to provide an account of control. These rules will end up accounting for NP-movement as well. The net result of the lexicosyntactic rules is that the subject or object of a verb will be associated with an unevaluated argument slot of another verb that is in the complement of the first verb.

4.2 A Modular Analysis of English

4.2.1 Assumptions
The following assumptions underlie the account being developed here:

(4.10)
Assumptions and terminology:
a. PS rules define hierarchical structure.
b. Case assigners (e.g., verbs, prepositions) syntactically sanction entities.
c. Clauses need not have case, but NPs must.[20]
d. There are no phonologically null elements in the syntactic string. (This is entailed by assumption (c).)
e. Pleonastic elements carry case and are not associated with an argument slot.
f. Overt NPs that are terms (i.e., that are not pleonastic elements) must be associated with an argument slot. (This is half of the θ-Criterion.)
g. Direct Evaluation mediates between lexical structure on the one hand and syntactic structure on the other hand, coindexing argument slots with overt syntactic elements (for example, direct object to direct object where these notions are defined in their respective domains).
h. Argument slots that are not assigned an index via Direct Evaluation are "unevaluated" argument slots.
i. Indirect Evaluation involves taking an index from a projection of a verb and using it as an index for an unevaluated argument slot.
j. Indexing is not assigned freely.

4.2.2 The Interpretation of Unevaluated Argument Slots
I will use the above assumptions to develop an account of the interpretation of unevaluated argument slots. The following rule of predication and lexicosyntactic rules will figure importantly in the account.

Modular Theory: English

(4.11)
Direct Evaluation
If β is an immediate constituent of γ in the following expressions and $\gamma = \alpha'$,[21]

$[_\gamma \ldots \alpha \ldots \beta]$
$[_\gamma \ldots \beta \ldots \alpha]$

then an index may be assigned to β and an *internal*[22] argument of α if:

  a. β is a case-marked NP or
  b. β is a clause.

(4.12)
Indirect Evaluation
If β is the second or predicate index on γ, and $\gamma = \alpha'$, then α may assign this index to an unevaluated argument slot of α.

(4.13)
Control
If α is a control verb, then α selects the index of either the subject argument slot (external argument) or the object argument slot (internal argument) and assigns it to β if:

  a. β is an immediate constituent of α' and
  b. β is a clause.

(4.14)
Predication
Given α and β, if α and β c-command each other and α = subject and β = a predicate, then coindex α and β. Condition: α must have case.[23]

This Predication rule, which involves a purely *structural* notion of predication, will be used to coindex the subject and the VP that c-commands the subject (NP). The data to be discussed are as follows:

(4.15)
a. John wants to leave.
b. John was wounded.
c. John seems to like women.
d. We persuaded John to play the piano.

Traditionally, (4.15a) is a case of subject control, (4.15b) is a case of passive or NP-movement, (4.15c) is a case of raising (NP-movement), and (4.15d) is a case of object control. Let us take each example in turn. The syntactic structure for (4.15a) is (4.16) (see note 18 concerning X):

(4.16)
John wants to leave.

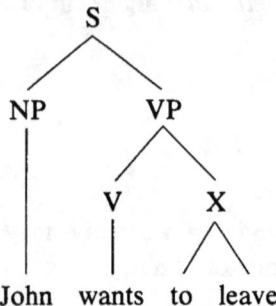

In order for evaluation to take place, the lexical structure of the verbs must be accessed. The PAS of the verb will be entered under the lexical item for ease of discussion.

(4.17)

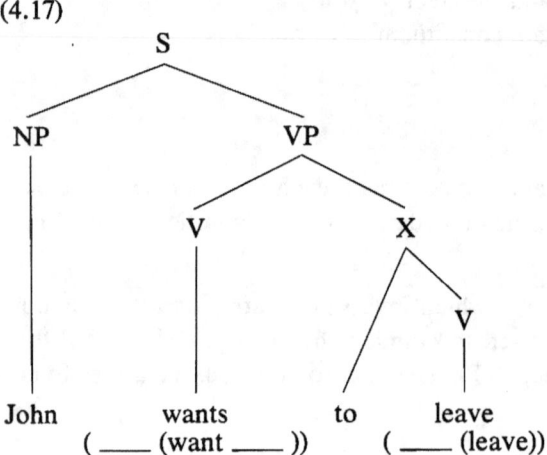

First syntactic sanctioning is taken care of. *John,* which is the subject or [NP, S], receives nominative case because the clause is finite. X is sanctioned by *want.* There is no syntactic sanctioning for the subject of *leave,* so nothing occurs in this position; in fact, no position is defined.

Modular Theory: English

Now Predication coindexes the NP *John* with the VP. Direct Evaluation follows. (4.18) illustrates the output of these two processes.

(4.18)
Predication and Direct Evaluation

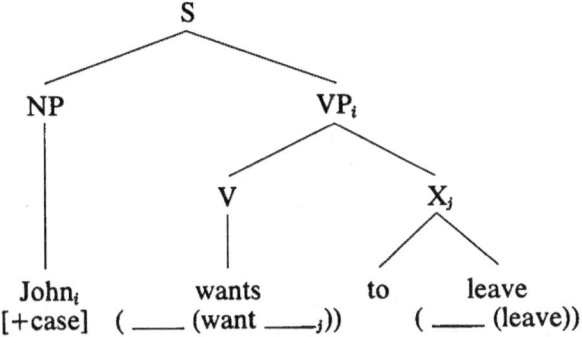

John$_i$ wants to leave
[+case] (___ (want ___$_j$)) (___ (leave))

The subject, or external argument, of *want* does not have an index; therefore, it is an unevaluated argument slot. (The subject of *leave* also does not have an index, but we will save that issue for a moment.) Indirect Evaluation now applies. The verb *want* takes the predication index, i, from its VP projection and assigns it to the unevaluated subject argument slot in its PAS. This argument now has an index, which enables the NP *John* to be interpreted as being associated with an argument slot; the argument slot, in turn, is linked to the NP *John*. Notice that the predication index has been removed. We will assume, until further notice, that the rule of Predication is a sort of well-formedness (maybe this is odd?) condition on predication that imposes the indexing relationship between subject and predicate, a relationship that must be expressed. If the index is removed for some reason, Predication simply establishes the indexing relationship again, reassigning the index of the subject to the VP.

(4.19)
Indirect Evaluation and Predication

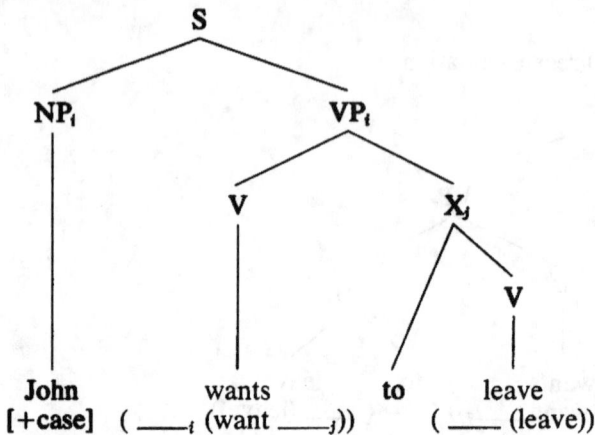

Turning to *leave*, we see that it has an unevaluated argument slot. *Leave* cannot take the index *j*, because if it does, the X will no longer have an index and will therefore become uninterpretable. Since *want* has already undergone Direct Evaluation, the argument slot associated with X has an index. So evaluation, direct or indirect, would no longer be motivated, or rather "driven." Consequently, the sentence would be left with one piece uninterpretable, and the subject of *leave* would be linked to the complement of *want*.

We know that *want* is a control verb. The rule of Control (4.13) stipulates that a control verb selects the index of either the subject or the object argument slot and assigns it to a constituent clause. In the case of *want*, the subject index, *i*, is selected and assigned. Control basically sets up a predication relation.

(4.20)
Control

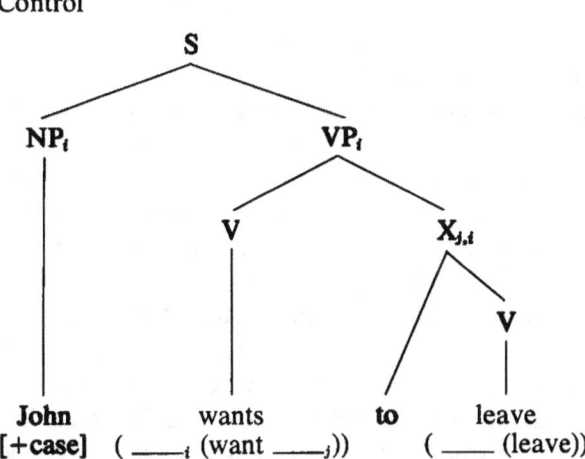

The subject argument slot of *leave* is unevaluated. Indirect Evaluation is now possible. The index i is "brought down" and is assigned to the unevaluated argument slot of *leave*. Note that in (4.20) only the rightmost index of the two may be used for Indirect Evaluation. *Leave* must take the *second* index if there is more than one, which means it is embedded. We are therefore assuming that indices are concatenated from left to right. Thus, Indirect Evaluation is in essence allowed to take only the index not being used as a *linking register* for the clause. Later, we will make Indirect Evaluation with one index optional. (4.21) shows the result of Indirect Evaluation.

(4.21)
Indirect Evaluation

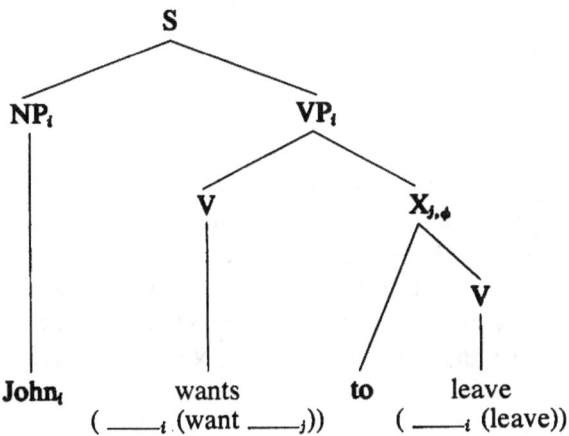

The interpretation of (4.15a) is now complete.

Notice that the lexicosyntactic rules, as well as Predication, are entirely local. This situation yields the same results as Subjacency, as we will see later on. "Control" is local.[24]

Before turning to the next examples, I would like to comment on the procedure being used for evaluation. Keeping track of indices that have already been used in evaluation or predication is an important technical problem. To simplify this record-keeping and to avoid positing any kind of pan-syntactic device that scans for indices within the sentence "further down" in the tree, I will assume for the moment that Direct and Indirect Evaluation and Predication proceed from left to right and from top to bottom, that they are ordered, and that they keep track of indices that have already been used. Predication comes first, followed by Direct Evaluation and then Indirect Evaluation. The Control indexing procedure involves moving from one indexing domain to another, often feeding Indirect Evaluation.[25]

The next example involves the passive.

(4.22)
John was wounded.

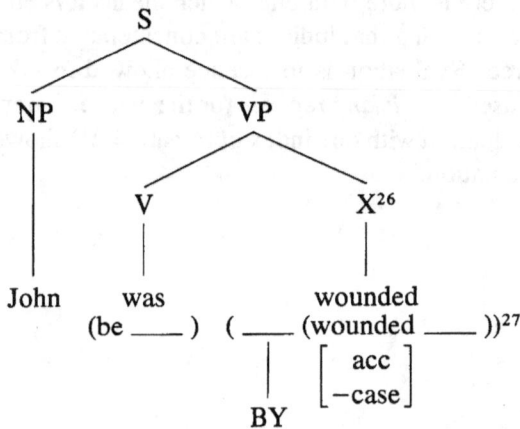

Following Chomsky (1981b), I will assume that the output of "passive" word formation is a "verb" whose subject is bound in some sense and is therefore not an "unevaluated" argument (i.e., is not construed as an unevaluated argument slot) and which has lost the ability to assign case to (i.e., syntactically sanction) its object. The only NP that can be syntactically sanctioned given the syntax is *John*. The NP subject *John* and

Modular Theory: English

the VP meet the requirements for Predication, so these two constituents of S are coindexed.

(4.23)
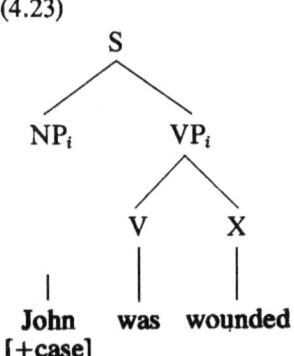

Moving on to *was*, Direct Evaluation indexes X with the clausal argument of *be*.

(4.24)
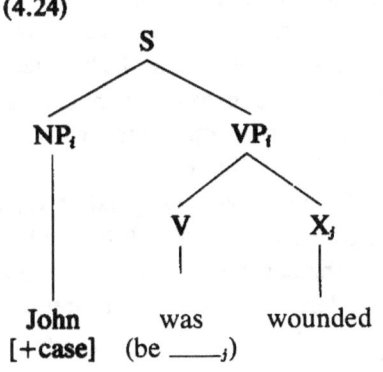

Indirect Evaluation will not apply, since *be* does not have any unevaluated arguments. But *be* does perform a kind of control, that is, it passes the index i (in this case) to its complement X. I will add an option to Control in order to handle this case which is illustrated in (4.26).

(4.25)
Revised Control
If α is a control verb, then α either (i) selects the index of the subject argument or the object argument slot and assigns it to β or (ii) takes the index from its projection and assigns it to β if:
    a. β is an immediate constituent of α' and
    b. β is a clause.

(4.26)

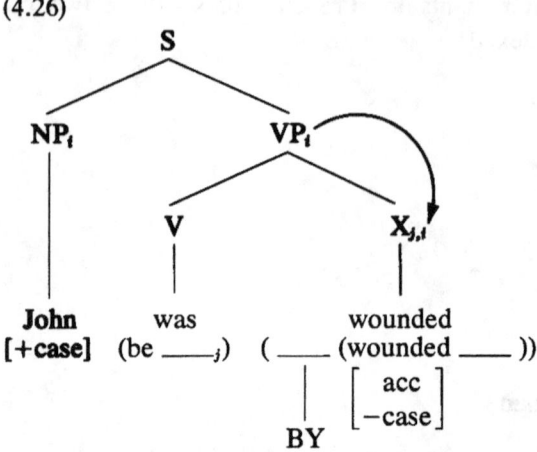

Now we move on to the next domain of indexing, the domain of *wounded*. Because *wounded* does not assign case, its direct object is not syntactically sanctioned and hence cannot appear in syntactic object position. Therefore, Direct Evaluation cannot apply, and we are left with an unevaluated argument slot. Recall the assumption that the "subject" argument of *wounded* is bound and hence not construed as an unevaluated argument slot. Indirect Evaluation is now an option for *wounded*. The index i is brought down and is used as a linking register for the object argument of *wounded*. Notice that we have never had to stipulate that the matrix subject evaluates or is associated with the embedded object. We rely on the "syntax" of the construction and the lexical properties of *wounded* to achieve this. The result of the interpretation of (4.15b) is (4.27):

(4.27)

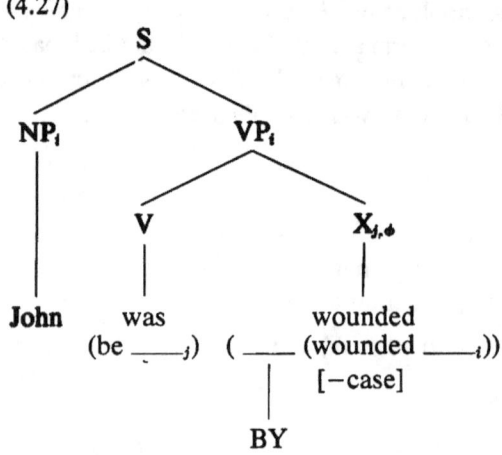

Modular Theory: English   125

In the absence of an overt BY-phrase, the subject of *wounded* is left undetermined by the grammar, to be fixed pragmatically.

The third example involves what has traditionally been called "raising."

(4.28)
John seems to like women.

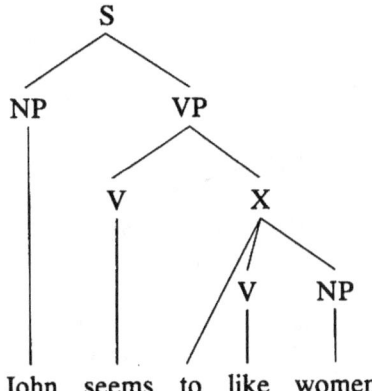

John receives nominative case because the sentence is finite. X is a complement of the monadic predicate *seem*. *Women* receives case from *like*. The subject of *like* receives no syntactic sanctioning. Next, Predication assigns identical indices to the NP *John* and the VP.

(4.29)
Predication

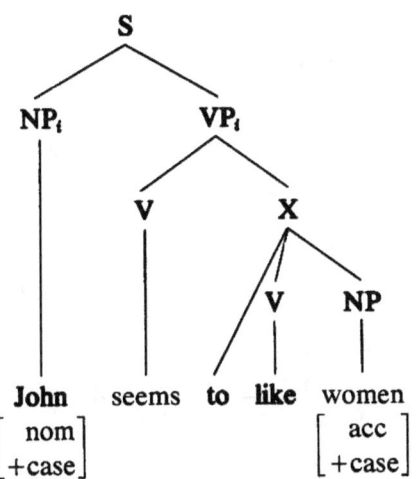

Direct Evaluation now assigns the complement X the same linking register as the only argument of *seem*:

(4.30)
Direct Evaluation

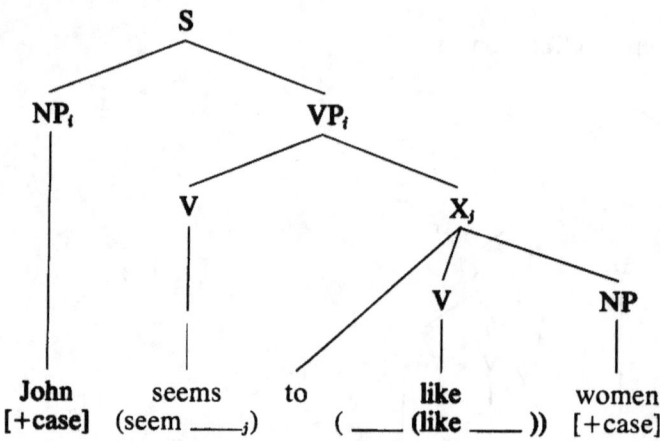

Indirect Evaluation does not take place, since *seem* has no unevaluated arguments slots. *Seem* is another predicate that triggers Control. Like *be* in the previous example, *seem* moves the index from its projection down onto its complement.

(4.31)
Control

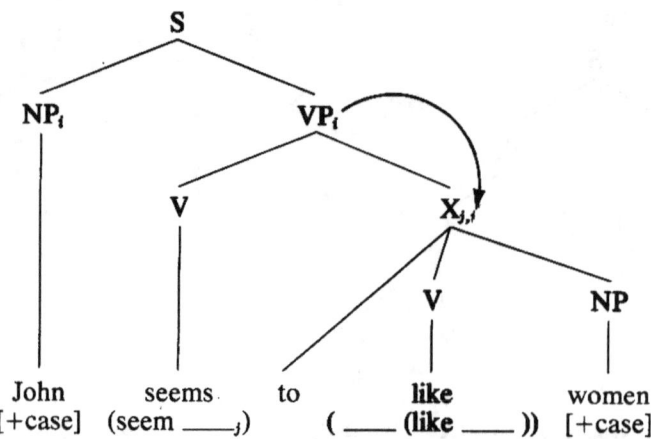

Modular Theory: English   127

The next domain of indexing is the domain of *like*. Since Predication is not relevant in this case, the next step is Direct Evaluation. An index is assigned to *women*, the syntactic object, and a linking register to the object argument slot of *like*.

(4.32)
Direct Evaluation

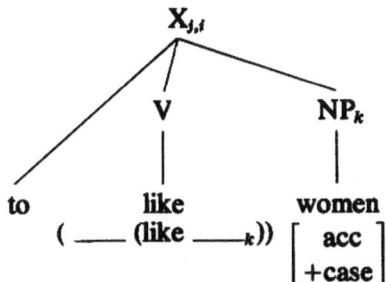

Indirect Evaluation will now take the index i and assign it to the unevaluated argument slot of *like*.

(4.33)
Indirect Evaluation

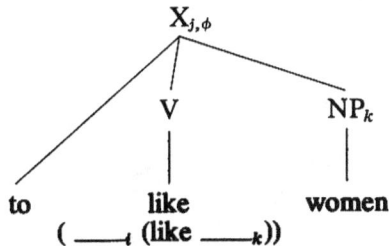

The NP *John* is now construed as linked to the subject argument of *like*.
The last example, (4.15d), is a case of object control:

Modularity in Syntax

(4.34)
We persuaded John to play the piano.

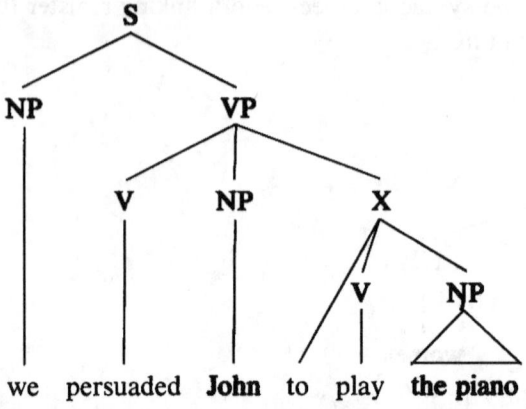

We, John, the piano, and perhaps X all receive case. After Predication, Direct Evaluation, and Indirect Evaluation, *we, John,* and X are all associated with a linking register.

(4.35)
Predication, Direct Evaluation, Indirect Evaluation

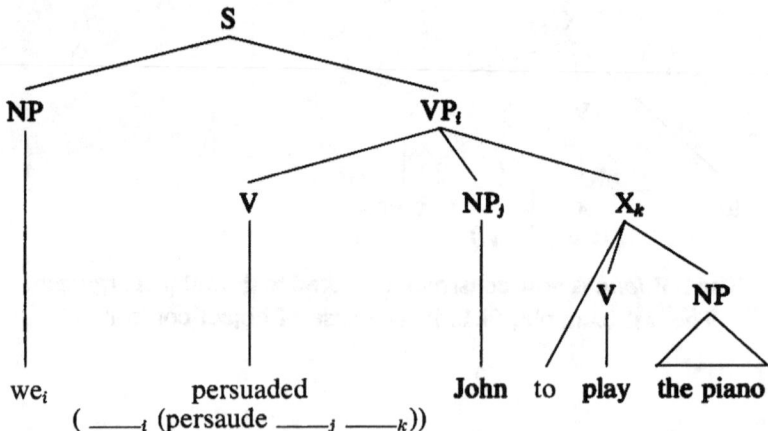

Persuade is another control verb. In this case the object argument slot is the one whose index is assigned to the X_k.

(4.36)
Control

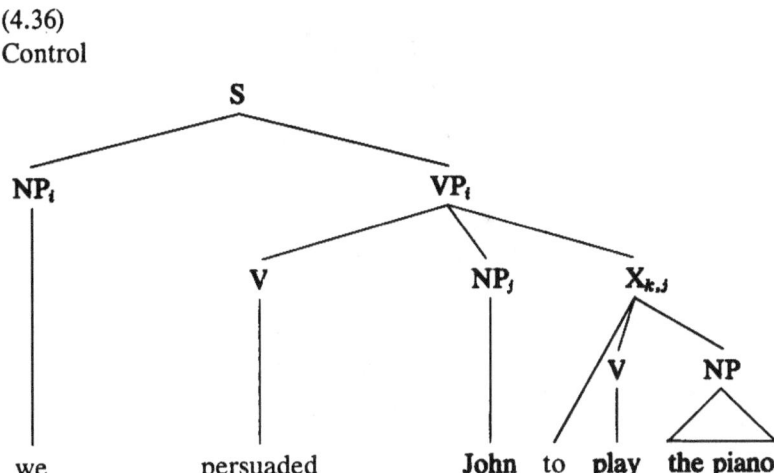

The next domain for indexing is the domain of the verb *play*. Predication is not relevant, but Direct Evaluation is; as a result, the NP *the piano* is linked to the object argument slot of the verb *play* (see (4.37)).

Since the subject argument slot of *play* is unevaluated and there is an extra index j, Indirect Evaluation assigns the index to that argument position (see (4.38)). The NP *John* is now construed as linked to the subject argument slot of *play*.

Sentences (4.15a–d) have illustrated the role of syntactic sanctioning (case assignment), Predication, and the lexicosyntactic rules of Direct and Indirect Evaluation and Control. The goal has been to construe certain dependencies in such a way as to simplify the form of rules in each domain. Syntactic sanctioning, via case, provides a syntactic position; those case-marked entities that are in the domain of a predicate are targets for Predication and the lexicosyntactic rules. If case must be assigned, then there must be an overt syntactic element to receive that case; and this element is then in turn available for Predication and evaluation. There is a dependency between overt elements and case and between case and evaluation, when it comes to NPs. Indirect Evaluation, Predication, and Control are stated in such a way as not to duplicate work accomplished by the "syntax" of a construction. Instead of stipulating which argument slot (i.e., subject, object) of the predicate is the target of Control, it simply assigns an index to the complement. This index in turn will be associated with an unevaluated argument slot of the embedded verb via Indirect Evaluation. In some

(4.37)
Direct Evaluation

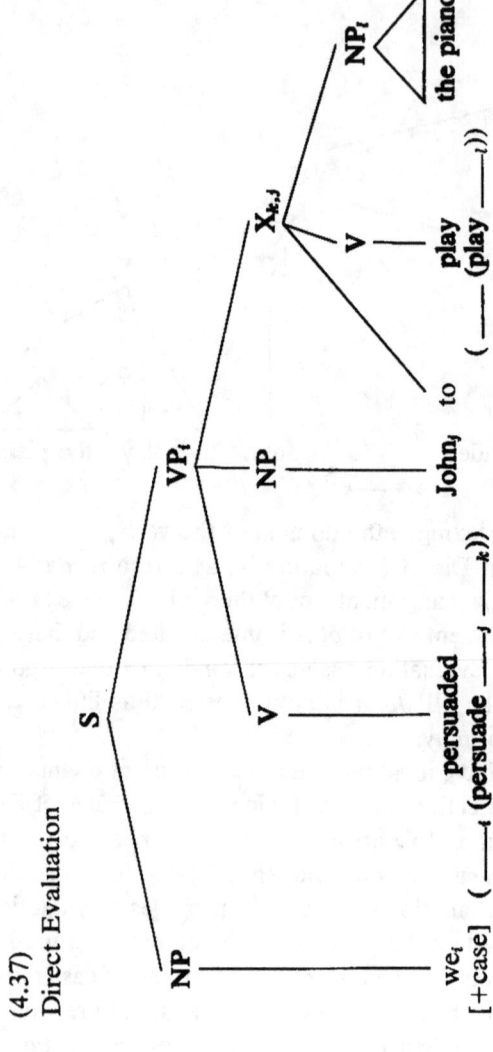

Modular Theory: English

(4.38)
Indirect Evaluation

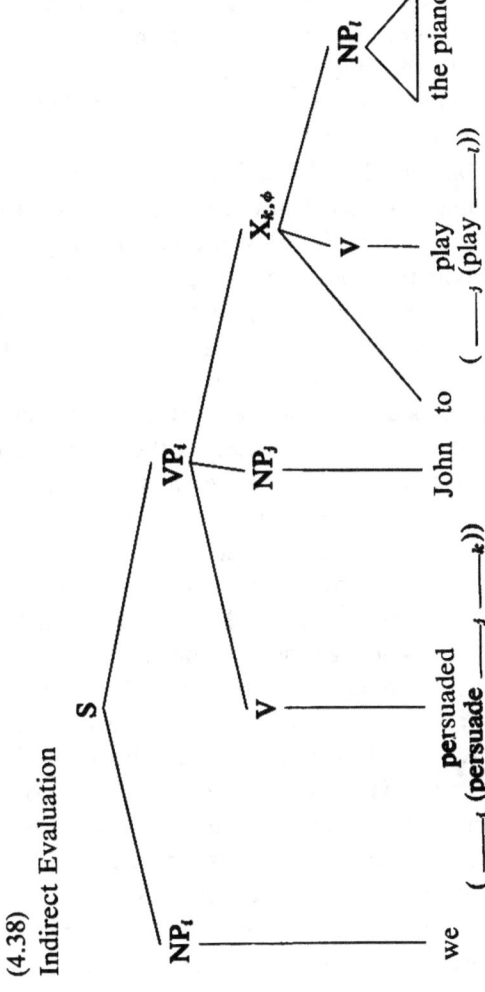

cases this argument slot will be the subject and in others it will be the object. Which one it is will depend on the syntactic environment, but it need never be stated explicitly which one is chosen.

Passive constructions provide a good example. In example (4.15b) it turns out that the subject in the domain of *was* is associated with the object of the "verb" *wounded*. No rule mediating between the syntax and lexical structure stipulates that it is the object that is targeted. How, then, was this accomplished? Following Chomsky (1981b), I have said that the case-assigning ability of the "passive verb" is taken away. This means that an overt [NP, VP] cannot occur, and Direct Evaluation will not assign an index to the object of *wounded* in the PAS. The argument slot will remain unevaluated. Recall that the subject argument slot has been bound and is not construed as an unevaluated argument of the same status as the object. Furthermore, there is a dependency between *wounded* and the verb *was*; it is *was* that triggers Control, which results, through Indirect Evaluation, in the linking of the [NP, S] with the object argument slot of *wounded*.

An interesting consequence of subsuming NP-movement under Indirect Evaluation and Control (which also handles the "traditional" control cases) is that the passive is now a case of "control of object."[28] An asymmetry between subject and object has been noted with respect to control. Subject-subject control and object-subject control have been recognized, but no subject-object or object-object control. But within this system there superficially is a case of subject-object "control." Control of object is possible only when a transitive verb loses the ability to syntactically sanction its object. Passive is precisely a case of this sort.[29] The asymmetry between subject and object is captured by the methods of syntactic and lexical sanctioning. I am adopting from Chomsky (1981b) the position that [NP, VP] is syntactically and lexically sanctioned by one entity, the verb, whereas [NP, S] receives its case from INFL and is lexically sanctioned via the predicate (VP in Chomsky's terms). Speaking in GB terms, the syntax of [NP, S] does not depend on the case-assigning properties of the entity that assigns it a θ-role, whereas the syntax of [NP, VP] does.

Another consequence of MG theory is that there is no syntactic distinction between NP-trace and PRO. Neither is a syntactic entity. Only one indexing procedure is needed. Actually, this must be qualified since there is a disjunction in the Control rule (4.25): "If α is a control verb then α either (i) selects the index of the subject argument or the object argument slot and assigns it to β or (ii) takes the index from its projection and assigns it to β." One disjunct involves the verb's passing an index down from one of its argument slots. I have joined these two cases because both involve passing an index down to a complement under the same environmental/structural conditions. I will return to the consequences and justification for this in chapter 5.

4.2.3 Pleonastic Elements

Since lexical sanctioning is dependent on case and not vice versa, it is conceivable that there could be a syntactic position that was associated with case and yet did not end up being lexically sanctioned. Given the discussion so far, it is obvious that there should be just such a case; it turns out to be, not surprisingly, [NP, S]. (4.39) involves a syntactic subject that receives case but is not lexically sanctioned.

(4.39)

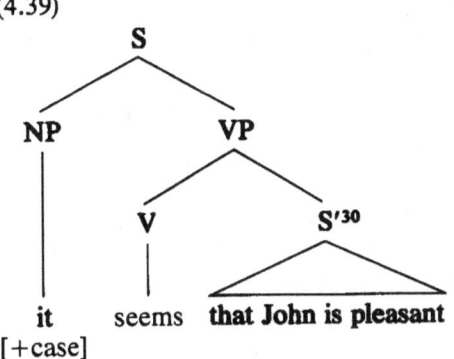

Here the *it* is functioning as a case carrier. Recall the view (for example, from Chomsky (1981b)) that the pleonastic element *it* is a placeholder. It occupies a position defined as obligatory by the PS rule S → NP INFL VP. The position taken here is that in this example it is case, and not the PS rule, that defines the syntactic position as obligatory.

4.2.4 Subject of an Infinitival

One type of subject has been referred to only briefly: the "subject" of an infinitival that has no θ-role. In GB theory such a subject would most likely be a trace of *it*, that is, a phonologically null element coindexed with a non-θ-bearing entity. In the theory being developed here it is not possible to define such an entity via phrase markers syntactically since there is no case, and case is required for NPs. I will develop an account of sentences like (4.40a,b) that does not involve positing a phonologically null subject that is not lexically sanctioned.

(4.40)
a. It seems ―― to be believed that Mike likes basketball.
b. It is likely ―― to be conjectured that Stevenson will lose the next election.

The question is, does ―― in (4.40a,b) have any syntactic status? If all Ss have an [NP, S], then there must be something in ――. This is the conclusion we reach if we adopt the rule S → NP INFL VP and, for example, *to be believed* is a sentential complement. But we are not adopting this rule. I have said that [NP, S] (or [NP, VP], for that matter) must have case. The place between *seems* and *to* has no case; therefore, there cannot be an [NP, S] in that position. Furthermore, we cannot justify an entity "semantically," since there is no argument slot (θ-role, in GB terms). Positing a trace of *it* is not unmotivated, given the assumptions of GB theory; after all, [NP, S] is obligatory and *seem* is a raising predicate. The modular analysis of (4.40a,b) will involve predication, evaluation, and Control—in other words, the same mechanisms that were intended to handle "NP-movement" and "control" of PRO. We will see that under this type of analysis there is no [−case, −θ-role] subject, i.e., [NP, S]. The job of this so-called subject is being accomplished by an index—not an indexed trace occupying a position defined by phrase markers. In section 4.3.5 this approach will be applied to other cases of successive cyclic "NP-movement."

Now consider (4.41), the representation of (4.40a).

(4.41)
It seems to be believed that Mike likes basketball.

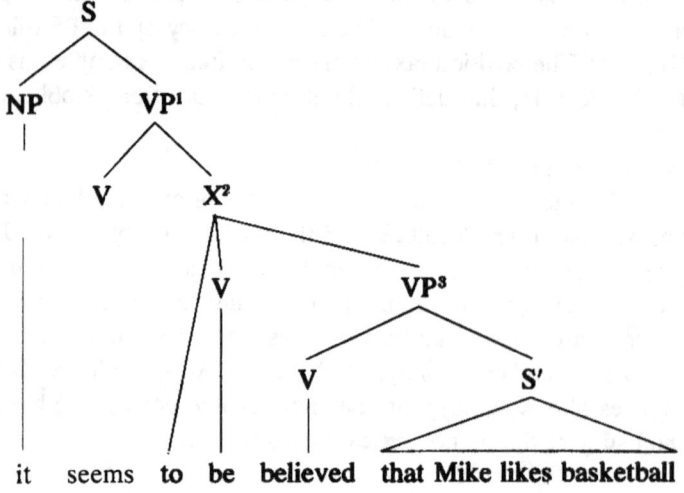

Modular Theory: English

The *it* receives case because the sentence is finite, and Predication coindexes the NP and the VP[1].

(4.42)
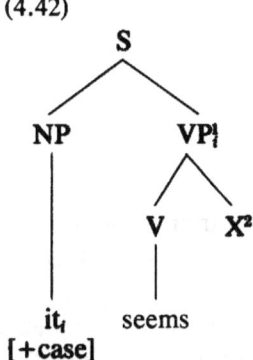

We now turn to the indexing domain of *seem*. X^2 and the argument slot of *seem* are assigned like indices.

(4.43)
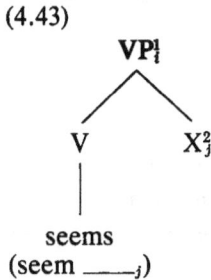

(seem ___$_j$)

Since *seem* is also a control predicate like *be*, it passes the index from its projection down to its complement.

(4.44)
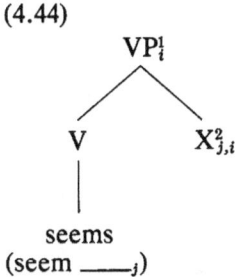

(seem ___$_j$)

The next domain for indexing is *be*. Direct Evaluation assigns a linking register to the sole argument position of *be* and to the VP[3]:

(4.45)

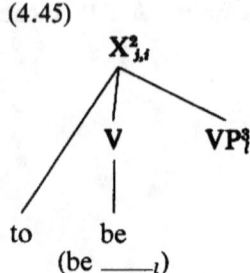

Being a control verb, *be* passes down the index i from its projection X^2. This brings us to the indexing domain of *believed* (see (4.46)). *Believed* evaluates the S' as the clausal argument in its PAS.

Believed, like *be* and *seem*, passes the index down to its complement, where it remains (see (4.47)). The index i does not enter into the indexing domain of the verb in the S' complement since the S' is not a projection of anything that is capable of passing an index down. Now the S' and the NP *it* are anaphorically related. Notice that if the S' were "preposed," (4.48) would result.

(4.48)
That Mike likes basketball seems to be believed.

Now *believed* does have an unevaluated argument position, so the S' and the argument slot of *believed* are anaphorically related.

Notice that GB theory and MG theory characterize the acceptability of (4.49) differently.

Modular Theory: English 137

(4.46)

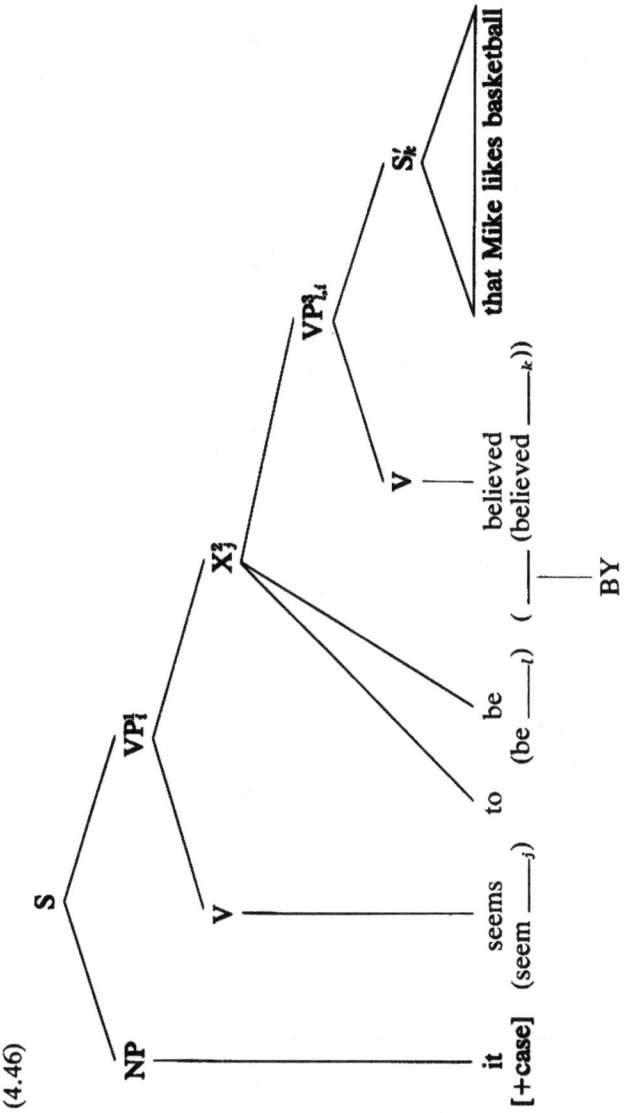

(4.47)

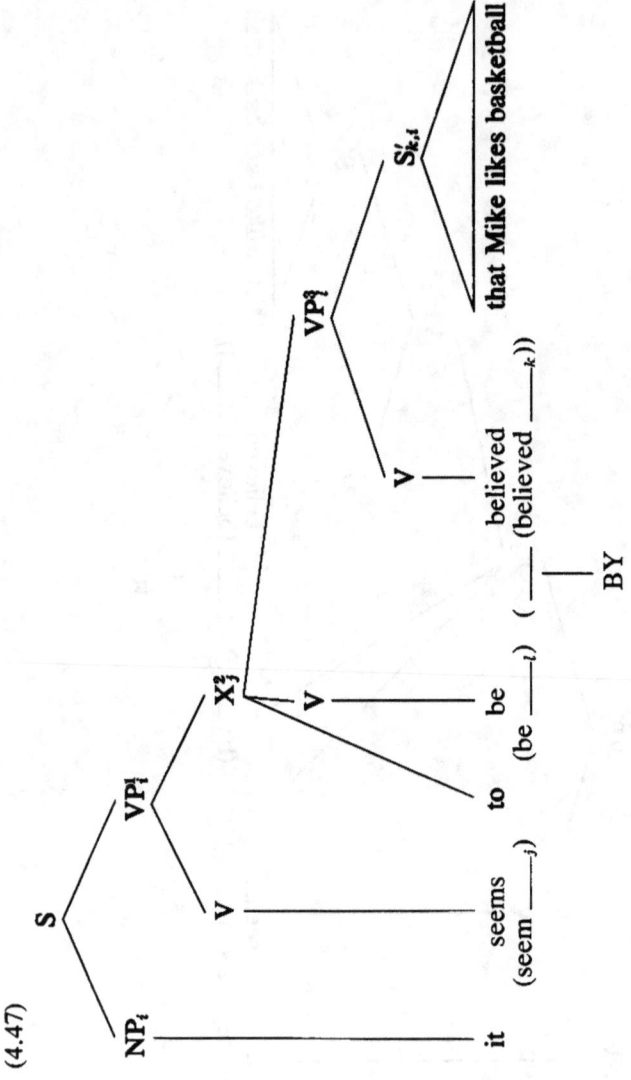

(4.49)
To seem to want to leave is rude.

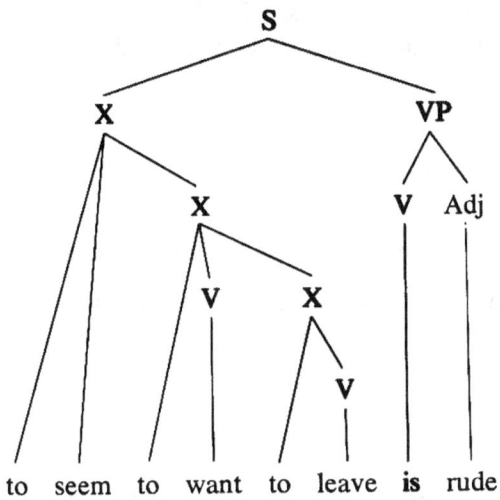

In GB theory X necessarily has a subject. In all likelihood, this subject would be PRO raised from the embedded complement. In MG theory, since PRO is not a syntactic entity, such an analysis is impossible. Since there is no case, there cannot be a syntactic subject. I cannot think of a principled reason in GB theory for attributing any peculiarity to (4.49). My own judgment is that it is in some way odd. We cannot know a priori what the particular oddity is, but MG theory offers an angle. In (4.49) there is no syntactic subject *or* index on the maximal projection of *seem*. *Seem* has no lexical subject, so there is "nothing" (no index) to pass on to the complement. This could account for the oddness of (4.49), if it is the case that *seem* must pass an index down.

To sum up this section, there is no syntactic entity that is [−case, −θ-role] (i.e., neither lexically nor syntactically sanctioned). The closest we come to such an entity is the index that first lands on the projection of a predicate having no unevaluated argument and in turn is passed on to its complement.

4.2.5 Alternative to Successive Cyclic NP-Movement

In this section we will pursue the line of argument developed in sections 4.2.2–4.2.4. We have been accounting for cases of NP-movement and control with one set of devices: Predication and the lexicosyntactic (indexing) rules. The environment for indexing and evaluation is "local"; that is, none of the proposed indexing procedures permits crossing any maximal projections in one step.[31] We will consider examples of different combinations of embeddings, that is, control verbs will be embedded under "raising" verbs and vice versa. Finally, in section 4.2.6, examples involving violations of "subjacency" will be discussed.

Consider (4.50) and (4.51).

(4.50)
Bill promised John to persuade Mary to seem to want to leave.

(4.51)
Tom persuaded Mary to want to be believed to like philosophers.

We will work through each example in order to see clearly how the indexing procedure works. For convenience, I repeat Predication and the lexicosyntactic rules:

(4.14)
Predication
Given α and β, if α and β c-command each other and α = subject and β = a predicate, then coindex α and β. Condition: α must have case.

(4.11)
Direct Evaluation
If β is an immediate constituent of γ in the following expressions and $\gamma = \alpha'$,

[$_\gamma$ ... α ... β]
[$_\gamma$ ... β ... α]

then an index may be assigned to β and an *internal* argument of α if:

a. β is a case-marked NP or
b. β is a clause.

(4.12)
Indirect Evaluation
If β is the second or predicate index on γ, and $\gamma = \alpha'$, then α may assign this index to an unevaluated argument slot of α.

(4.25)
Revised Control
If α is a control verb, then α either (i) selects the index of the subject argument or the object argument slot and assigns it to β or (ii) takes the index from its projection and assigns it to β if:

Modular Theory: English

a. β is an immediate constituent of α' and
b. β is a clause.

Turning to the first example, (4.50), we will proceed with evaluation (see (4.52)). The three NPs, *Bill*, *John*, and *Mary*, all have case. Starting at the top and left, the first indexing procedure that applies is Predication.

(4.53)

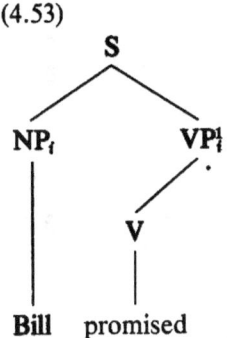

The next domain for indexing is that of *promised*. Direct Evaluation assigns indices to the NP *John* and to X^2:[32]

(4.54)

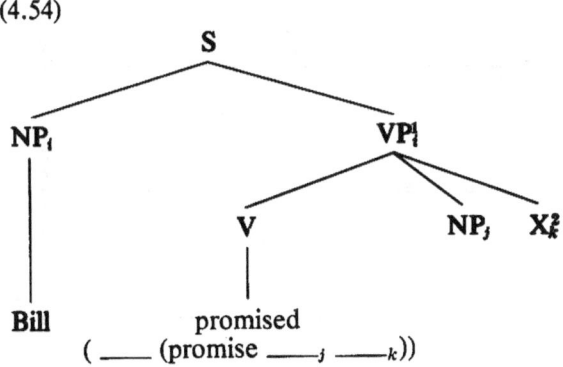

Indirect Evaluation now allows the verb *promised* to take the index i from the VP projection of the verb and assign it to any unevaluated argument slot in its PAS.

(4.52)
Bill promised John to persuade Mary to seem to want to leave.

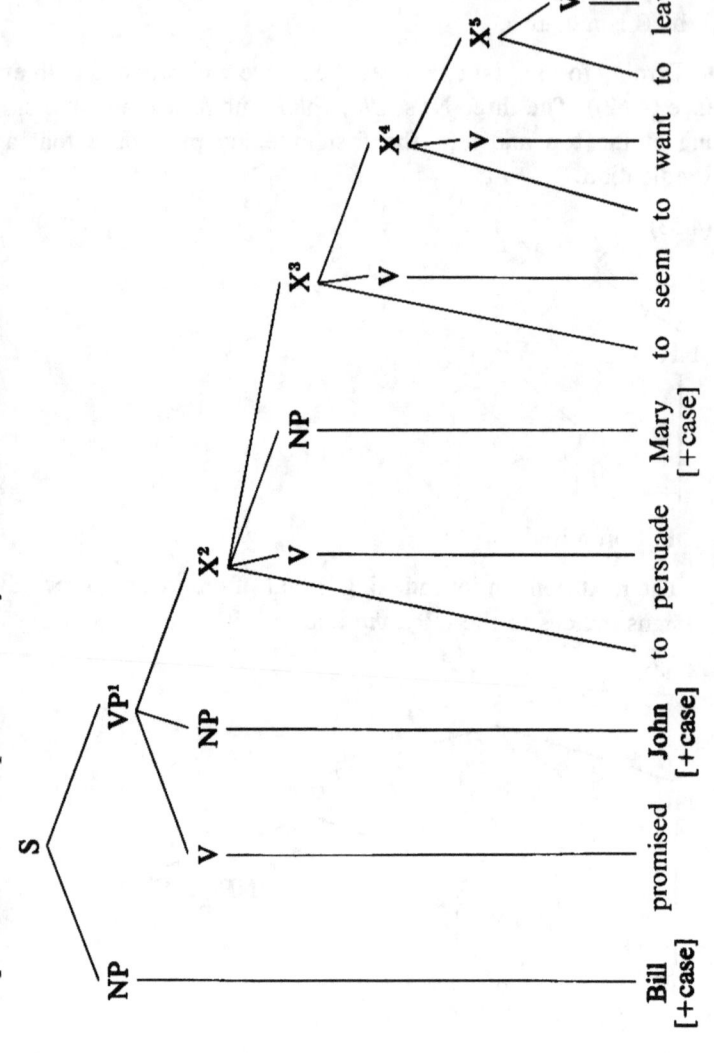

Modular Theory: English

(4.55)

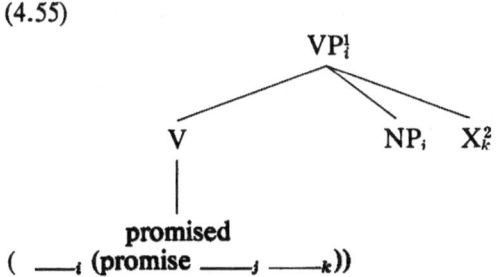

$$(\underline{\quad}_i (\text{promise} \underline{\quad}_j \underline{\quad}_k))$$

Promise is a control verb. The index of the subject or external argument is assigned to X^2: $X^2_{k,i}$.

This brings us to the next domain of indexing, that of *persuade*. Direct Evaluation assigns indices to the NP *Mary* and to X^3.

(4.56)

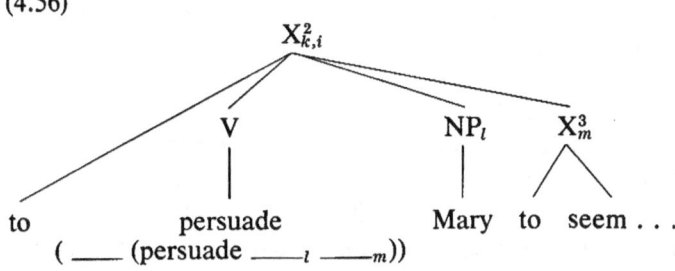

$$(\underline{\quad} (\text{persuade} \underline{\quad}_l \underline{\quad}_m))$$

Indirect Evaluation takes the index i from the maximal projection of *persuade* and assigns it to any unevaluated argument slot of the verb: $(\underline{\quad}_i (\text{persuade} \underline{\quad}_l \underline{\quad}_m))$. *Persuade* is also a control verb, but this time object control is involved. *Persuade* assigns the index of its object to X^3: $X^3_{m,l}$.

Seem is the next domain of indexing. Direct Evaluation assigns an index to X^4 so that it is coindexed with the argument slot of *seem*:

(4.57)

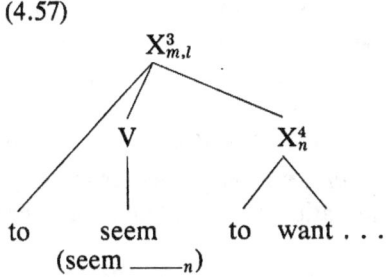

$$(\text{seem} \underline{\quad}_n)$$

The index l cannot be used to evaluate an unevaluated argument slot of *seem*. *Seem*, we must recall, is also a "control" verb insofar as it passes an index (from its projection) down to its complement. Thus, X_n^4 is associated with the index l: $X_{n,l}^4$.

In the domain of *want*, Direct Evaluation assigns an index to X^5 in order to associate it with the internal argument of *want*.

(4.58)

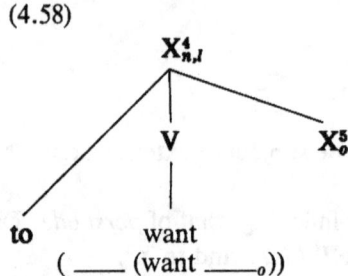

to   want
(_____ (want _____$_o$))

Indirect Evaluation takes the index l from the maximal projection of *want* and assigns it to the unevaluated argument slot of that verb: (_____$_l$ (want _____$_o$)).

Next we should consider *want*'s properties as a control verb. Williams (1980) characterizes *want* as a case of *nonobligatory control* (NOC).[33] One of his tests for NOC is to check whether the PRO of the embedded complement can be substituted for a full NP. This is certainly true for *want*, since examples like (4.59) are perfectly good:

(4.59)
a. Mary wants to leave.
b. Mary wants Bill to leave.

Another reason for claiming that *want* is a case of NOC is that even in a sentence like *Mary wants to leave*, which contains an unevaluated argument slot, *Mary* need not be obligatorily construed as solely satisfying that argument slot. An easy interpretation for *Mary wants to leave* is that Mary wants *us* to leave or *Mary and some other group* to leave. For example, *Mary wants to leave together* accommodates this interpretation. Because of these facts, I will suggest that *want* passes the index of its subject argument slot on to X^5; then the unevaluated argument slot of *leave* will be construed as being linked to the NP *Mary*. If *want* does not pass the index on, the subject argument slot of *leave* remains unevaluated. The grammar leaves the interpretation of this argument position open. (I will discuss the interpretation of unevaluated argument slots in the next chapter.)

Returning to (4.50), we see that (4.60) is the end result of all the indexing procedures.

(4.60)

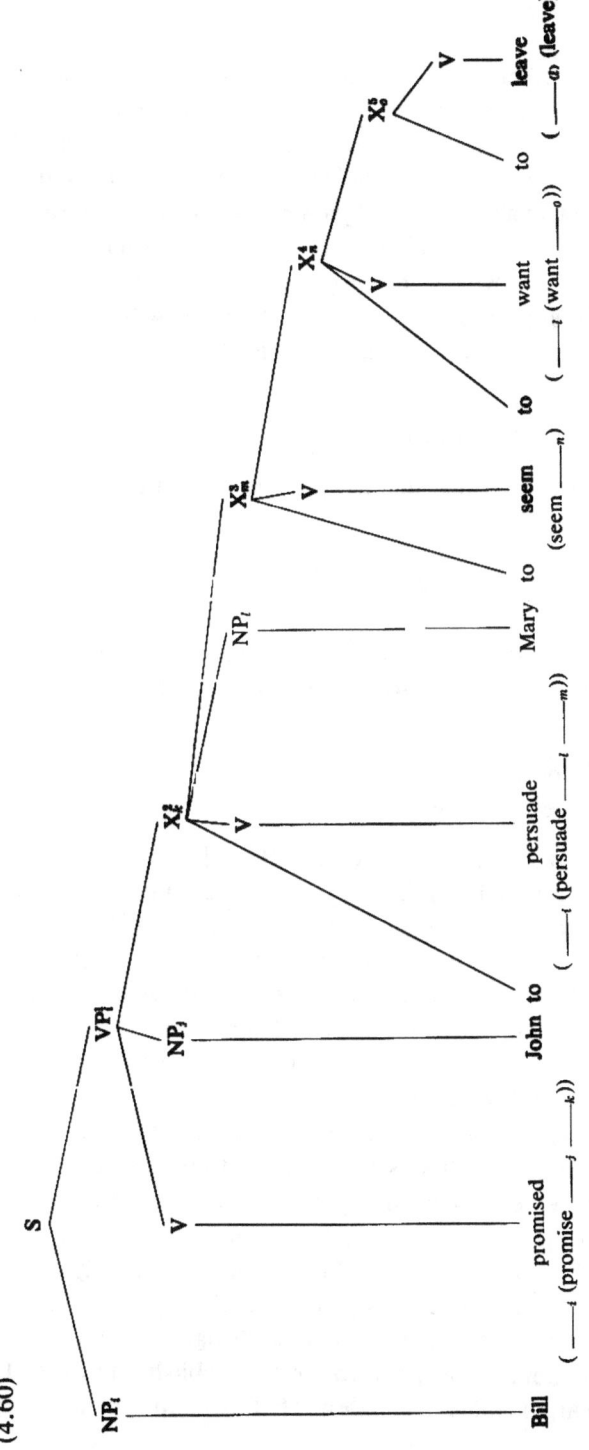

To summarize the points made by this example: NP-movement and control of PRO have been accounted for by the assignment and manipulation of indices. An important notion here is "domain of indexing." Indices cannot be accessed outside of a verb's domain of indexing for the purposes of evaluation or of passing down (i.e., control). An interesting point raised by the NOC verb *want* is that some verbs *optionally* pass the index down. So far, argument slots have received indices by virtue of there being an overt NP or clause in the domain of indexing of the verb. But what about examples like (4.61)?[34]

(4.61)
Mary wants to try to leave together.

Clearly *Mary* cannot be construed as satisfying the subject argument slot of *leave*:[35]

(4.62)
*Mary left together.

The subject of *leave* has to be construed as being plural or as involving more than one entity, as the words *group* and *committee* imply.

(4.63)
a. The group left together.
b. The committee left together.

But there is no overt NP in (4.61) to serve as the subject of *leave*. In this case *want* does not pass down the subject argument index to the X *to try* . . . Thus, the subject of *try* will not receive an index through Indirect Evaluation and hence will remain unevaluated. *Try*, unlike *want*, is an obligatory control verb and therefore does pass down an index. But there is no index to pass down. How do we handle control in this case? One possibility is that the control verb assigns an index to its subject so that it has one to pass down to the projection of *leave* (i.e., X). Indirect Evaluation then assigns this index to the subject argument slot of the verb *leave*. (Indirect Evaluation is not sensitive to the "source" of the index—that is, whether it was simply passed down (i.e., by a *seem*-type control verb) or whether it was the index of an argument of a *want*-type control verb.) In this case, Control does not simply copy an index—instead, an index is actually produced. This index is not associated with any overt element in the syntactic string. Its sole function is to satisfy the requirement of the verb *try* to establish control.[36] The result is that two arguments are coindexed but have no syntactic manifestation. At the level of sentence grammar, the subject of *try* and *leave* is not fixed. We must look at the content of utterance to fix an interpretation. This, of course, is not determined entirely in the grammar; that is, the grammar narrowly construed simply indicates that whatever ends up satisfying the subject argument slot of *try* will also satisfy the subject argument slot of *leave*.[37]

4.2.6 Subjacency and NP-Movement

Subjacency is a theory-dependent condition on movement rules (i.e., Move α in the Revised Extended and GB theories) that restricts a rule from moving an element across two bounding nodes (e.g., NP and S, which are cyclic nodes). Subjacency can be viewed as a condition on a relation between an antecedent and a syntactic gap, i.e., a condition that does not entail "movement." In this section I will consider Subjacency with respect to NP-movement and control (leaving WH-movement and extraposition aside).

Without a rule of NP-movement, or more accurately, without phonologically null entities like *t* (trace) or PRO, which define syntactic gaps, Subjacency cannot be invoked to handle cases like (4.64a,b), from Chomsky (1981b, 58 (9vii); 82, (7ii)):

(4.64)
a. *John seems [that it is certain [t to like ice cream]]
b. *they seem that [t feed each other] would be difficult

Chomsky states (1981b, 59) that ". . . we may think of the rule move-α a bit more abstractly as expressing the configuration . . . β locally binds α and β is not in a θ-position." Examples (4.64a,b) exhibit nonlocal binding; that is, they violate Subjacency. However, since without movement we cannot use Subjacency to explain why they are ungrammatical, we will instead invoke the MG theory analogue of the θ-Criterion to handle them. In the first example, (4.64a), *John* will end up not being associated with the subject argument slot of *like*.

(4.65)

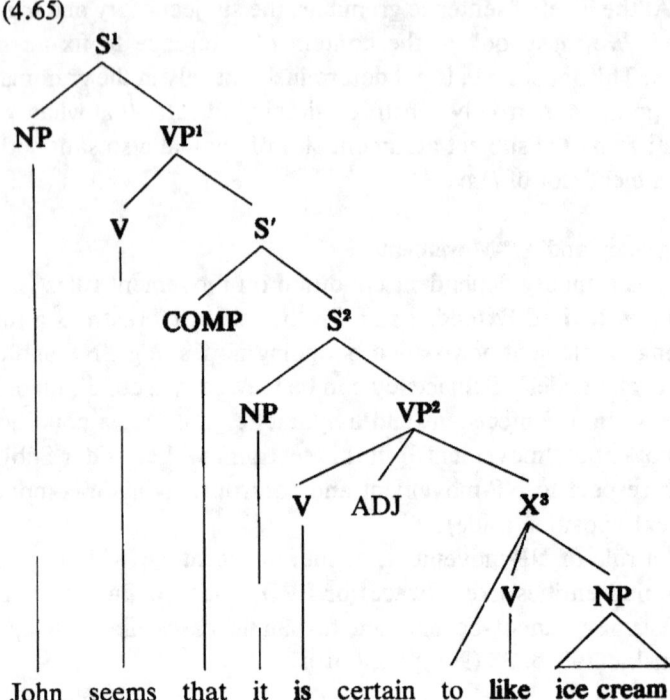

John seems that it is certain to like ice cream

The NP *John* is coindexed with VP^1, via Predication:

(4.66)

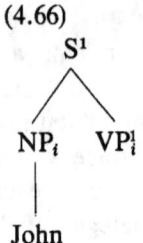

John

The verb *seems* directly evaluates the S' complement and then passes the index *i* on to the S':

(4.67)

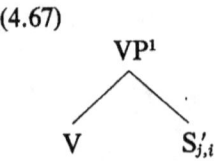

seems
(seem ___$_j$)

Modular Theory: English

Since S' is not a projection of the verb *is*, the index *i* is not accessible to the verb for the purpose of passing it on to X^3. The index remains on S', where it is unable to act as a "conduit for a θ-role." In MG theory terms the NP *John* is not construed with an argument slot.[38] Since all non-pleonastic elements must be associated with an argument slot, (4.64a) is therefore rendered anomalous. An acceptable variant involves ridding the structure of the S'.

(4.68)
John seems to be certain to like ice cream.

Here the VP^2 is the complement of *seem* and X^3 is a complement of the V *be*. The index *i* can now successfully reach X^3 and be indirectly evaluated by *like*.

According to the theory developed here, example (4.64b) (**they seem that [t feed each other] would be difficult*) has two problems. First, there is nothing in the clause *[feed each other]* to carry nominative case. Recall that this is the role of *it*. If the clause is made infinitival, this is no longer a problem, though the sentence is still odd.

(4.69)
*they seem that [to feed each other] would be difficult

Once again the θ-Criterion is violated. The NP *they* will not be associated with an argument slot because its index (say, *j*) will land on S' or S with no way of being passed down to the projection of the verb *feed*. Other variants of (4.64b) are acceptable once this violation is factored out:

(4.70)
a. it seems that [to feed each other] would be difficult
b. [to feed each other] would be difficult

Violations of Subjacency end up being violations of the MG theory analogue of the θ-Criterion because an NP has failed to be construed with an argument slot of a verb. Since NP-trace and PRO are not distinct syntactic entities in this theory, it is claimed that all instances of "grammatical" control should "obey" Subjacency. That is, whenever a PRO or NP-trace in GB theory is coindexed with another NP in the sentence, it will involve "local" binding; and whenever the "antecedent" of PRO is *not* local, the sentence cannot involve the kind of control we have been discussing. The prediction made here is that in cases involving "violations" of Subjacency one will always be able to interpret the PRO alternatively as being pragmatically controlled—that is, as involving "speaker," "hearer," or some other contextually salient entity. We will consider these cases in detail in the next chapter.

4.2.7 On the Nonpassivizability of *Promise*

It has often been pointed out that subject control verbs like *promise* do not appear to passivize.[39]

(4.71)
a. John promised Bill to leave.
b. ??Bill was promised (by John) to leave.

Example (4.71b) would have the following syntactic structure:

(4.72)

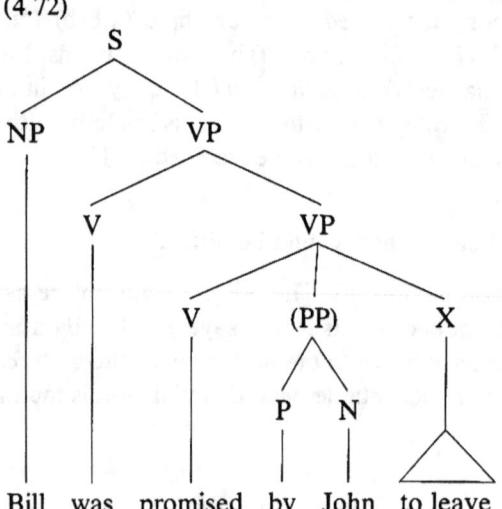

Recall that the formation of *promised* from *promise* involves some modification of the PAS; that is, the subject of *promise* is bound. In MG theory this offers a plausible reason why subject control verbs do not passivize. By the indexing procedure developed here, the index of *Bill* will end up being linked to the object argument slot of *promised*. When it comes to control, however, the situation is abnormal: the subject is bound. We can explain the oddity of (4.71b) as follows: although bound subjects cannot be used for control, the infinitival is forcing a "control" interpretation; tension results because a controller is needed where none is available.

4.2.8 Other Consequences of the Predication-Evaluation Theory of NP-Movement and Control

An important result of EST has been its ability to account for the left-right asymmetry of movement rules. Chomsky (1975) and Fiengo (1974) suggest that, for English, the requirement that the NP precede its trace follows from a general constraint on the antecedent-anaphor relation: the antecedent must precede and command the anaphor. If NP-trace is an anaphor and the moved NP is the antecedent, it follows quite naturally that NP-movement, in order not to violate this condition on anaphora, can operate only upward and leftward. Many of the finer points of this theory of movement have been dealt with in such works as Dresher and Hornstein (1979).

Useful as these results are, they are unavailable here because the present theory does not use the notion "trace of NP." Instead, an analysis of leftward NP-movement appears to follow from a property of Predication (which, along with Evaluation, is one of the analogues of NP-movement). Williams discusses several cases of predication (1980, 206, (14)):

(4.73)
AP: John made Bill *sick*.
NP: John made Bill *a doctor*.
PP: John kept it *near him*.
VP: John *died*.

Williams posits the following rule of Predication and an accompanying C-Command Condition (1980, 206, (13) and (15)):

(4.74)
a. *Predication*
   Coindex NP and X.
b. *C-Command Condition on Predication*
   If NP and X are coindexed, NP must c-command X or a variable bound to X.

All the cases of predication in (4.73) appear to involve the NP being to the left of the X-phrase that is predicated of it, except (superficially) those examples involving "movement" that leaves a variable-trace behind. Thus, if Predication requires that the NP be to the left of X, as Williams's account seems to imply and as assumed here, then leftward NP-movement follows a structural requirement attributable to the predication relation. Since "regular" control cases also involve predication, it is not surprising that the "antecedent" of "PRO" shares the property of the NP-trace antecedent; that is, it c-commands the "PRO" and is to its left.[40]

4.3 Defining the Base: Problems of Constituency and the Content of the S-Node

In developing a procedure of evaluation, I have used conventional node labels such as VP and S and have put aside the issue of the node label that dominates *to* and V (i.e., infinitival complements). In this section I turn to this and related issues, showing how the evaluation procedure requires posing certain questions in certain ways. First I will discuss the status of S, and then the infinitival complement problem.

4.3.1 The Relation of S to V

What is the relation of S to V? Is S a projection of V? Bresnan (1982, 353), following Hornstein (1977) and McCloskey (1979), says that "S and $\bar{\text{S}}$ [S'] are considered to be major categories which are projections of no lexical category . . ." Those who argue that S is a projection divide into two camps: those who claim that S is a projection of V (e.g., Jackendoff (1977) and Marantz (1980)) and those who claim that S is a projection of INFL (e.g., Chomsky (1981b) and Stowell (1981)). To say that S forms a separate system, which is Bresnan's and Hornstein's position, is not really possible here. As in Stowell (1981), the PS rules assumed here are allowed only to define the position of the head with respect to "specifiers" and "complements"; they contain no reference to categories. Recall that we are adopting Stowell's X-bar principles, of which the following one is relevant to this discussion (1981, 87, (5)):

(4.75)
Every phrase is endocentric.

S, therefore, is a projection of *something*. It turns out that in MG theory S is, strictly speaking, a projection of either Modal, *have*, *be*, or the main verb. That is, S is a projection of whatever carries tense and/or modality.[41] An example should make this clearer:

(4.76)
John should have been renting the piano.

Given the PS rules $X'' \rightarrow (X'') \ X'$, $X' \rightarrow X \ X''^*$, (4.76) receives the following syntactic analysis:

(4.77)

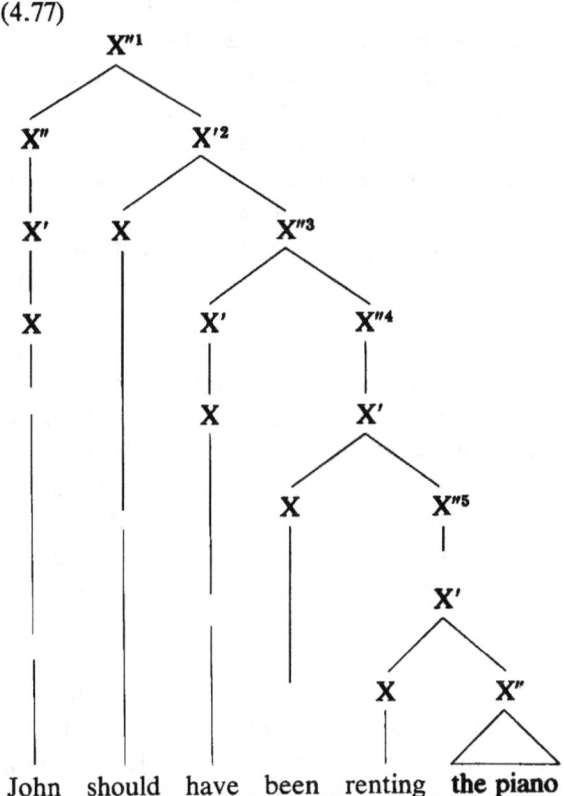

John   should   have   been   renting   **the piano**

After feature percolation all the Xs have received categorial content.

Except for the modal, *should,* the above structure is similar in many ways to Akmajian, Steele, and Wasow's (1979) account of Modal, *have,* and *be*. The structure states the following relations: *have* is a complement of *should*, *been* is a complement of *have*, and *renting*, or X'''^5, is a complement of *been*. I am assuming that, for example, *have* takes complements headed by elements that carry a certain type of "verbal" morphology (*-en, -ed,* or vowel ablaut). *Be* takes complements headed by elements that carry *-ing*. Since this analysis does not include Affix Hopping, I am assuming that the relevant (morphological) features percolate with the rest of the categorial features. This is strikingly similar to Gazdar, Pullum, and Sag's (1982) account of Affix Hopping.[42]

Returning to the problem of the status of S, notice that (4.77) represents X'''^1 as a projection of *should*. Does this mean that S is a projection of some modal? Strictly speaking, that is what the analysis claims.[43] Recall that S is identified as present when the subject of the verb is syntactically realizable. In the above example it is the modal, *should,* which harbors "modality," that is syntactically sanctioning the subject, the NP *John*. In short, I am claiming that entities that syntactically sanction the subject also involve the construal of S. This entity is not a separate constituent; it resides in the verb or in one of the "auxiliary" elements. This means also that the presence of an uninflected verb like *go* does *not* involve the construal of a syntactic S, since the relevant feature (say, tense) is missing.[44]

Having determined the status of S, we must now examine its effects on MG theory. One involves the statement of Predication and another the statement of Indirect Evaluation. Under this analysis, Predication takes an NP and an adjacent element that may be X″ or X′ and assigns indices to them. Indirect Evaluation must be stated so that the verb is allowed to take an index that shows up anywhere along the path of its projection, i.e., X″ or X′. Another point that must be clarified is how nominative case is assigned; this is taken up in section 4.3.3.[45]

4.3.2 Infinitival Complements

Throughout this chapter I have treated *to* and V as constituents of a mystery node, X. In sentences like *John wants to go,* I have treated *to go* as though it were a complement of the verb *want*. The question is, How does *to* fit into the analysis? There are two choices: (i) *to* is a specifier of V or (ii) *to* takes a V″ complement. I choose the latter course for the following reason: some verbs select infinitival complements specifically, and if *to* were a specifier of V, then the fact that *to* occurred in the complement would not show up on the projection of that complement.[46] The structure for *John wants to go* would be as shown in (4.78).

Modular Theory: English   155

(4.78)

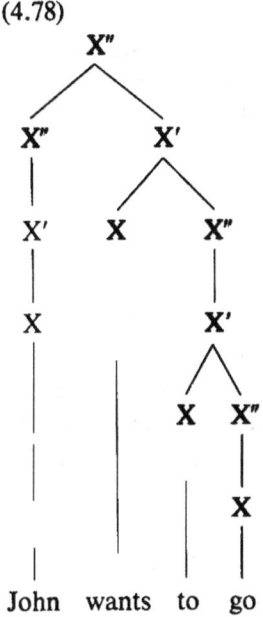

John   wants   to   go

The question immediately arises, What happens to Indirect Evaluation? If *want*, which is an optional subject control verb, assigns the index of its subject to the X" complement, how does the verb *go* in turn receive it? It appears that *to*, like *seem* and *be*, passes the index down to its complement.

4.3.3 Subject-Auxiliary Inversion
Culicover (1976, 67) notes that

there are three generalizations that any analysis of yes-no questions should capture:
  1. In yes-no questions, the sequence of elements that precedes the subject NP consists of TENSE attached to a verbal element—M [Modal], *have,* or *be.*
  2. If the presence of the subject NP is ignored, the sequence before and after the NP has precisely the appearance of an expansion of AUX followed by a verb phrase.
  3. The affixes in a yes-no question appear precisely where they would appear if Affix Hopping had applied everywhere in the sentence, including the sequence that precedes the subject NP.

We need to explore how the theory presented here accounts for these generalizations, without benefit of PS rules expressing ordering dependencies and transformations "moving" constituents. A question immediately arises concerning Tense. Here, since Tense is not introduced via a rewrite rule, we cannot rely on that rule to limit a simple sentence to a single instantiation of Tense. This is where the potential trouble arises: since Tense (i.e., tense and modality) sanctions the syntactic subject, what is to prevent the following string from being generated?

(4.79)
*John should Mary has Paul was renting the piano.

I have already alluded to the obvious solution: to rely on the subcategorization properties of the Aux elements themselves to rule out this sentence.[47] *Have, be,* and the modal *should* do not take tensed complements. Consequently, if *have, be,* and the main verb should end up as complements to an Aux element, it must be tenseless. Another reason for rejecting (4.79) is that two of the subjects would not be associated with argument slots.

Culicover's generalizations state, then, that the element to the left of the subject carries Tense, that the order of the Aux elements remains the same even after "inversion," and that the dependencies expressed by the PS rules are maintained even when the subject changes position. The following examples (from Culicover (1976, 63)) will aid discussion.[48]

(4.80)
a. Has John written?
b. Is John writing?
c. Will John write?

(4.81)
a. Has John been writing?
b. Will John be writing?
c. Will John have written?

(4.82)
Would John have been writing?

Examples (4.80)–(4.82) would be associated with the following structures.

Modular Theory: English

(4.83)

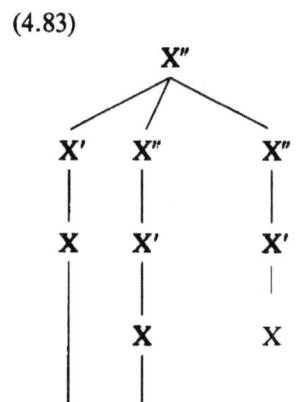

```
a. has      John   a. written
b. is              b. writing
c. will            c. write
```

(4.84)

```
a. has   John   a. been    a. writing
b. will         b. be      b. writing
c. will         c. have    c. written
```

(4.85)

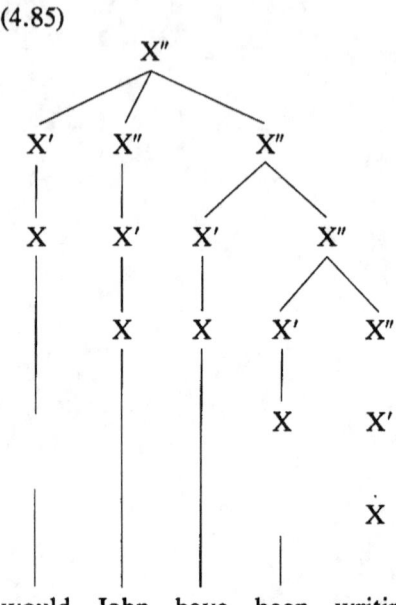

would John have been writing

The Aux expansion rule of earlier generative literature was an ingenious way of expressing at once all the order dependencies of Modal, *have,* and *be,* making them available at a single point in the grammar. Since we are not using a PS rule to express the relative order of these elements, we must assume that this information is part of the subcategorization information of each of them—that is, that perfective *have,* for example, can have "progressive" *been* as a complement.

Examples (4.83)–(4.85) illustrate one structural possibility. Another would be to put the subject *John* down with the other complement (that is, to make *John* the syntactic subject of *written* in (4.83a)). This is the alternative Ken Hale suggests (personal communication). Taking such a tack would entail revising more extensively the nominative case-assignment rule. If *John* were embedded, some kind of "exceptional case marking" would be needed. The case-assignment rule would have to ignore the fact that an X″ boundary intervened between the case-assigning element and the target of case assignment, i.e., *John*. Thus, *John* is best left where it is, within easy reach of *has, is,* and *will.* Now it is necessary to modify how case assignment works when it comes to these Aux elements. I will assume that certain elements can assign nominative case either to the left or to the right. In (4.83)–(4.85), where the Aux elements assign nominative case to the right, the case-receiving element must be *immediately* to the right; therefore, some kind of adjacency condition is needed.[49] In sum, therefore, we see that this theory crucially relies on the subcategorization properties of the Aux elements to yield Culicover's generalizations 1–3. Inversion in this theory is simply the property that certain elements may assign nominative case either to the right or to the left.

I could be accused at this point of missing an elementary generalization involving the category affiliation of the invertible elements. If there is in fact a rule of Subject-Aux Inversion that need only know category affiliation in order to work, this would be a serious criticism. But, as Susan Steele has pointed out (personal communication), such an approach would require that every inverted case have (as input to the inversion rule) a corresponding uninverted string. There do appear to be cases where no uninverted version exists. Steele reports that only (4.86b) is possible for her, and not (4.86a).

(4.86)
a. I shall help.
b. Shall I help?

Correspondingly, there are cases that resist Subject-Aux Inversion.

(4.87)
a. Thou shalt not kill.
b. Shalt thou not kill?

(4.87b) is definitely odd. Granted, we cannot necessarily know ahead of time what kind of oddity is involved; but it seems fair to say that if *shalt* is a modal, then Subject-Aux Inversion can invert it. We do not seem to be dealing with subtle intuitions here, though; (4.87a) seems to involve a fairly fixed order, which (4.87b) violates. In any event, although such examples are not conclusive evidence for our approach, they do raise doubts about the generality of a syntactic Subject-Aux Inversion rule.

To conclude this section on subject-aux inversion, note that the subject *John* in (4.83)–(4.85) ends up being coindexed with the X" complement via Predication. Indirect Evaluation applies in case the complement is headed by a main verb and associates the index of *John* with the subject argument slot of that verb. If the complement is headed by *have* or *be,* the index is passed on to the complement. Hence, the elements that pass on Predication indices include Modal, *have, be, to,* and "raising" verbs like *seem.*

4.4 Final Remarks

Many topics and constructions remain to be discussed; for example, I have considered neither WH-movement nor relative clauses. I leave these and other issues for the future, turning instead to explore further ramifications of the analyses proposed so far. A crucial assumption concerning the status of certain phonologically null elements is not being carried over into this theory, a decision that has some fundamental consequences. Recall that in this analysis the "subject," [X″, X″], is not obligatory, by virtue of the PS rules. This leaves the option of not assuming that PRO is an entity in the syntax (that is, syntax in the narrow sense and not in a sense that includes all levels of representation). Therefore, unlike Stowell, who is another advocate of an impoverished PS system, I am not positing PRO in the syntax. This decision raises certain problems and questions, to which the next chapter is devoted.

Chapter 5
Consequences for Anaphora in English

In this chapter I will reassess the status of NP-trace and PRO. Previously I have suggested that there are not two distinct syntactic entities, one an anaphor (NP-trace) and the other a pronominal anaphor (PRO).[1] Such a position entails rethinking the question of anaphora in general, since it has been assumed and argued that NP-trace (unlike PRO) falls under a general set of binding principles that also account for the construal and distribution of overt anaphors, pronouns, and referential expressions (R-expressions) and at the same time explain why most "movement" rules operate leftward.[2] In section 5.1 I will briefly review the development of the anaphora question with respect to overt pronouns and anaphors. In section 5.2 I will present a hypothesis about the organization of the language system, with its various interacting components, that will, in concert, constitute an account of some of the properties associated with NP-trace, PRO, and overt pronouns and anaphors. This approach is similar in spirit to that of Reinhart (1980) and also adapts some aspects of binding theory (Chomsky (1981b)). Section 5.3 involves motivating an extension of bound anaphora to so-called empty categories (or unevaluated argument slots). Section 5.4 gives an account of empty categories, drawing heavily on the approach to control and binding discussed in chapter 4.

5.1 Anaphora and Coreference

5.1.1 "Pronominalization"
The problem of accounting for the behavior of pronouns has been the focus of much research in linguistics and has played a crucial role in developing and deciding between competing theories. Approaches have varied. The earliest work (Lees and Klima (1963), Langacker

(1969), Ross (1969), Lakoff (1968, 1970), Postal (1970)) was most concerned with accounting for the anaphoric, coreferential interpretation of pronouns, utilizing a pronominalization/reflexive transformation that replaced full NPs with a pronoun, subject to satisfaction of an identity condition. The problems with such an approach are well known (see, for example, Helke (1973), Bach (1970), Bresnan (1970), Wasow (1979)). Later, although the theoretical mechanism was changed from a transformational rule to an interpretive one, the problem was still viewed primarily as one of accounting for the anaphoric use of (now base-generated) pronouns (Wasow (1979), Dougherty (1969), Jackendoff (1972)). Jackendoff (1972) introduced a rule of noncoreference operative whenever coreference is not established between two NPs. Lasnik (1976) redefined the problem. He argued that only a rule of noncoreference (or disjoint reference) is needed and that coreference is handled pragmatically. This new approach was heralded as a breakthrough (for example, in Bresnan (1978)).

However, Lasnik's noncoreference rule has come under criticism (Evans (1980), Bach and Partee (1980)). The most notable problem seems to involve a confusion among "... three notions associated with the term *coreference*" (Evans (1980, 360)). Lasnik's noncoreference rule is intended to rule out cases of "accidental" coreference, which occurs when a pronoun is used indexically (deictically) to refer to some individual who turns out to be a person already referred to (say, by name) in the sentence. However, this is a case of extensional coreference and, as Evans points out, does not yield an ungrammatical sentence. Yet this is just the kind of case that Lasnik argues is, and should be, proscribed by a grammatical rule. Because of this sort of problem, later studies have moved away from the noncoreference rule (see Chomsky (1981b), Reinhart (1980)).

5.1.2 Three-Valued Indexing Systems and Their Consequences

Writing on coreference and bound anaphora, Reinhart (1980, 4) points out that the following "... 3-valued indexing system is assumed, at least implicitly, in all current analyses of anaphora within interpretive semantics." ((5.1a–c) are Reinhart's (6a–c).)

(5.1)
a. *Obligatory (stipulated) coreference*, e.g.:
   (i) Zelda bores herself.

Anaphora in English   163

b. *Obligatory (stipulated) noncoreference,* e.g.:
   (ii) Zelda bores her.
   (iii) She adores Zelda's teachers.
c. *Optional (free) coreference,* e.g.:
   (iv) Zelda adores her teachers.
   (v) Those who know her adore Zelda.

Reinhart offers an informal statement of the anaphora conditions that reflect the three-valued system (her examples (10a–c)).

(5.2)
a. A nonpronominal NP must be interpreted as noncoreferential with any NP that c-commands it. (This entails that a pronoun must be interpreted as noncoreferential with any full NP it c-commands.)
b. A reflexive or reciprocal pronoun (an R-pronoun) must be interpreted as coreferential with (and only with) a c-commanding NP within a specified syntactic domain.
c. A non-R-pronoun must be interpreted as noncoreferential with any c-commanding NP in the syntactic domain which is specified for [(5.2b)].

(5.2c) stipulates that nonanaphors (i.e., pronouns and R-expressions) are noncoreferential with "any c-commanding NP in the syntactic domain which is specified for [(5.2b)]." For example, in Chomsky (1981b) each NP in (5.3) would have a "referential" index that is freely assigned.

(5.3)
He_i loves $Bill_j$.

In GB theory the indices cannot be identical because of Binding Condition (5.4c), shown here in Koster and May's formulation (1982, 137).

(5.4)
Binding Conditions
a. Anaphors must be bound in their governing category.
b. Pronouns must be free in their governing category.
c. All other NPs must be free in all governing categories.

Bill, therefore, cannot have the same index as *he*.[3]

In (5.3) this "disjointness" is not a fact about actual speaker reference. When (5.3) is embedded in a conversation, it is entirely possible for *he* and *Bill* to refer to the same individual. The speaker can, in fact, be intending to refer to one individual:

(5.5)
Speaker A: Does Bill love anyone?
Speaker B: Well, he loves Bill.

Evans discusses another example in which binding theory would require noncoreference. For example, because of (5.4c) the two instances of *Bill* in (5.6) would be deemed noncoreferential.

(5.6)
Bill^1 thinks that Bill^2 is terrific.

But, as Evans demonstrates, Bill^1 and Bill^2 can be used to refer to the same individual (example from Evans (1980, (49)).[4]

(5.7)
I know what John and Bill have in common. John thinks that Bill is terrific and Bill^1 thinks that Bill^2 is terrific.

5.1.3 The Problem Redefined

Reinhart (1980) argues that the grammar is solely responsible for cases of bound anaphora, where "... all pronouns can be interpreted as bound variables, regardless of whether the antecedent is a quantified NP or not ... ," and *not* responsible for establishing noncoreference or coreference. She posits the following optional coindexing procedure (1980, 34, (54)):

(5.8)
Coindex a pronoun P with a c-commanding NP α (α not immediately dominated by COMP or S').
Conditions:
a. If P is an R-pronoun, α must be in its minimal governing category.
b. If P is a non-R-pronoun, α must be outside its minimal governing category.

An R-pronoun such as *himself* is only interpretable as a bound variable; thus, if (5.8) does not apply, the sentence will not be interpretable. When a non-R-pronoun is coindexed, it is then bound; otherwise, the pronoun is considered to be an indexical. Thus, a non-R-pronoun can potentially be construed as a bound variable (or as referentially dependent) or an indexical, depending on the binding situation. Names, on

Anaphora in English

the other hand, are never targets for binding and therefore have no potential bound variable interpretation. Non-R-pronouns exhibit properties associated with both anaphors and names. What is crucial for our purposes is that there are not, under this view, two types of non-R-pronouns (i.e., bound variable non-R-pronouns and indexical non-R-pronouns). This view of the role of binding in determining the properties associated with a given entity will figure importantly in our discussion of "empty categories."

5.2 Anaphora: A Modular Account

I have briefly reviewed the various accounts of the interpretation of pronouns and anaphors, raising certain questions about (for example) the status of "disjoint reference" or the meaning of "referential index." Much of this may seem like terminological quibbling, but in fact it is more than that. Depending on one's understanding of the terminology or interpretation of, say, the role of indices, a particular picture of the grammar, or language system, emerges. At the outset I will clarify certain distinctions, present some data, and show how certain "facts" are attributable to principles of well-formedness stated over lexical structure or over syntactic structure, etc. Just what kind of "fact" is involved is not something that can be known pretheoretically; therefore, the characterization "is a 'fact' of X" is necessarily theory dependent. My approach is guided by the following intuition: what may look like a *single* "fact" may derive from a number of different properties of the language system that interact in such a way as to yield a result that is the "fact." That is to say, there is no single level of representation over which a rule or principle is stated that accounts for all the "facts" related to anaphora. Though this approach should not be controversial, the theory that results—not being obvious—should be so.

5.2.1 The General Framework
The following sentences will form a basis for discussion.[5]

(5.9)
a. Michael saw Robert.
b. Michael saw him.

(5.10)
a. Sam believes he is brilliant.
b. Sam believes him to be brilliant.

(5.11)
a. Michael saw himself.
b. Michael saw herself.

(5.12)
a. Wash yourself!
b. Wash himself!

(5.13)
a. I lost my way.
b. We lost my way.

(5.14)
a. We expected me to like John.
b. We expected John to like me.

(5.15)
Carter voted for every Democrat.

(5.16)
The soldiers think that the officers are competent.

(5.17)
We think that the officers will be sent to the front.

    The general framework to be developed here will be modular "in the sense that it will posit distinct principles working in distinct parts of the description of English which interact in such a way as to account for the facts . . ." (Harnish (1982, 39)). The goal will be to account for (oddity) judgments of certain sentences using pragmatic and semantic principles that interact with various levels of the grammar. Since the goal is to develop an account of interpretation that includes reference, we must move to the interface of the "grammar" and language use. The proposed system will be set up in the following way: there are three levels of representation (lexical, syntactic, and semantic) over which pragmatic inferences and principles are stated. In the end, the point of these pragmatic inferences will be to account for successful linguistic communication.

    According to inferential theories of communication (see Bach and Harnish (1979)), communication is successful if an intended addressee (a "hearer") infers the speaker's actual communicative intent. The nature of communication and the role that linguistic structure plays in it will be important in our account of reference, coreference, and anaphora, because we will want to sharply distinguish the contribution of linguistic meaning from the contribution of referential intent to the total communicative intent of a speaker.

Before we discuss examples (5.9)–(5.17), certain terms must be defined and distinguished. Much could be said—indeed, much has been said—about the proper vocabulary for describing the word-world relations we are interested in. The important distinction for our purposes is between what is in the *extension* of a predicate (or *denotation* of a term) and what is the *referent intended* in the utterance of an expression. The former is a *semantic* (word-world) relation, and the latter a *pragmatic* (speaker-world) relation. The extension of a predicate (or term) consists of the objects that the predicate is *true of*. Thus, all male objects are in the extension of the word *(is) male*. These are the objects the predicate is *literally* true of. Something can be literally called *male* only if *male* is (literally) true of it.[6] On the other hand, many nonmale things can be *referred* to with the word *male*, if the circumstances are right, though such uses of language will be *nonliteral*. For instance, nonliteral reference is common when the speaker knows the hearer is mistaken about the object of reference. Thus, imagine that a speaker knows that Jones is a plumber, not a famous playwright; but because Jones often wears dark turtleneck sweaters, the hearer *thinks* Jones is a playwright. The speaker might very well not want to bother to correct the hearer about his misapprehension, instead playing along with the mistaken belief and referring to Jones with the phrase *The playwright over there* . . . Thus, the speaker could very well successfully communicate his message concerning Jones to the hearer using a phrase that does not *denote* Jones at all. The crucial point for our purposes is that the object of referential intention need not belong to the extension (denotation) of the term used to refer to it.

The potential problem now is that linguistic devices for signaling aspects of the message can be reflecting either semantic or pragmatic information. There is no a priori reason why a device should not develop in a language for signaling the fact that the speaker of the expression containing the device intends to refer to different (or identical) entities in the utterance of that expression. Likewise, there is no a priori reason why a language should not have a device for signaling the fact that a relational predicate must, can, or cannot contain the same object as arguments for distinct slots in its predicative structure. Thus, if we encounter a device in a language that seems to be constraining the class of potential communicative intentions one can have in uttering its expressions communicatively, we are free to ask whether the constraint exists at the semantic or pragmatic level. In what follows I will argue that different constraints can apply in English at the same levels, and because of this it can look at first glance as though semantic principles are involved when in fact pragmatic principles are.

I will divide the principles into groups depending on the maximal level of structure needed to state them. I have not ordered these principles.

Lexical Level
Structural
P1. *Predicate Argument Principle*
The lexicon provides the argument structure of predicates (e.g., verbs).
Semantic
P2. *Co-satisfaction Principle* (defined over lexical structure)
The semantics of some predicates is such that if xVy, then $x = y$. For example, if "x cranes y's neck" or "x loses y's mind" or "x nods y's (own) head," etc., then $x = y$.
Pragmatic
P3. *Disjoint Reference Principle* (defined over lexical structure)
The arguments of a predicate are intended to be disjoint, unless marked otherwise.

Lexical-Syntactic Levels
Semantic
P4. *Co-satisfaction Principle* (defined over lexical and syntactic structure)
The semantics of *self* is such that if xVy (pro)+*self*, then $x = y$.

Syntactic Level
Structural
M1. *Binding Mechanism*
Coindex a pronoun P with a c-commanding NP α (α not immediately dominated by COMP or S'). Condition: if P is a non-R-pronoun, α must be outside its minimal governing category.[7]
Pragmatic
P5. *Coreference/Disjoint Reference Principle* (defined over syntactic structure)
If an NP α is bound (i.e., coindexed with a c-commanding NP) by an NP β and NP α is referential, then (a) they are intended to be coreferential or (b) they are intended to at least overlap in reference

if one index ranges over a set (as in the case of we_i). However, if NP α and NP β are not coindexed, then they are intended to be disjoint if NP α is referential and NP β c-commands NP α.

P6. *Imperative Principle* (from Harnish (1983))
The literal and direct use of the imperative form is to direct the hearer H to perform some act A mentioned by the main verb of the sentence.

Figure 5.1 is a schematic representation of the syntactic and lexical components, their associated rules and principles (boxes 1 and 2), and the rules and principles that mediate between them. In addition, a pragmatic component is depicted (box 3) that utilizes both lexical and syntactic (as well as sematic) information in order to assign representations a literal and direct (illocutionary) force and content.

Principles P1–P5 and M1 all bear discussion, though I will mention only a few points here. Note, for instance, the use of both disjoint extension and disjoint reference principles. If these principles were not distinguished, coreference and disjoint reference would become coextension and disjoint extension (the pragmatic would equal the semantic), and any violation of the principles would induce *nonliterality*. However, it seems intuitively wrong (and theoretically cumbersome) to view sentences such as (5.18a–c) as being nonliteral if they are not disjoint:

(5.18)
a. *John* likes *John*.
b. *He* said that *John* is brilliant.
c. *John* believes *him* to be a genius.

What sort of theory would say that uttering (5.19)

(5.19)
John likes himself.

could involve a literal use of *John, likes,* and *himself,* where a speaker would thereby be speaking literally, but if the speaker should decide as in (5.18a) to refer to John (the same John) *twice* instead of *once* with John's (literally usable) name, somehow the utterance magically becomes nonliteral? But this raises the question, What feature of nonliterality has entered the communicative act? Embracing a theory that posits such nonliterality is a dubious alternative when a perfectly sound one is available. I turn now to developing just such an alternative. This

Modularity in Syntax 170

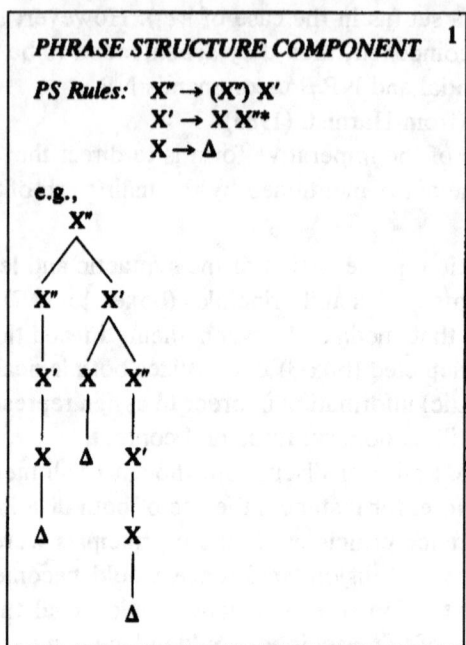

Provides syntactic structures

Lexical insertion
and feature climbing

Example:

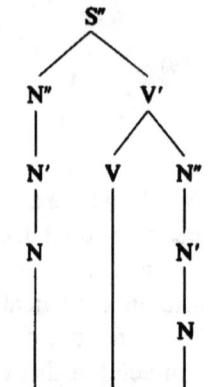

Figure 5.1
A tentative model of the language system (English)

> **LEXICAL COMPONENT** 2
>
> Contains:
> a. List of nondecomposable items
> b. Lexical entries (e.g., PASs)
> c. Principles of word formation and operations on PASs
> d. The Co-satisfaction Principle (P2.) (e.g., if x cranes y's neck then $x = y$)

Provides PAS (P1.
Predicate Argument Principle)

Example: (___$_i$ (saw ___$_j$))

Figure 5.1
(continued)

Modularity in Syntax

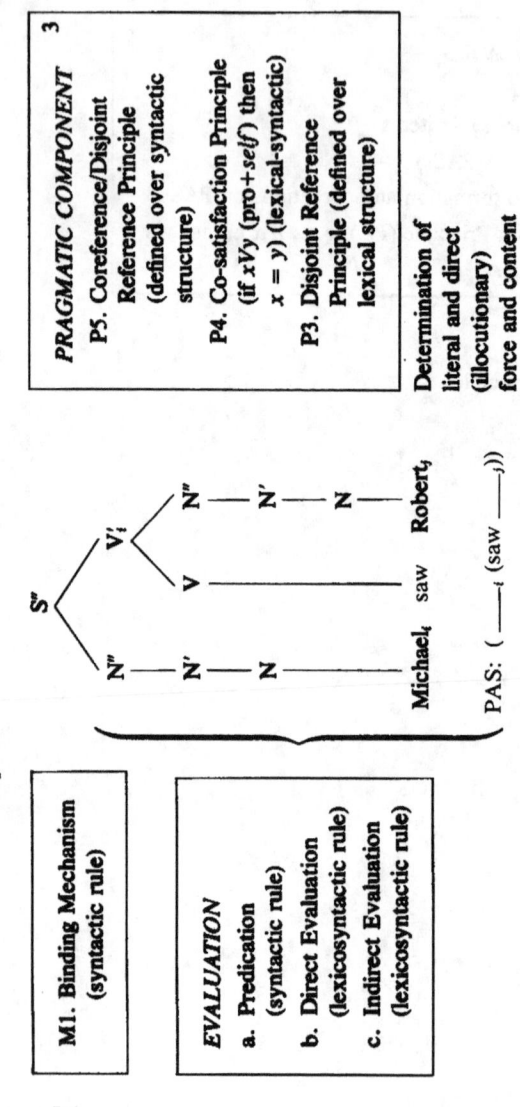

Figure 5.1
(continued)

Anaphora in English   173

requires making some assumptions about particular facts of English. Roughly stated, they are:

F1.
(Lexical semantic) The pronoun *he* is literally and directly used indexically to denote something only if it is male and neither speaker nor hearer.

F2.
(Lexical pragmatic) The pronouns *I* and *my* are literally and directly used indexically to refer to something only if it is the speaker.

F3.
(Lexical pragmatic) The pronouns *you* and *your* are literally and directly used indexically to refer to something only if it is the hearer.

Here I will leave aside any qualification or elaboration of these assumptions; but see Farmer and Harnish (in preparation) for discussion.

5.2.2 The Account: A First Approximation

Returning to (5.9)–(5.17), let us see how the proposed theory would characterize each one.

  Michael saw Robert (5.9a) has the following syntactic and lexical structure:[8]

(5.20)

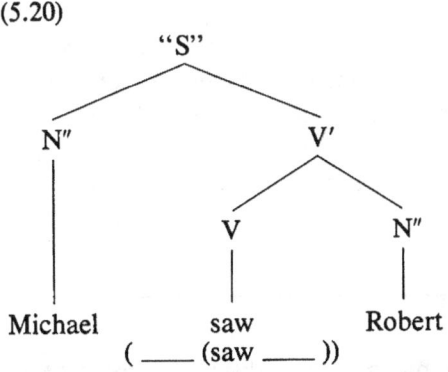

We know, furthermore, that after Predication and evaluation *Michael* is coindexed with the subject argument slot and *Robert* with the object argument slot. Recall that the Predicate Argument Principle (PI) provides the lexical structure of the verb, which has been used for the purposes of evaluation. The Co-satisfaction Principle (P2) does not apply, since *saw* does not stipulate that its arguments are identical. The Binding Mechanism (M1) and the Co-satisfaction Principle (P4) also do not apply, since the sentence contains neither pronouns nor instances of (pro)+*self*. This leaves only P5, the Coreference/Disjoint Reference Principle. Roughly, P5 states that if two NPs are bound (i.e., coindexed), then they are intended to be coreferential; but if they are not bound, then they are intended to be disjoint in reference. *Michael* and *Robert* are not coindexed, since M1 could not and did not apply; thus, they are intended to be disjoint in reference. The following list summarizes these steps:

(5.21)
P1: PAS provided by the lexicon
P2: Not applicable
P3: Argument slots of *saw* intended to be disjoint unless otherwise indicated[9]
P4: Cannot apply
M1: Cannot apply
P5: Concludes that *Michael* and *Robert* are intended to be disjoint in reference

Typically, P5 will be overridden if there is some contextual reason to suppose that a single individual is being referred to with the names *Robert* and *Michael*. Notice that literality can be preserved if the individual is named both *Robert* and *Michael*, since the individual is in the extension of both names.

Michael saw him (5.9b) is quite similar to *Michael saw Robert*, except that it involves a pronoun, *him*, instead of the name *Robert*. Despite the presence of a pronoun, the Binding Mechanism (M1) still does not apply since the NP Michael is within the minimal governing category of the pronoun. Since the Binding Mechanism has not coindexed *Michael* and *him*, P5 concludes that the two NPs are intended to be disjoint.

(5.22)
P1: PAS provided by the lexicon
P2: Not applicable
P3: Argument slots of *saw* intended to be disjoint unless otherwise indicated
P4: Cannot apply
M1: Cannot apply
P5: Concludes that *Michael* and *him* are intended to be disjoint in reference

Anaphora in English

Sam believes he is brilliant (5.10a) has the following syntactic structure:[10]

(5.23)
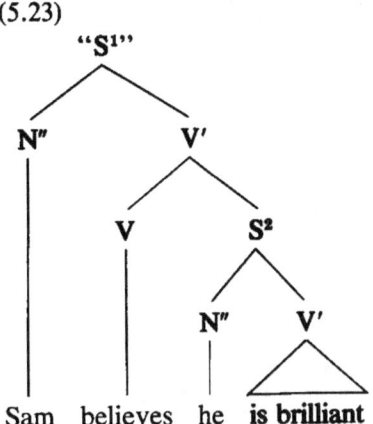
Sam believes he is brilliant

(5.24)
P1: PAS provided by the lexicon
P2: Not applicable
P3: No effect
P4: Cannot apply
M1: Can apply, coindexing *Sam* with *he*
P5: If M1 has applied (the condition is met), then *Sam* and *he* are intended to be coreferential.

P3 does not have any visible effect on reference, since one of the argument slots is associated with a clause. M1 *can* apply in this sentence, since *Sam* is outside the minimal governing category of *he*, which is S^2. P5 would conclude that *Sam* and *he* are intended to be coreferential. If M1 does not apply, than P5 concludes that *Sam* and *he* are intended to be disjoint in reference.[11]

Sam believes him to be brilliant (5.10b) is associated with a structure that differs slightly, but significantly, from that of *Sam believes he is brilliant*.[12]

(5.25)

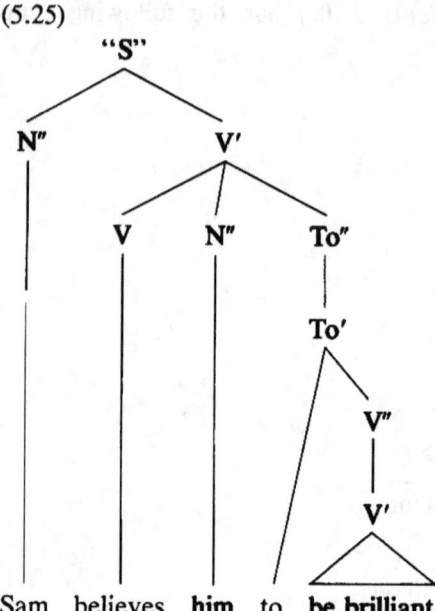

Sam believes **him** to **be brilliant**

The difference lies in the relation between *him* and *Sam*. Since they both have the same minimal governing category, the topmost "S", the Binding Mechanism cannot apply and P5 will conclude that *Sam* and *him* are intended to be disjoint in reference.

(5.26)
P1: PAS provided by the lexicon
P2: Not applicable
P3: No effect
P4: Cannot apply
M1: Cannot apply, since *Sam* is not outside the minimal governing category of *him*
P5: Concludes that *Sam* and *him* are intended to be disjoint in reference

Michael saw himself (5.11a) has the following syntactic and lexical structures associated with it, after Predication and evaluation:

Anaphora in English

(5.27)

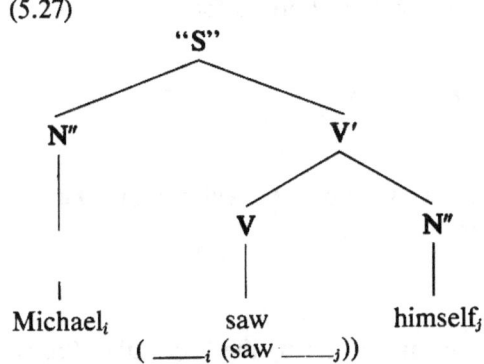

In this case P4 finally comes into play. P4 says that "the semantics of *self* is such that if xVy (pro)+*self*, then $x = y$." For terminological convenience I will talk about slots of a predicate being satisfied by objects in the world; thus, the argument slots of the predicate in (5.27) must be satisfied by the same object in the world.

(5.28)
P1: PAS provided by the lexicon
P2: Not applicable
P3: No effect
P4: Stipulates that the argument slots of the predicate must be satisfied by the same object in the world
M1: Not applicable
P5: Not applicable

Recall the specification of P5 to the effect that if two NPs are not bound, then they are intended to be disjoint in reference, if NP α is referential. I am assuming that *himself* is not a referential NP; therefore, P5 cannot apply.[13]

Michael saw herself (5.11b) is very similar to the previous sentence except that the pronoun, *her*, has female entities in its extension. In order for this sentence to be literally true, it must be the case that *Michael* is being used as a name for a woman (i.e., a female). If some oddity is to be ascribed to this sentence, it is that *Michael* tends to be used as a name for males. If, however, we replace *Michael* with a name such as *Lee*, then either form of the pronoun yields a normal situation:

(5.29)
a. Lee (Remick) saw herself.
b. Lee (Marvin) saw himself.

The principles for *Michael saw herself* are as follows:

(5.30)
P1: PAS provided by the lexicon
P2: Not applicable
P3: No effect
P4: Stipulates that the argument slots of the predicate must be satisfied by the same object in the world
M1: Not applicable
P5: Not applicable

Wash yourself! (5.12a) is accounted for by the Imperative Principle, P6. Recall also F3, which states that the pronouns *you* and *your* are literally and directly used to refer to something only if it is the hearer. The following is the syntactic structure and also the lexical structure (after evaluation):

(5.31)

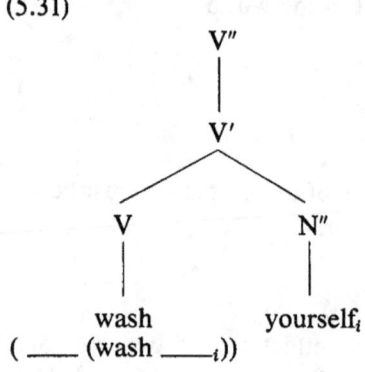

In this case P4 stipulates that the argument slots of the predicate must be satisfied by the same object in the world, i.e., $x = y$. We know from F3 that the hearer satisfies the y argument slot. Since $x = y$ and y = hearer, then x must also be the hearer. All of this is compatible with P6, which says that the literal and direct use of the imperative form is to direct the hearer to perform some act mentioned by the main verb, i.e., x = hearer.

(5.32) summarizes the effect of the principles with respect to (5.12a).

(5.32)
P1: PAS provided by the lexicon
P2: Not applicable
P3: No effect

P4: Stipulates that the argument slots of the predicate must be satisfied by the same object in the world
M1: Not applicable
F1: *Your* used literally and directly to refer to the hearer
P6: Imperative form used literally and directly to direct the hearer
P5: Not applicable

Wash himself! (5.12b) is odd. Harnish (1982) has claimed that the oddity of this sentence can be reduced to a conflict between the Imperative Principle (P6) and F1 in conjunction with the Co-satisfaction Principle (P4). F1 states that the pronoun *he* is literally and directly used indexically to denote something only if it is male and neither speaker nor hearer. P4 fixes $x = y$. Since y is associated with the pronoun *him* and $y = x$, x is also associated with the pronoun *him*. But now there is a conflict between the Imperative Principle and F1-P4. The Imperative Principle requires that x be construed as being satisfied by the hearer, but F1 and P4 require that x be satisfied by some third person; hence the oddity.

(5.33)
P1: PAS provided by the lexicon
P2: Not applicable
P3: No effect
P4: Stipulates that the argument slots of the predicate must be satisfied by the same object in the world
M1: Not applicable
F1: Stipulates that *he* and *him* are used literally and directly to denote something only if it is male and neither speaker nor hearer
P5: Not applicable
P6: Imperative form used literally and directly to direct the hearer

⎫
⎬ ← conflict
⎭

I lost my way (5.13a) illustrates the Co-satisfaction Principle (P2), which is defined over lexical structure.[14] The semantics of *x lost y's way* is such that $x = y$; that is, the x slot and the y slot must be coextensive. F2 states that the pronouns *I* and *my* are literally and directly used to refer to something only if it is the speaker. Since *I* and *my* are coextensive, there is no conflict between P2 and F2.

(5.34)
P1: PAS provided by the lexicon
P2: The semantics of x lost y's way is such that $x = y$
P3: No effect
P4: Not applicable
M1: Not applicable
F2: States that the pronouns *I* and *my* are literally and directly used indexically to refer to something only if it is the speaker
P5: Concludes that *I* and *my* are disjoint in reference

Since *I* and *my* are referring expressions and M1 has not coindexed them, P5 designates them, wrongly, as disjoint in reference. This is clearly not the result we want. I will assume, therefore, that when it comes to coextension and coreference, the semantic principle has primacy over the pragmatic principle. (In Farmer (in preparation) P5 is modified in such a way so as not to yield a conflict between P5 and P2.)

We lost my way (5.13b), like the previous example, invokes P2; that is, $x = y$. However, a conflict arises because the pronouns *we* and *my* are not coextensive, as the predicate requires. *We* and *my* certainly overlap in reference, but this is not sufficient to satisfy the requirement that the objects that satisfy x be identical to those objects that satisfy y.

We expected me to like John (5.14a) also presents a conflict. Here, M1 would not coindex *me* and *we*, since *we* is in the minimal governing category of *me*. Since *we* and *me* are referring expressions, P5 would conclude that they are disjoint in reference.[15] However, there is a conflict between P5 and a lexical fact. That is, P5, which is defined over syntactic structure, stipulates that *we* and *me* are intended to be disjoint in reference, whereas it is a semantic fact of these two words that they overlap in extension, because they both include the speaker. Thus, one principle requires disjointness, while a fact about the semantics of these pronouns results in overlapping reference.

We expected John to like me (5.14b) differs from the preceding example in the following crucial way: *we* and *me* can be coindexed by M1, *we* being outside the minimal governing category of *me*. P5 concludes that since *we* and *me* are coindexed and since *we* denotes a set that includes the speaker (i.e., the index "ranges over a set"), then *we* and *me* must at least overlap in reference. It is not necessary that the two NPs be coextensive as in the case of *We lost my/our way*.

Carter voted for every Democrat (5.15) presents a problem. It is not entirely clear what the facts are concerning this sentence. It feels as if there is some sense of disjointness that needs to be captured. In the present theory this disjointness cannot be captured by P5, since P5 requires that NP α be a "referring expression." Following Chomsky, I will assume that quantified NPs are not referring expressions. In any case, quantified NPs seem to behave differently. The relevant principle is P3, which says that arguments of a predicate are intended to be disjoint in reference unless otherwise marked. Here, there is no such "otherwise." This entails that the values of the variable bound by *every* should be distinct from *Carter*. In other words, the set containing just *Carter* is disjoint from the set containing every Democrat voted for by Carter. This account makes the following prediction: if an NP α is a nonreferring expression outside the predicate structure of an NP β, then disjointness is not a necessary presumption. That is, P5 will fail to mark the two NPs as intended to be disjoint in reference.[16] There do appear to be cases supporting this prediction:

(5.35)
a. John believes everyone in the room.
b. John believes that everyone in the room is healthy.

Speaking loosely, in (5.35a) *John* appears to be disjoint in intended reference from *everyone in the room*, whereas in (5.35b) *John* and *everyone in the room* can be construed as "overlapping" in reference.

As for the so-called reflexive interpretation, in which Carter votes for himself, this clearly involves certain nonlinguistic facts like "Carter is a Democrat" and "Carter was on the ballot." It is therefore not my goal here to capture this kind of coreference.

The soldiers think that the officers are competent (5.16) was discussed by Lasnik (1976), who claimed that *the soldiers* and *the officers* had to be disjoint in reference. I agree that the presumption, based on P5, is that these two NPs are intended to be disjoint in reference. However, unlike Lasnik, I am assuming that this presumption can be overridden by an appropriate context. That is, actual speaker reference may involve the intention that the hearer recognize overlapping reference. The next example perhaps makes this point clearer.

We think that the officers will be sent to the front (5.17), in isolation, lends itself to the following interpretation: that *we* and *the officers* are intended to be disjoint in reference. However, if the speaker, for example, is an officer, then at least overlapping reference is involved. Once again, a nonlinguistic fact is invoked to yield nondisjointness. Hence, the pragmatic principles defined over lexical and syntactic structures involve presumptions. These presumptions may well not coincide with actual speaker reference. This aspect of the communicative chain will not be developed here; I mention it simply to isolate it from the main concern, which is defining the contribution of linguistic structure to recognizing the referential intent of the speaker if the speaker is speaking literally and directly.

This concludes the discussion of anaphora. It has not been my intention to develop a complete account of anaphora phenomena here;[17] instead, I have offered an account of some well-known, albeit limited, cases that have posed problems for theories that use indices for both coreference and disjoint reference.

5.3 The Status of Empty Categories

Viewing indexing as only expressing instances of bound anaphora and not "disjointness" requires rethinking free indexing and the Binding Conditions.[18] In Chomsky (1981b, 1982) free indexing is assumed. All NPs, including ECs,[19] are freely assigned a "referential" index. Once indexing has taken place, the Binding Conditions are in effect and act as a kind of filter. For example, if an anaphor is free in its governing category, then Binding Conditions (5.4a) designates the string (structure?) as ill formed. Although this approach is elegant, I do not adopt free indexing here, for a number of reasons.[20] The indices in GB theory are assigned at S-structure, a level of representation that includes both empty categories and phonologically realized NPs. In MG theory there is no single level of representation corresponding to S-structure that includes both phonologically null and phonologically realized entities. If we were to index the MG theory analogue of PRO and NP-trace, free indexing would involve two different levels of representation. This is because these two so-called ECs are argument slots of predicates and do not occupy a phrase marker position in the tree, which I am assuming to be a syntactic representation corresponding to phonologically realized elements. Thus, it should be noted that I am using the two terms *PRO* and *NP-trace* sometimes to refer to two different theoretical entities as defined by GB theory and sometimes, in MG theory, to refer to entities that are not distinct and are not defined at the syntactic level of representation (narrowly construed).

Anaphora in English

5.3.1 The GB Claim and Some Questions

Recall that previous analyses view PRO and NP-trace as being two entities, the former a pronominal anaphor and the latter an anaphor. NP-trace thus falls under Binding Condition (5.4a) (Chomsky (1981b)). PRO cannot be subject to the Binding Condition, since a contradiction then arises; it is therefore designated as ungoverned, with the result that none of the conditions apply to it. Such an account is an attempt to capture the similarities between other anaphors and NP-trace, on the one hand, and the pronominal anaphor properties of PRO, on the other. For example, like other anaphors, NP-trace (i) always has a local antecedent, (ii) occurs in the subject position of infinitivals, (iii) has no inherent reference, and (iv) occurs in governed positions. PRO, unlike other anaphors, can have a nonlocal antecedent and occurs in ungoverned positions.

So far the approach has been to posit several entities, classifying them according to their behavior. Such an approach has treated anaphors and NP-trace as a natural class. In contrast, PRO shares properties of both anaphors and pronominals, and hence cannot fall under the same conditions as the other entities. My proposal will be that there are overt anaphors, pronominals, and unevaluated argument slots that are all targets for coindexing or targets of an identity condition. The properties traditionally associated with NP-trace and PRO will follow from the evaluation procedure and the nature of the overt NP that is coindexed with the argument slot.

5.3.2 Properties to Be Accounted For

The following list summarizes the properties associated with anaphors, PRO, NP-trace, and pronominals.

(5.36)
a. *"Bound variable"*

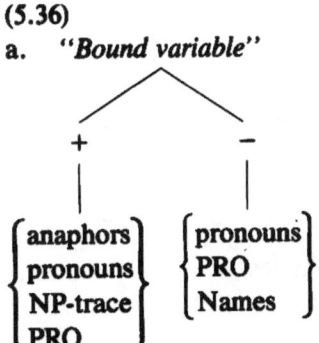

b.   *Antecedent local*

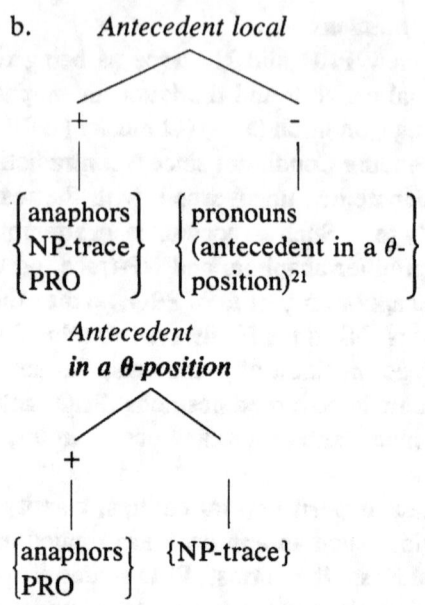

Anaphors, pronouns, PRO, and NP-trace can all be "bound variables" (i.e., coindexed by some c-commanding element), unlike Names (5.36a). Pronouns and PRO do not have to be bound (5.36a). The antecedent of anaphors, PRO, and NP-trace is local, whereas the antecedent of pronouns is not (5.36b). And anaphors and PRO both have antecedents in θ-positions, whereas NP-trace does not (5.36c). The following examples illustrate the properties diagrammed in (5.36a–c).

(5.37)
"Bound variable"
a. Anaphors
   The men$_i$ like each other$_i$.
   Mike$_i$ works himself$_i$ to death.
b. Pronoun
   Kathleen$_i$ thinks that she$_i$ can retire next year.
c. NP-trace
   John$_i$ seems t$_i$ to like oysters.
d. PRO
   Stan$_i$ wanted PRO$_i$ to go to the Olympics.

Anaphora in English

(5.38)
Not a "bound variable"
a. Pronoun
   He visited Bill at the hospital.
b. Name
   *Bill$_i$ believes that Bill$_i$ doesn't understand the situation.
c. PRO
   It's unclear what PRO to do.

(5.39)
Antecedent local
a. Anaphor
   *The men$_i$ think that Mary likes each other$_i$.
   Mary thinks that the men$_i$ like each other$_i$.
b. NP-trace
   *They$_i$ seem it is believed t_i to be fools.
   versus:
   It seems they$_i$ are believed t_i to be fools.
   They$_i$ seem t_i to be believed t_i to be fools.
c. PRO
   I told Mary$_i$ PRO$_i$ to leave.

(5.40)
Antecedent nonlocal
Pronoun
The men$_i$ think that Mary likes them$_i$.

(5.41)
Antecedent in a θ-position
a. Anaphor
   Mike$_i$ washed himself$_i$.
   $+\theta$
b. PRO
   Mike$_i$ wanted PRO$_i$ to wash himself.
   $+\theta$

(5.42)
Antecedent not in a θ-position
NP-trace
They$_i$ seem t_i to like philosophers.
$-\theta$

As far as I can tell, the only property I have listed that does not follow Chomsky (1981b) is the claim that if PRO is bound, its antecedent is local and never remote. Chomsky claims that the antecedent for PRO can be remote, which further distinguishes it from NP-trace (since NP-trace is derived via Move α and is subject to Subjacency).

Chomsky (1981b, 78) discusses several cases of long-distance control where "... PRO may be controlled by a remote antecedent ..." He contrasts this with the antecedent of NP-trace. He gives the following two examples to illustrate his point:

(5.43)

a. They$_i$ thought (that I said) that [$\begin{Bmatrix} \text{PRO}_i \text{ feeding each other} \\ \text{PRO}_i \text{ to feed each other} \end{Bmatrix}$] would be difficult.

b. *They$_i$ seemed (that I said) that [$\begin{Bmatrix} t_i \text{ feeding each other} \\ t_i \text{ to feed each other} \end{Bmatrix}$] would be difficult.

(5.43a) at first looks like a case of control (i.e., binding as determined by the grammar narrowly construed). If this is correct, then changing *they* to *Mary* should yield an ungrammatical sentence (if control is obligatory).

(5.44)
Mary$_{(i)}$ thought that Bill said that PRO$_i$ to feed each other$_i$ (feeding each other$_i$) would be difficult.

Each other is coindexed with PRO. But what is PRO bound by? At least two interpretations are available. PRO can be construed as referring either to Mary and Bill or to Bill and some other third person. (For the second interpretation it is perhaps necessary to provide some context.)[22]

In conclusion, if it can be maintained that cases of long-distance control are all instances of pragmatically determined control, then the oft-cited distinction between NP-trace and PRO is spurious; namely, that PRO, unlike NP-trace, can have a remote antecedent and in effect violate Subjacency. I will assume, then, that all cases of binding or coindexing of PRO are instances of local binding, and that the grammar does not distinguish for the purposes of binding between NP-trace and PRO.

5.4 Accounting for the Properties of NP-trace and PRO

I have claimed that any distinctions that can be drawn between NP-trace and PRO are derivative and play no role in determining binding possibilities. I view NP-trace and PRO as one entity. NP-trace is a case of an argument being bound by (i.e., coindexed with) an NP in a $\bar{\theta}$-position, and PRO is an argument slot that is possibly bound by an NP in a θ-position. Both seem to involve [−case] "gaps"; for example, while a verb may be transitive (subcategorize for an object argument), the "passive" form corresponding to that verb does not assign case to the object NP (hence a [−case] "gap"), and the NP cannot occur in the tree as an [NP, VP]. This object argument is construable, however. As Chomsky notes (1982, 33),

... any theory will somehow have to explain the fact that in the sentence *John was killed,* *John* is assigned the θ-role that *kill* assigns to its direct object in . . . *kill John,* and that the passive participle in this case does not have a direct object in the position of the associated active form.

Chomsky states that Move α can be viewed in a more theory-neutral way as expressing a relation between an antecedent (in this case *John*) and a gap (object of *killed*) where the following relations hold ((5.45) = Chomsky's (46)):

(5.45)
a. The antecedent lacks an independent θ-role (and is therefore in a $\bar{\theta}$-position).
b. The gap is properly governed (if it is trace . . .).
c. The relation is subject to bounding theory (Subjacency).

This relation is supposed to hold between NP-trace and its antecedent and, crucially, not between PRO and its antecedent if there is one. This is certainly true of (5.45a); the antecedent of NP-trace lacks an independent θ-role (in MG terms, is not associated with another argument slot) and is therefore in a $\bar{\theta}$-position. But now comes the important question: do other distinctive properties follow from (5.45a)? For example, if the antecedent lacks an independent "θ-role," does it follow that the gap is properly governed and that the relation (antecedent-trace or gap) is subject to bounding theory (i.e., Subjacency)? If there is any content to the distinction between NP-trace and PRO beyond the definitional one, then the answer to this question must be yes. At least one expects distinctions to exist, even if (5.45b,c) aren't quite correct.

Since MG theory does not distinguish between NP-trace and PRO beyond the observation that some "antecedents" occur in θ-positions and some in $\bar{\theta}$-positions, it is necessary to show that no further distinctions fall along these lines that affect these gaps.[23] That is, it must be shown that there are no properties that depend on drawing a distinction between entities with θ-position antecedents and those with $\bar{\theta}$-position antecedents. I will show that the properties mentioned in (5.45b,c) do not entail positing two entities, one that is [−pronominal, +anaphor] and the other [+pronominal, +anaphor].

5.4.1 Subjacency

Subjacency can be said to express a condition on a relation between two coindexed entities, α and β, such that two bounding nodes (i.e., S or NP and perhaps S') may not intervene between α and β. The Move α relation, which in GB theory expresses the relation between NP-trace and its antecedent, is subject to Subjacency, whereas the PRO-antecedent relation, presumably, is not. What must be shown is that whatever corresponds to Subjacency in MG theory constitutes a condition that holds between θ-position antecedents and $\bar{\theta}$-position antecedents and their respective bindees. In section 5.3 I suggested that all cases of long-distance control could be given a pragmatic explanation; that is, the proper terminology for identifying the antecedent for PRO in (5.46) involves pragmatic notions like "speaker," "hearer," etc., and not syntactically defined notions like NP or [NP, S].

(5.46)
a. I thought that you said that PRO feeding each other would be difficult.
b. They thought that you said that PRO feeding each other would be difficult.

The PRO in (5.46a,b) is not coindexed with any of the other NPs in the sentence. PRO in (5.46b) is not coindexed with the NP *they*, though the subject of *feed* may be construed pragmatically as the same group of people the speaker is using the word *they* to refer to. There is no syntactic difference between (5.46a) and (5.46b) as far as the interpretation of the subject of *feed* is concerned.

In a case like (5.47) (from Chomsky (1981b, 57)), Subjacency has been violated:

(5.47)
*John$_i$ seems [$_{S'}$ that [t$_i$ to feed himself] will be difficult]

In our terms the MG theory analogue to the θ-Criterion has been violated. If Subjacency is violated, this entails that the antecedent in a $\bar{\theta}$-position will not be associated with an argument slot (θ-role, in GB theory). Recall that *seem* passes the index of Predication down to its complement, *[that [to feed himself] will be difficult]*. The index has landed on an S', which is not a projection of *feed*. The index is inaccessible to that verb, or to any verb, for that matter. *That* does not pass the index down to the "S". *John* cannot be construed as the subject argument of *feed*. This suggests that Subjacency in MG theory amounts to the following statement: an NP outside the domain of a predicate cannot be construed as being linked to an argument slot of that predicate unless the index of that NP has been passed down. What keeps NPs from entering the domain of a predicate is any intervening node that is not the projection of a verb, an Aux element, or *to*. In (5.47) the S' intervenes, blocking the index of *John* from entering the domain of the verb *feed*. Since the procedure of indexing adopted here for construing overt NPs with arguments is subject to Subjacency, in the sense just described, and since the construal of PRO has not been treated differently from that of NP-trace, it follows that the PRO-antecedent relation must also "obey" Subjacency in the present theory.

5.4.2 Proper Government

Another distinction that is drawn between NP-trace and PRO is that NP-trace must be *properly governed*, whereas PRO must not be governed at all. The following definitions are important. ((5.48) is from Chomsky (1981b, 165), (5.49) from Jaeggli (1980, 20).)

(5.48)
Government
$[_\beta \ldots \gamma \ldots \alpha \ldots \gamma \ldots]$, where
a. $\alpha = X^0$
b. where ϕ is a maximal projection, if ϕ dominates γ then ϕ dominates α
c. α c-commands γ[24]

(5.49)
Proper Government
α properly governs β iff α governs β and
a. $\alpha = [\pm N, \pm V]$, i.e., is a lexical category
or
b. α is coindexed with β.

The definition for *government* basically states that the head governs its complements, and that the subject (i.e., [NP, S]) is *not* governed by the verb. *Proper governors* are lexical categories. The AGR element of INFL is not a proper governor for trace. If something like the Empty Category Principle (ECP: [$_\alpha$ e] must be properly governed) is operative as a condition on NP-trace, then—given the definition of proper government—it should be the case that gaps associated with $\bar{\theta}$-position antecedents should appear in different structural positions than gaps associated with θ-position antecedents.

Let us examine several cases where NP-trace and PRO supposedly contrast.

(5.50)
a. John wants to leave.
b. John seems to like baseball.

In GB theory the subject of *leave* is a PRO, whereas the subject of *like* is an NP-trace. The subjects of *leave* and *like* must be PRO and trace, respectively, so as not to violate the Extended Projection Principle (the Projection Principle coupled with the requirement that clauses have subjects; see Chomsky (1982, 10)). Notice that they are both subjects of an infinitival. The structures must differ, however, since NP-trace must be properly governed while PRO cannot be. In GB theory it is assumed that complements are clausal, that is, that even infinitivals are S's. This is all right for (5.50a), which has the structure in (5.51):

(5.51)
John wants [$_{S'}$[$_S$ PRO to leave]]

The PRO is in an ungoverned position. The S' protects the PRO from being governed by *want* (since government cannot cross a maximal projection), and the structure contains no other eligible governor. But what about (5.50b)? The NP-trace must be properly governed, but the S' blocks government by the only potential governor, *seems*.

(5.52)
John$_i$ seems [$_{S'}$[$_S$ t$_i$ to like baseball]]

In order to achieve proper government of t_i, Chomsky (1981b, 66) proposes that ". . . English has a marked rule of $\bar{S}$-deletion [S'-deletion] for complements of verbs of the *believe*-category, permitting the verb to govern the subject of the embedded complement . . ." *Seem* is just such a verb, so it utilizes the rule of S' Deletion, yielding the following structure:

(5.53)
John$_i$ seems ϕ [$_S$ t$_i$ to like baseball]

Thus, depending on the matrix verb, the subject of an infinitival can be either NP-trace or PRO. Two questions arise at this point: (i) what are the formal properties of S' Deletion? and (ii) how are cases like (5.54a–c) handled?

(5.54)
a. It is probable that John will win.
b. *John$_i$ is probable t$_i$ to win.
c. *It is probable PRO to win.

(5.54a) shows that *probable* takes an S' complement; the subject is a $\bar{\theta}$-position, which should allow raising. But (5.54b) shows that *probable* does not delete the S', hence not allowing the trace to be properly governed. Thus, *probable* has the following properties: (i) its subject is a $\bar{\theta}$-position, (ii) it takes an S' complement, and (iii) it does not delete S'. This predicts that (5.54c) should be acceptable:

(5.55)
*It is probable [$_{S'}$[$_S$ PRO to win]]

The fact that (5.54c) is also odd suggests that the explanation for the oddity of (5.54b) is wrong. One possible explanation is that the subject of the infinitival is governed, but not properly governed. This would rule out both NP-trace *and* PRO, since the only position where neither NP-trace nor PRO can appear is one that is governed but not properly governed. Within GB theory, subcategorization cannot be relied on to handle this problem because one of the theory's assumptions is that all complements are subcategorized for as Ss (or S's). That is, VP complements are not subcategorized for.[25] I have not, however, adopted this assumption. Necessarily the lexical entry is enriched, though in one sense the enrichment is nothing more than encoding the "S' Deletion" property of a predicate in a different way (i.e., by subcategorization). The solution for the oddity of (5.54b,c) is simply that *probable* does not take *to* infinitival complements. Indeed, it would be nice to have this "fact" follow from some other properties, which is exactly what Chomsky's analysis is intended to accomplish, but the ECP does not seem to work straightforwardly here. In general, my analysis can-

Modularity in Syntax 192

not take advantage of such an approach, since it cannot construct S′ complements without the requisite complementizer. Consequently, under the definition of proper government, both PRO and NP-trace are properly governed in MG theory.

To summarize, I am claiming that arguments with corresponding overt NPs, whether that NP is in a $\bar{\theta}$-position or a θ-position, will be properly governed and the relation will "obey" Subjacency. We will now see that when an argument slot is coindexed with an overt NP, that argument exhibits anaphoric properties, and when it is not, it behaves like a deictic (or indexical) pronoun. For example, in (5.56) and (5.57) the subjects of *wounded* and *leave* are both bound within the minimal governing category.[26]

(5.56)
John was wounded.

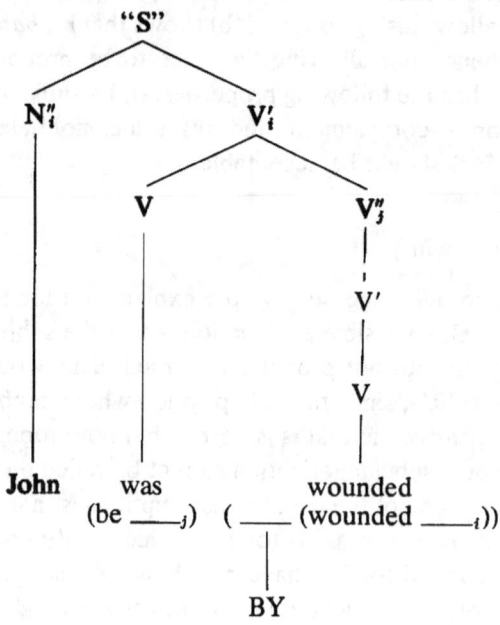

(5.57)
John tried to leave.

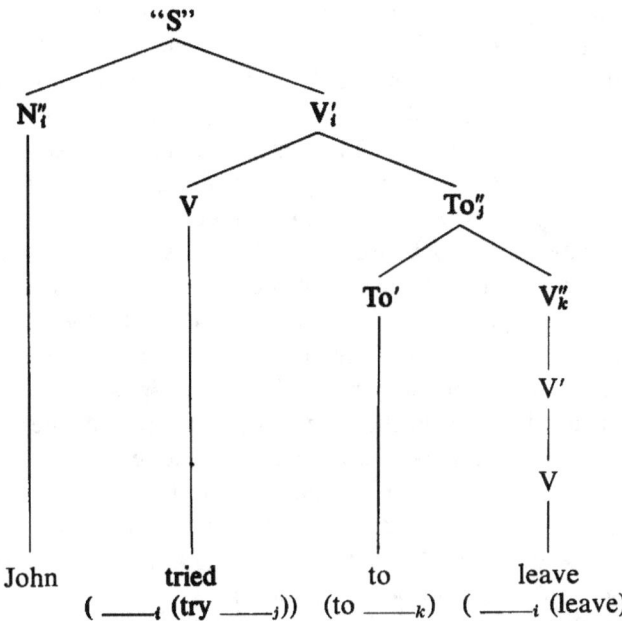

In neither case does an NP or S' intervene between the overt NP and the argument slot. On the other hand, when an argument goes unevaluated, it appears to violate Subjacency, thus exhibiting a pronominal property. I am not invoking the Subjacency Condition to achieve this result, since it follows from the indexing procedure and the θ-Criterion. I am not invoking the condition that ECs must be properly governed, since this is a consequence of the proposed analysis and need not be independently stated. I am not adopting the Binding Conditions to account for the distribution of ECs in part because I am not using the notion "is an anaphor" when it comes to ECs; these "anaphoric" properties follow from the indexing procedure outlined in chapter 4.

5.5 Summary

The brief account of anaphora presented in this chapter is by no means complete. More comprehensive analyses can be found in Chomsky (1981b, 1982), Huang (1982), or Higginbotham (1980); Farmer and Harnish (in preparation) also undertake a more detailed study of reference and anaphora. In writing this book, I did not originally intend to address the anaphora question. However, this became necessary once it became clear that I could not adopt wholesale the very popular GB theory account of anaphora. Since I am *not* assuming that NP-trace and PRO are syntactic entities in the narrow sense—that is, they do not occupy a position at the phrase marker level of representation—I am not able to assume that free indexing and binding conditions will account for their distribution. Rather, I have been claiming that the NP-trace and PRO of GB theory are in fact argument slots of predicates and that their anaphoric properties follow from the indexing procedure implemented by Predication and Evaluation. I have assumed that some entities pass indices down to their complements (*seem, to,* etc.) and some do not (*that, believe,* etc.). I have argued that in MG theory the differences between GB theory's NP-trace and PRO can be reduced to differences in the nature of the antecedent (i.e., in a θ-position or in a $\bar{\theta}$-position). It also follows from the indexing procedure that the NP-trace and PRO will be c-commanded by their respective antecedents.

My decision not to include NP-trace and PRO at the syntactic level does not rule out adopting free indexing for the overt NPs, but I have chosen not to. Instead, I have chosen to accept Reinhart's view that the indexing involves only cases of *bound* anaphora.

I have just begun to set out constructing a grammar that will provide structures, principles, and facts about the language, which then determine presumptions concerning intended reference. I have attempted to account for certain types of oddities in terms of tensions between pragmatic and semantic principles and facts.

Chapter 6
Implications for Language Typology

Throughout this work I have been concerned with identifying which overt expressions at the phrase structure level of representation are linked to which argument positions at the level of lexical structure. I have been assuming a rather impoverished PS system similar to that of Farmer (1980) and Stowell (1981), and have implemented a procedure called *evaluation* to associate overt expressions with argument slots, an association signaled with "identical" indices. The evaluation procedure developed for Japanese is sensitive to (case) particles; the procedure for English is sensitive to structural position. In what follows I will speculate on just how these slightly differing procedures may, in part, account for some of the typological differences between English and Japanese.[1]

6.1 Some Differences between English and Japanese

We will be concerned with three well-known and observable differences between English and Japanese. The first involves word order. In Japanese the N' constituents that are associated with a predicate can be in any order to the left of the head V. In English, while there is some freedom of order, PS positions are more strictly determined. A second difference involves NP-movement. English is said to have such "movement," whereas Japanese does not.[2] A third difference involves what is referred to in the literature as *null-anaphora*. In Japanese it is quite common for the subject and/or the object to be missing at the PS level of representation. Farmer (1980), Kitagawa (1982), and Hale (1983) have claimed that argument slots not associated with overt expressions are pronominal in nature. As for English, it appears that the object cannot be missing syntactically, whereas the subject can be. The nature of "missing" is, obviously, open to theoretical interpretation. Chapter 5 of this book was devoted to defending a particular interpretation, namely, that "missing" means *not* present at the PS level in this case.[3] The question then is, Why is there an asymmetry, so far as it actually exists, between subject and object in English and not in Japanese? In the next section I turn to accounting for these differences, using the theory developed in this book.

6.2 Speculation on Certain Typological Differences

6.2.1 Word Order

The nature of the evaluation procedure may well determine, in part, whether or not word order is "free." These remarks should be taken as speculative in nature, since I have not attempted to identify all the factors that may be influencing word order. For example, I have ignored the notion of "preferred word order," assuming that this is a contextually determined matter and not necessarily a province of the grammar, though this is not entirely clear. In any case, I have developed an account of evaluation in Japanese that uses the (case) particles as the mediators between the phrase structure level of representation and the lexical level. The only structural requirement is that the N' be a sister to the Verb. For English, on the other hand, the evaluation rules, coupled with Predication, are sensitive to location relative to the predicate. If function is determined by way of location, then it is not surprising that for an entity to be construed as functioning in a particular way it must be traceable to a particular position. I am not going so far as to suggest that if a language utilizes case particles, or the equivalent of case particles, the order is always free; nor am I suggesting that if (case) particles are not used, the language will have rigid word order. The most that can be said is that if location plays any role in evaluation, then word order variation will be distinctly different in nature.

6.2.2 NP-Movement

It has often been pointed out that so-called configurational languages like English involve NP-movement, whereas so-called nonconfigurational languages like Japanese do not. In the theory developed here, to say that English has NP-movement is simply to speak metaphorically. The question now is not "Why doesn't Japanese have NP-movement?" but rather "Can we extend the movement metaphor to Japanese, and if so, what are we picking out?" The discussion of the topic construction, *tough* sentences, and indirect passives in chapter 3 pointed out that the particles, specifically *ga* and *wa*, seem to function in a manner similar to the [X", S] position in English. That is, an expression marked by *ga* might not be associated with an argument slot that is also associated with the particle *ga*. Analogously, an [NP, S] in English may end up being linked to an object argument slot of a predicate. To extend the movement metaphor to Japanese, I have looked to the nature of evaluation to find the proper vocabulary—that is, the proper vocabulary involves "(case) particles" as opposed to "location in PS." For both languages I have used Predication and Indirect Evaluation in those instances where the movement metaphor applies. In MG theory terms, then, NP-movement involves something like the following situation: an overt expression (i.e., something in PS) is associated with an argument slot via Predication and Indirect Evaluation.

6.2.3 Null-Anaphora

It is well known that in Japanese the argument slots of a predicate need not be associated with an overt expression. Put differently, the subject or object can be missing at the PS level. In English, on the other hand, it appears that an "argument" may be missing only under very particular circumstances, and only subject arguments may be absent. Why is there a subject/object asymmetry in English and not in Japanese? Once again, we turn to the nature of evaluation for clues. In Japanese any argument slot may be directly associated with an overt expression. It is not necessary to first directly evaluate for the object argument slot and then proceed to the other argument positions. For English, on the other hand, the evaluation procedure is slightly different. Recall that Direct Evaluation involves associating [NP, VP] with the object argument slot of the predicate, and that Direct Evaluation occurs before Indirect Evaluation. Indirect Evaluation, in both English and Japanese, involves taking a "predication index" and associating it with any unevaluated argument slot. In English this usually amounts to linking the subject argument slot. Linking the object argument slot first avoids the need for stipulating which argument slot is linked when Indirect Evaluation applies. Such a state of affairs characterizes a certain subject/ object asymmetry. But this is not yet the whole story. Recall also the assumption that if a verb syntactically sanctions (assigns case to) [NP, VP], an overt expression, then it will occur at the PS level.[4] This, coupled with Direct Evaluation's effect of linking up syntactic objects with object argument slots before Indirect Evaluation, yields only unevaluated subjects. If the element that syntactically sanctions subject—that is, Tense and/or Modality—is missing, then the subject argument slot will go unevaluated unless an index is passed down from another predicate. In a sense, then, the asymmetry between subject and object in English is also due, in part, to the assumption that what syntactically sanctions object is different from what syntactically sanctions subject and that what syntactically sanctions subject isn't always present. This suggests that there actually should be cases of "missing" objects in English. These would be cases of infinitival passives like *To be admired is nice*. Here, *admired* does not syntactically sanction the [NP, VP] and there is no Tense to syntactically sanction a subject, so the argument remains unevaluated.

There are indeed differences between Japanese and English. Some of these differences may reduce to the nature of evaluation. Perhaps the next question is, Can the nature of evaluation be reduced to some universal parameter? That is, is there a parameter that yields different types of evaluation procedures, depending on how it is set? On the basis of the results described here, I would suggest that investigating the interface of levels of representation may well offer some insights into the nature of typological differences among the world's languages.

Notes

Chapter 1

1. Examples (1.2) and (1.3) are to be distinguished from other examples in the literature for which a structural ambiguity has been claimed. For example, McCawley (1968) suggests that a sentence like *John and Mary went to Chicago* is ambiguous with regard to whether John and Mary went together or separately. Two different structures were assigned to this string to capture this "ambiguity." However, as Harnish (1976) points out, claiming ambiguity for such a sentence would lead to the absurd conclusion that it is n-ways ambiguous because John and Mary could have met halfway to Chicago, or a quarter of the way, etc. Such examples are therefore not ambiguous, but indeterminate. That is, one cannot tell from the structure of the sentence whether John and Mary were together at any point during their trip(s) to Chicago.

2. The following are other versions of the "command" condition:

Reinhart (1976) C-command (Klima (1964) In construction with)
"X C-commands Y if every branching node dominating X dominates Y."

Reinhart (1983) c-command
"A node A c(onstituent) commands a node B iff the first branching node α that dominates A either dominates B, or is immediately dominated by a node α' which dominates B, where α and α' are of the same category type (e.g., S & $\bar{S}$)."

Lasnik (1976) kommand
"A *kommands* B if the minimal cyclic node dominating A also dominates B." (where NP and S are the cyclic nodes)

See also Chomsky (1981b) for numerous versions of c-command.

3. The **following rule** schemata introduce the complex symbol, CS (from Chomsky (1965, 97)):

$$[+V] \rightarrow CS \, / \, \begin{Bmatrix} \alpha\!\frown\!\text{AUX} \underline{} \\ \underline{} \text{Det}\!\frown\!\alpha \end{Bmatrix}$$

where α is an N, α being a variable ranging over specified features . . . The rules abbreviated by the schemata . . . assert . . . that each feature of the preceding and following Noun is assigned to the Verb and determines an appropriate selectional subclassification of it.

4. For historical perspective on the issues addressed in "Remarks on Nominalization," see Newmeyer (1980, 192–195). For a review of the arguments presented in "Remarks," see Jackendoff (1977, chap. 2).

5. Jackendoff (1977, 36) offers the following phrase structure for English:
(i)
$$X^n \rightarrow (C_1)...(C_j)-X^{n-1}-(C_{j+1})...(C_k)$$
where $1 \leq n \leq 3$, and for all C_i, either $C_i = Y'''$ for some lexical category Y, or C_i is a specified grammatical formative.

6. See Hale (1980, 1983) for discussion of this idea.

7. See Chomsky (1981a,b), Bresnan (1982), Hale (1983), Farmer (1980, 1981b), and Brame (1979) for discussion of this point.

8. See Taylor (1971) for a lexical approach to N/case affiliation.

9. See Marantz (1980) for a discussion of S as a projection of V. In chapter 4 I return to the question of whether or not S is a maximal projection in English.

10. The term *specifiers* will be used to pick out nonhead constituents of X''.

11. The term *category-neutral* is taken from Stowell (1981).

12. Questions keep arising. When do we know that two elements E^1 and E^2 belong to the *same* category, differing only in some idiosyncratic way, and when do we know that E^1 and E^2 in fact belong to different categories? Presumably another test would involve seeing whether maximally general syntactic or lexical rules ever picked out E^1 *and* E^2 or not. I will not pursue these questions of category affiliation, however.

13. Kuno's work will be discussed at length in chapter 2, which reviews major issues in Japanese syntax and examines some of the prevailing accounts.

14. Care is needed in using the term *syntactic level of representation*, because it is used to refer to several levels. For example, when describing the Projection Principle, Chomsky (1981b, 29) says that "Representations at each *syntactic level* (i.e., LF, and D- and S-structure) [emphasis mine/AKF] are projected from the lexicon, in that they observe the subcategorization properties of lexical items." Even domain D is a *syntactic* level of representation. In this book, the term *syntactic level of representation* refers specifically to the level that has both phrase markers *and* words in it. This level is thus distinct from predicate argument structures, for example. Indeed, predicate argument structures, which have argument slots associated with them, have categorial information associated with them as well, i.e., "subcategorization" information.

One really cannot be too careful on this point. For example, Chomsky (1981b, 132–133) states in reference to Japanese,

We may think of D- and S-structures as being pairs (α, β), where α is a formal syntactic structure and β is a representation of associated GFs such as (11)–(13) [examples are from p. 131]:

Note to Page 23   201

(11)
[$_{S_1}$ NP$_2$, [$_{VP_1}$ NP$_3$, [$_V$, tabe]]]
(12)
[$_{S_2}$ NP$_1$, [$_{VP_2}$ (11), [$_{V_2}$ sase]]]
(13)
[$_{S_2}$[$_{VP_2}$[$_{S_1}$ NP$_2$, [$_{VP_1}$ NP$_3$, [$_V$, tabe]]] [$_{V_2}$ sase-rare]]]

For English, β is derived from α by abstraction from order, etc. For Japanese, α is a "flat" structure formed by (1) [i.e., X' → W* X] and β is essentially the same as the corresponding element in English. Case and binding theory crucially consider the element of β of the pair (α, β) in both types of language, but we need not make the distinction in English since β is a simple abstraction from α. Function chains are similar in the two cases.

What is happening here is that β in Japanese, which corresponds more or less in Modular Grammar to predicate argument structures, is considered to be the same as β in English; β in English is S-structure, and S-structure is a *syntactic level of representation*. It is for this reason that I am being cautious in my use of the term *syntactic level of representation*. If my usage was not made explicit, it would appear that my comments would be trivial concerning the interplay between levels of representation.

15. *Flattened out* means that structures like (i) are converted to (ii):
(i)

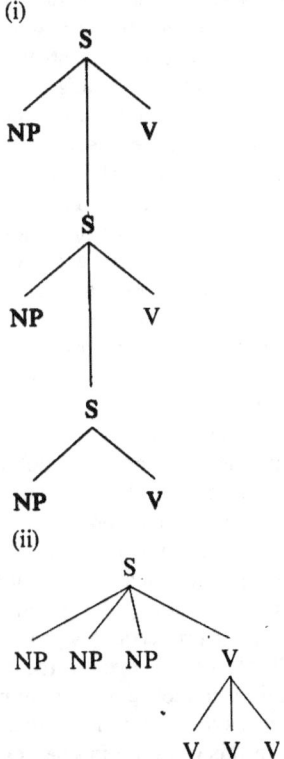

(ii)

16. For extensive discussion and arguments against the position that has been called "lexicalism," see Kuroda (1981).

17. This is not an uncontroversial position to take. For a different point of view, see Bresnan (1971, 1978), Brame (1976), Gazdar (1981), Morin and Wehrli (1978), Steele (1981). For some criticisms of these accounts, see Koster and May (1982) and Chomsky (1981b).

18. The literature on this topic is growing exponentially. I recommend Jaeggli (1980) for an introduction to and lucid discussion of the status of phonologically null elements. Also, there is a fourth element called "pro" (little pro) which is supposed to be present in so-called pro-drop languages (cf. Chomsky (1982)).

19. This appears to be Stowell's (1981) position. See also Stowell (to appear).

20. See Bresnan (1982) for a theory that differs from Chomsky (1981b, 1982) in some of the respects just discussed.

While my position runs counter to Chomsky (1981b) and Jaeggli (1980), it actually begins to merge in some respects with the Chomsky (1982) conception of PRO. There, PRO and the other empty categories receive a functional definition and no longer have intrinsic content.

21. Actually, as I understand it, this is almost what S-structure is in GB theory; however, one level (D-structure, which reflects the argument structure of the verb) is *mapped* onto another level of representation (S-structure, which is closer to what the surface string is like). Also, S-structure is an abstraction away from "stylistic" rules, i.e., scrambling. Since Modular Grammar does not have a scrambling rule, it does not make use of this abstraction. "S-structure" in this theory does not involve "transforming" one level of representation into another (for example, D-structure into S-structure). Such a relationship suggests that S-structure contains all the information represented at D-structure. The theory assumed here will characterize the surface string as reflecting some aspects of, say, the argument structure of a verb but not all aspects. So, for example, in order to identify "empty categories," the argument structure must be accessed. Such a theory does not, speaking loosely, involve a derivation from D- to S-structure. This position is not unlike what Chomsky (1981a,b) suggests for Japanese, namely, that D- and S-structures in Japanese are actually a pair α,β. For a discussion of this point see note 14.

Numerous other questions arise. For example, what is the status of deletion rules in this theory? If they go the way of scrambling, another "stylistic" rule, then there would not necessarily be any deletion rules. I will not be pursuing this question here, however. Another question involves anaphora. This question arises if one is using Government-Binding theory as a point of reference or departure. In GB theory the distribution of the phonologically null entities, PRO, NP-trace, and WH-trace, is accounted for by binding theory. Binding theory also accounts for the indexing (i.e., binding) properties of pronouns, anaphors, and "names." Empty categories fall into one of these three types (pronoun, anaphor, or name) or some combination thereof (e.g., pronominal/anaphor). However, if PRO and NP-trace are not syntactic entities, then the whole anaphora question is broached. I return to this question in chapter 5.

Chapter 2

1. The parenthesized consonants in these suffixes surface in the derived word depending on whether the verb stem ends in a consonant or not.

2. The distinction between the *o* causative and the *ni* causative will be discussed in the section on case marking. For some historical perspective on the problem, see Farmer and Kitagawa (1981) and Hinds and Howard (1978).

3. I will not go into the difference between the *wa* and *ga* particles. Chapter 3 contains some discussion of how to incorporate an account of particle-*wa* in a modular theory.

4. *Hatarak-ta* is realized as *hataraita*.

5. I will adopt the terminology of Kuno and others writing in the same tradition. It should not be inferred that by using this terminology I am assuming the same theoretical underpinnings.

6. Realized as *sikatta*.

7. The indirect passive is also referred to as the "adversity passive."

8. GA-marking of a direct object is extensively discussed in Farmer (1980) and will not be taken up again in this work.

9. Throughout this work I will be concerned primarily with these three case particles. I will not, for example, examine instances of the genitive particle *no*.

10. For an example of an exception to (i), see Bedell (1973). Also, this is an abstraction away from the use of particle-*wa*.

11. For some challenging remarks, however, see Kitagawa (1981).

12. Since the use of * is not consistent among linguists, I should mention that in the following examples I use * and ?? to indicate not that the sentences are ungrammatical, but that they are not entirely without problems.

13. The following convention has been adopted: *ni/o* means that either particle may appear. This will be glossed 'let/make', with 'let' corresponding to *ni* and 'make' corresponding to *o*. When *ni* is translated as 'let (make)' or as 'make (let)', this means that either reading is acceptable.

14. For a more extensive discussion of these double nominative constructions, see Kuno and Tonoike (1980).

15. The RCC makes the prediction that multiple occurrences of *zibun* in a sentence must have the same antecedent (Howard and Niyekawa-Howard (1976, 203)).

(i)
Taroo wa Hanako ga zibun no heya de zibun no sigoto, o site, ita to itta.
                                  self 's room in self 's work   do be say
'Taro said that Hanako was doing self's work in self's room.'

(ii)
a. Taro said that Hanako was doing his work in his room.
b. Taro said that Hanako was doing her work in her room.
c.,d. *Taro said that Hanako was doing $\begin{Bmatrix}\text{her}\\\text{his}\end{Bmatrix}$ work in $\begin{Bmatrix}\text{his}\\\text{her}\end{Bmatrix}$ room.

16. Other quite plausible accounts of case particles in Japanese have been developed that share the assumption that word formation takes place prior to lexical insertion. Among them are Miyagawa (1980), Inoue (1981), and Hasegawa (1981). Miyagawa, in particular, argues for a similar conception of the role of semantic linking.

17. For an account within this general framework of the case arrays in (i) and (ii), see Farmer (1980).

(i)
N'-ga N'-ga
(ii)
N'-ni N'-ga

These correspond to such sentences as (iiia,b), (iva–c).

(iii)
a. Mary ga nihongo ga wakaru. (stative–simple verb)
   'Mary understands Japanese.'
b. Mary ga nihongo ga hanseru. (potential–derived verb)
   'Mary can speak Japanese.'

(iv)
N'-ni N'-ga
a. Mary ni nihongo ga wakaru. (stative–simple verb)
   'Mary understands Japanese.'
b. Mary ni nihongo ga hanaseru. (potential–derived verb)
   'Mary can speak Japanese.'
c. Taroo ni zibun no ketten ga wakaranai.
   'Taro does not understand self's shortcomings.'

((ivc) is from Shibatani (1978, 56).)

18. In Farmer (1980) *PAS* stood for *propositional argument structure*. This, it turns out, is misleading. For the level of representation that I am discussing, the term *predicate argument structure* is more appropriate.

19. An argument slot corresponds in some theories to a thematic relation. I will not be concerned with *how* "θ-roles" are assigned to the argument slots, assuming that so long as no claims are made about *how* θ-roles are to be used in the theory, they can safely be ignored for the time being.

20. Contrary to Farmer (1980), I am not assuming that there is a thematic hierarchy that (p. 89) ". . . roughly incorporates such relations as: agent, source, goal, theme." These notions are elusive, defying definition. I hesitate, therefore, to state any generalizations using this vocabulary.

21. I am no longer assuming the first of the following conditions that I assumed in Farmer (1980, 92):

(i)
After evaluation has been completed [an evaluation is *completed* when either no more argument positions or no more NPs remain to be indexed], all NPs in the clause are indexed.

(ii)
Only one NP per argument position and only one position per NP.

In Farmer (1980) I was attempting to use the evaluation procedure as the major "filtering" device in the grammar. My views have changed on this. While evaluation plays an important role, it is not the last word.

22. It is not clear that this *ni* is in fact a dative *ni*. It could be that *aw* is not a transitive verb and that the *ni* is the semantic *ni*.

23. Notice that this controller/controllee relationship requires that there be a "Like Subject Constraint." In other words, Equi-NP Deletion is obligatory in configurations like [$_s$ NP NP [$_s$ NP V] V].

24. Recall that this structure is the one used by Kuno to characterize the *o* causative. See Farmer and Kitagawa (1981) for relevant discussion of these points.

25. See Jaeggli (1981) for a modular account of the passive in Romance languages.

26. See Aronoff (1976) for one version of the organization of the lexicon (i.e., that words are listed in the lexicon) and Lieber (1980) for another (i.e., that stems and affixes are listed).

27. I am not assuming that lexical structures universally have internal versus external arguments (cf. Williams (1981b), Vergnaud and Zubizarreta (1982), Hale (1983), Marantz (1981a)). By this, I do not claim that making such a distinction is necessarily wrong; but, for example, Marantz's oft-cited arguments for the distinction are not valid. (In this regard, see Bresnan (1982). Note, though, that one aspect of her argument against Marantz's position is not quite correct; that is, to say that an abstract noun phrase cannot be the object of *on* in *The ceiling caved in on John's dream* is false. True, the ceiling is literally caving in (this is the literal interpretation Bresnan is concerned with); but surely *John's dream*, which she calls an abstract NP, can be used nonliterally to refer to an individual, say, John's girlfriend.) Hale (1983) also offers arguments for a more highly articulated lexical structure that depends on viewing c-command as the single most important condition on anaphora. I leave extensive consideration of these arguments for Farmer (in preparation).

28. Farmer (1980, 1981a,b) and Hale (1980) discuss these results at length.

29. One could broaden the definition of *syntax* to include lexical structure, but I am using this term in the narrower sense of identifying the level of representation that is an analysis of strings of words.

30. My use of the term *unevaluated argument* differs from Hale's (personal communication). Hale assumes for Japanese that all argument slots of a predicate are assigned an index regardless of whether or not there is a corresponding NP in the syntax. Hence, all argument positions are "evaluated"; there is no such thing as an "unevaluated argument." Both theories say that there are argument slots that do not have a corresponding NP in the syntax.

31. I would like to thank Natsuko Tsujimura for suggesting these examples.

Chapter 3

1. I would like to thank Bill Poser for bringing this kind of case to my attention.

The example itself is from Marantz (1981b, 137), where the reader will also find a different account of these data.

2. Ueda (1981) discusses many related case array problems (namely, examples that are similar to the "double-*o* constraint"), arguing that only surface filters can account for the ungrammaticality of sentences like (i) (= Ueda's (25) (1981, 112)):

(i)
*Taroo kara Otaru kara Katoo-san ni   hon o   okut-ta.
         from   from   dat book-acc send-past
'Taro sent a book from Otaru to Mr. Kato.'

Ueda claims to have shown that the only way to handle such cases in the framework of Farmer (1980) is to (a) modify the operation of the case-linking rules (as noted in the text) and (b) adopt the following principle (p. 112):

(ii)
More than one argument position may not be assigned the same linking register.

Ueda says that (ii) expresses a "contextual dependency of case linking rule, (which) obviously (is) an undesirable complication of the grammar" (p. 113). First, I would not adopt (ii) because it would wrongly rule out any PAS that had more than one dative *NI*. Second, I would in any event not want to make the case-linking rules sensitive to what else may be in the sentence independently. Ueda's attempt to handle (i) involves positing the following filter (p. 118):

(iii)
The Double-Case Filter
*[$_S$ ...NP$_1$ Y NP$_2$...]
where (a) NP$_1$ and NP$_2$ are lexical and in the same case and (b) Y does not contain an S-boundary or a conjunction.

Ueda notices a number of problems that his proposal faces, namely, the many "apparent" counterexamples to it. For example (p. 120; Ueda's (36a), (37a)):

(iv)
Fuyuko *ga* suugaku *ga* suki-da.
'Fuyuko likes mathematics.'

(v)
Boku ga Haruko *ni* Taroo *ni* aw-ase-ta.
'I had Haruko meet Taro.'

His solution is to invoke the notion of "markedness" and to say (p. 122) that the above

> marked constructions are derived by relaxing the autonomy thesis of grammatical components in such a way that the information in the semantic representation may weaken the effect of surface filter [iii] under certain conditions. These conditions are the cost at which the marked constructions are free from the effect of surface filter [iii].

As Bill Poser (personal communication) points out,

> If markedness is involved, we should expect to find languages rather like Japanese in which multiple datives and nominatives are not permitted. Of course, due to the special character of the double nominative constructions these are indeed rare, but multiple datives are rather common, I think.

Concerning another problem with Ueda's filter, Poser notes that

> It is also problematic how to define the notion *same* case. Since both structural and semantic accusative count as "accusative" for the purposes of the [Double-Case Filter], we cannot say that two homophonous case morphs are the same only if they are assigned in the same way. On the other hand, there appear to be no [Double-Case Filter] effects when instrument *de* is combined with locative *de*, for instance, so these do not count as instances of the same case.

To summarize, although the theory presented in Farmer (1980) and here is not against positing surface filters—that is, filters are not incompatible with the theory—filters are viewed as a means of earmarking a problem area and not necessarily as a solution. In Farmer (1980) I suggested that evaluation plays much of the role of filters. Indeed, I still hold this view, though it becomes increasingly clear that the process of evaluation is much more complex than was described in that work. Since Ueda's proposed filter simply earmarks a problem, and since it appears that evaluation cannot handle it either, I am in agreement with Ueda on this point.

3. Ueda (1981) discusses similar examples (p. 110, (18)):

(i)
a. Boku ga Hanako ni Taroo ni aw-ase-ta.
   I-nom   dat   dat meet-cause-past
   'I had Hanako meet Taro.'
b. Boku ga Hanako o Taroo ni aw-ase-ta.
   I-nom   acc   dat meet-cause-past
   'I made Hanako meet Taro.'

The framework of Farmer (1980) could easily accommodate (ia), but (ib) remained problematic. Now that the application of the grammatical linking rules has been modified, this problem is resolved. Recall that *au* 'meet' is among the verbs that idiosyncratically assign NI to their object argument slot. This NI is assigned via semantic linking and carried over. After *-sase* is attached, the

Note to Page 82

derived PAS undergoes the grammatical linking rules, where the argument slots are assigned GA and O. This process is shown in (ii).

(ii)
a. Semantic linking
($\underset{S}{\underline{\quad}}$ $\underline{\text{NI}}$ au)
b. *-Sase* word formation
($\underset{S}{\underline{\quad}}$ ($\underset{S}{\underline{\quad}}$ $\underline{\text{NI}}$ au) sase)
c. Output of grammatical case linking
($\underset{S}{\underline{\text{GA}}}$ ($\underset{S}{\underline{\text{O}}}$ $\underline{\text{NI}}$ au) sase)

Now (ib) presents no problem. Given this new approach, however, we see that the account of (ia) is more refined than before. Farmer (1980) offered two ways of accounting for (ia): (a) via NI Linking (there called NI Causative Linking)—"Link second argument slot: $\underline{\text{NI}}$" or (b) via part (c) of Regular Case Linking—"Elsewhere link: $\underline{\text{NI}}$." Under this new account, only alternative (a) is viable. That is, part (c) of Regular Case Linking will not have a chance to apply, because *au* 'meet' has caused the object argument to be marked with NI and because the NI Linking rule has marked the subject of *au* with NI (that subject being the second argument of the PAS). We therefore conclude that (ia) involves NI Linking, which seems to agree in any event with the noncoercive interpretation of that sentence. The procedures involved in the PAS of *awase-ta* are as follows:

(iii)
a. PAS of *au* 'meet'
($\underset{S}{\underline{\quad}}$ $\underline{\quad}$ au)
b. Semantic linking
($\underset{S}{\underline{\quad}}$ $\underline{\text{NI}}$ au)
c. Causative word formation
($\underset{S}{\underline{\quad}}$ ($\underset{S}{\underline{\quad}}$ $\underline{\text{NI}}$ au) sase)
d. Semantic linking (NI-causative)
($\underset{S}{\underline{\quad}}$ ($\underset{S}{\underline{\text{NI}}}$ $\underline{\text{NI}}$ au) sase)
e. Grammatical Case Linking (only part (a) of Regular Case Linking will apply)
($\underset{S}{\underline{\text{GA}}}$ ($\underset{S}{\underline{\text{NI}}}$ $\underline{\text{NI}}$ au) sase)

Example (iiie) gives the PAS that is appropriate for (ia).

4. For English Williams utilizes the following coindexing procedure, which he calls *Predication* (1980, 206, (15)):

(i)
Coindex NP and X.

5. These sentences are taken from Kitagawa (1982, 185–187).

6. These sentences are taken from Saito (1981, 1) and Tomoda (1982). I would like to thank Shizuko Tomoda for discussing the properties of this construction at length with me.

7. Many of these examples are taken from Oehrle and Nishio (1981). I would like to thank both authors for discussing with me the problems associated with this construction.

8. Kitagawa offers the following formal definition of *topic* (1982, (14a,b)) (bars are changed to primes throughout Kitagawa's examples):

(i)
a. "Topic" in Japanese is X'-*wa*, where X is [−V].
b. *Wa* indicates that the immediately preceding X' is outside of the domain of "evaluation" in terms of the PAS of the nucleus V.

He also introduces a schema that legislates the structure of topic constructions, along with a well-formedness condition that accompanies it (1982, (15), (16)):

(ii)
[$_{Top}$ X'-wa] [$_{Pred}$ X'* V]

(iii)
Topic Binding
The Topic X' must be bound pragmatically to an X' which is in the domain of Predication (Pred).

Kitagawa assumes (pp. 184–185) that

each specific analysis of topic construction may be presented as a triplet composed of: (i) the surface string of overt arguments with semantic evaluation completed in terms of the PAS; (ii) the PAS with evaluation completed; and (iii) the topic structure assignment with pragmatic evaluation completed by means of Topic Binding.

Kitagawa gives the following analysis of (3.14) (examples (17), (18)):

(iv)
Naomi wa udon o   tabe-ta.
   top noodle-acc eat-past
'Naomi ate udon noodles.'

(v)
a. [$_V$[$_{N'}$[$_N$ Naomi]] wa [$_{N'}$[$_N$ udon]] o$_m$ [$_V$ tabe-ta]]
b. PAS: (<u>GA   O</u>$_m$ tabe-)
c. [$_{Top}$[$_{N'_i}$ Naomi] wa] [$_{Pred}$ [$_{N'_i}$ Pro] [$_{N'}$ udon] o [$_V$ tabe-ta]]

The O argument slot of *tabe* is associated with *udon o*. This is indicated by means of the index *m*. The GA argument slot remains unevaluated, since there is no matching N' that is marked with *ga*. Following Farmer (1980), Kitagawa assumes that unevaluated arguments are interpreted as pronouns. These so-called pronouns ". . . participate in the operation required for the satisfaction of Topic Binding." This is represented in (vc).

The next example illustrates a slightly different binding relation. This binding relation is, however, affected by the principle exhibited in (vc), namely, that all overt arguments must be evaluated in some sense. (Examples (vi), (vii) are from Kitagawa (1982, (19), (20)).)

(vi)
Taroo wa Hanako ga   ieda-si-ta.
    top   nom   leave-home-do-past
'As for Taro, Hanako ran away from home.'

(vii)
a. [$_{V'}$[$_{N'}$[$_N$ Taroo]] wa [$_{N'}$[$_N$ Hanako]] ga$_m$ [$_V$ iede-si-ta]]
b. PAS: (<u>GA</u>$_m$ iede-sita)
c. [$_{Top}$[$_{N'_i}$ Taroo] wa] [$_{Pred}$[$_{N'_i}$ Hanako] ga [$_V$ iede-si-ta]]

In this example, *Taroo* and *Hanako* are coindexed. Kitagawa notes (p. 185–186) that

with Topic Binding connecting *Taroo* and *Hanako*, what [(viic)] says is that Taro's and Hanako's identities are somehow closely related to each other, e.g., husband and wife, father and daughter, etc. Topic Binding . . . is thus a pragmatic linking operation based . . . on the real world knowledge of the speech act participants.

9. I put aside the question of the incorporation of various postpositional phrases like *-de, -ni,* etc.

10. For an introduction to the inferential system of these works, see Akmajian, Demers, and Harnish (1983, chap. 9).

11. My account draws on work by Tomoda (1982) and Saito (1981).

12. Recall that it is not my intention here to provide a complete account of the conditions that satisfy this notion of relevance. I leave the working out of such a notion for future research.

13. For a rather different account of the indirect passive in a closely related theory, see Marantz (1981b).

14. Tomoda (1982) discusses many interesting examples that I have not touched on here. I refer the reader to her paper for a more extensive survey of this construction.

15. Inoue (1976) does away with any account based on using a cyclic transformation or a cyclic interpretive rule.

The following is Inoue's *zibun* interpretation rule (1976, 161, (97)).

SD:
$$\left\{\begin{matrix}\# \\ //\end{matrix}\right\} X \left(\begin{bmatrix}+H \\ NP\end{bmatrix}\right) X \left(\begin{bmatrix}+H \\ NP\end{bmatrix}\right) X \begin{bmatrix}+Refl \\ NP\end{bmatrix} X \; V \left\{\begin{matrix}\# \\ //\end{matrix}\right\} X \left(\begin{bmatrix}+H \\ NP\end{bmatrix}\right) X \; \#$$
1 2   3   4   5   6   7   8 9 10 11   12   13 14

Conditions: (i) $\begin{bmatrix}+H \\ NP\end{bmatrix}$ commands $\begin{bmatrix}+Refl \\ NP\end{bmatrix}$.

(ii) 3 = Subj, 5 ≠ Subj.

(iii) 2, 4, and 11 do not contain $\begin{bmatrix}+H \\ NP\end{bmatrix}$

Interpret (optional):

$$7 = \begin{cases} 3. & \text{(a)} \\ 5. \text{ Condition: 9 has } [-\text{Like Subj}]. & \text{(b)} \\ 12. \text{ Conditions: } 11 = \phi, \begin{bmatrix}+\text{Refl}\\ \text{NP}\end{bmatrix} \neq \text{Subj unless bounded by} \\ \quad \text{more than one pair of } //\text{'s, } 3 = \phi \text{ unless} \\ \quad 5 = \phi \text{ and } 9 = [-\text{Like Subj}]. & \text{(c)} \\ 12. \text{ Condition: If 11 contains Subj-conj, 11 contains no NP.} & \text{(d)} \\ 3. \text{ Conditions: (i) does not hold, and } 6 = Y \begin{Bmatrix}\# \text{ Co-conj } \# \\ // \text{ Co-conj}\end{Bmatrix} \\ \quad Z, \left(\text{where } Z \neq \begin{bmatrix}+H\\ \text{NP}\end{bmatrix}\right). & \text{(e)} \end{cases}$$

This rule has a number of properties that simulate the cycle. One involves Inoue's use of the feature [−like subject], which is a feature on the verb. For example, *-sase* 'cause' has the feature [−like subject], which means that the second NP can, potentially, be an antecedent. Another property involves the use of two different types of boundaries: # (sentence boundary) and // (internal sentence boundary). It is clear that any account will incorporate the notion "cyclic" subject in order to identify certain antecedents for the purposes of interpreting *zibun*. Inoue's version of the *zibun* interpretation rule uses a nonstructural concept ([−like subject]) and a structural concept (# versus //) as a way of encoding this antecedent. My approach amounts to breaking up Inoue's single rule into different rules and/or principles that can be generalized over different levels of representation.

16. Some theorists (for example, Quine (1953)) deny that there is a principled distinction between the semantic information associated with an expression and general factual information. In Quine's terms this would simply be a factual oddity.

17. Kitagawa (1981) also discusses cases where the antecedent is a nonsubject and where a subject is not a plausible antecedent for *zibun*.

18. See Washio (1981) for the opposite position on this point.

19. See Farmer (1980) for extensive discussion of Oshima's work and for an alternative account that, unlike Oshima's, requires neither the Tensed-S Condition nor the A-over-A Condition to govern the application of the Disjoint Reference rule.

20. Strictly speaking, argument slots do not "refer."

21. It is not at all clear to me why Washio finds (186) unacceptable. I would like to thank Sachiko Tsugihara and Natsuko Tsujimura for discussing these cases with me.

Chapter 4

1. In some senses, evaluation in Modular Grammar theory is analogous to θ-theory of Government-Binding. Since MG theory does not yet use thematic

relations (though I do not deny the possibility that they may play some role in the grammar), to avoid confusion I will refer to thematic roles (θ-roles) only when discussing GB theory in conjunction with MG theory. However, I would like to make it clear at this point that much of the work accomplished by θ-theory is accomplished here by the system of evaluation. At this point, the issue is purely terminological. The difference in the two theories with respect to the notion "θ-role" would only come out if, in GB theory, the notion "agent" were used in a rule or principle (say, as opposed to "experiencer"). Williams has done this in his work on argument structures. But in terms of the task of lexically sanctioning an overt NP, either vocabulary will suffice to express whether or not the NP is associated with an argument slot of the verb.

Hale (1983) offers a way of incorporating the notion "θ-role" that is compatible with the present theory. Hale associates arguments in lexical structure (LS) with variables, and these variables in turn are associated with variables in the "dictionary definition," or meaning, of the verb. Thus, θ-roles are factored out of LS. Therefore, since it is the LS that undergoes evaluation, and if overt NPs are assigned θ-roles, then it is the LS (or PAS, in MG theory) that is the conduit for the θ-roles.

2. Hale (1983) appears to be taking a similar position, at least for nonconfigurational languages, when he says that ". . . arguments in LS (Lexical Structure) belong to the class of linguistic elements to which the terms 'pronoun' and 'anaphor' are appropriately applied . . . ," though I will not refer to argument slots as "pronouns" or "anaphors." Other proposals that appear to be similar at least in spirit, if not in form, are Bresnan (1982), Brame (1976), and Hasegawa (1981). (Note, though, that Bresnan uses the term *functional anaphor* when talking about PRO and discusses this entity as though it can be used to "refer." Here, argument slots cannot be used to "refer.")

3. See Hale (1983) for extensive discussion of the "configurational/nonconfigurational" distinction. See also Hasegawa's (1981) account of the differences between English and Japanese within a lexical framework.

4. This will turn out to be quite similar to deriving the case filter from the θ-Criterion in GB theory. For discussion of this point in GB theory, see Chomsky (1981b, chap. 6).

5. I will not speculate on the status of INFL as a constituent of S at this point. In MG theory, INFL cannot be a syntactic node without some further assumptions that I am not prepared to make. INFL, then, is to be construed as standing for tense, agreement, or whatever feature of the verb (in the examples to follow in the text) allows the subject NP to emerge. I am thus speaking loosely when positing the INFL constituent, but will include it in tree structures for the time being, for ease of explication. Later I will return to this question, when speculating on the status of S.

6. Here I put aside the issue of the head of S, but will return to it in section 4.4.

7. I have adapted aspects of Williams's (1980) proposal. The term *predication* is used in a number of works (see Wilkins (1981), Hasegawa (1981)), though many of the assumptions that underlie those works differ from the ones made here.

8. Subject and object are identified in the PAS as well as in the PS. I am assuming, following Williams and also Hale (1983), that subject is an external argument and object an internal argument. I am not assuming that grammatical relations are primitives (unlike Bresnan (1982) and many references cited there, Perlmutter (1978), and Perlmutter and Postal (1977)).

9. Only case-marked NPs are "visible" for evaluation and predication. This idea is loosely adapted from Chomsky (1981b).

10. I cannot appeal directly to the θ-Criterion because it has a different sense. According to the θ-Criterion, not only must NPs have a θ-role, but in addition all θ-roles must be assigned to one and only one "argument." The analogue of the θ-Criterion in MG theory would be something like (i):
(i)
All argument slots must be indexed and all nonpleonastic elements must be associated with an argument slot.
I am using only the second half of the condition.

11. See Hale (1983) for the status in English of NPs as argument positions. Hale argues for construing NPs as arguments.

12. The following is a formal statement of the Projection Principle (Chomsky (1981b, 36, 38)).
(5)
 (i) $[_\gamma \ldots \alpha \ldots \beta \ldots]$
 (ii) $[_\gamma \ldots \beta \ldots \alpha \ldots]$
(6)
 (i) if β is an immediate constituent of γ in (5) at L_i, and $\gamma = \bar{\alpha}\ [\alpha']$, then α θ-marks β in γ
 (ii) if α selects β in γ as a lexical property, then α selects β in γ at L_i
 (iii) if α selects β in γ at L_i, then α selects β in γ at L_j
The variables L_i, L_j range over what we are considering . . . to be the "syntactic levels": LF, D-structure, S-structure.

13. Bresnan (1982) also does not posit a syntactic entity PRO: "*Anaphoric control relations* arise from the presence of a functional anaphor ('PRO') which is not expressed in c-structure" (p. 379). It is not at all clear, however, that this "functional anaphor" ('PRO') is analogous to unevaluated argument slots of MG theory, because it ". . . is created by an optional functional schema . . ." The theory proposed here incorporates no such device.

14. For further discussion and criticism of the VP' (complement) hypothesis, see Koster and May (1982). They argue against such proposals as those in Bresnan (1978), Brame (1976), Morin and Wehrli (1978), and Wehrli (1980). Also, see Steele (1981, chap. 4) for a discussion of the status of infinitival complements.

15. See Jaeggli (1980), Aoun (1982), Iwakura (1982), Stowell (1981), for example. For some objections to the GB account of PRO, see Bresnan (1982), who approaches these questions from a rather different point of view from the one taken here, i.e., a "lexical-functional" theory of syntax.

16. It may well be true that utilizing a "richer" vocabulary for "subcategorization" is redundant in GB theory, but such a criticism does not carry over into MG theory. "Subcategorization" is viewed here as being a statement about what kinds of syntactic entities may be associated with what argument slots. In this sense, semantic linking in Japanese has this property also.

17. Chomsky (personal communication) has pointed out this [$-\theta$-role, $-$case] entity to me. The reason I question its status is that this "anaphor" shares none of the other properties of other anaphors beyond the definitional one, "bound by an entity in an A-position."

18. Throughout this section I will label the node dominating *to* and *leave* or V with an X. In section 4.4 I will explore the actual status of X.

19. This is certainly not the first time that NP-trace and PRO have been "collapsed." For accounts in other theoretical paradigms, see Hasegawa (1981) and Koster (1978, chap. 5).

20. See Stowell (1981) for discussion of the pertinent differences between NPs and clauses.

21. The environment for Direct Evaluation defined here is virtually identical to the environment stated in the Projection Principle of Chomsky (1981b).

22. Contrary to the analysis of Japanese, I am treating the argument slots asymmetrically with respect to evaluation.

23. This rule of Predication is a liberal modification of Williams's (1980) Predication rule.

24. This is at variance with the oft-cited claim about the control of PRO. In chapter 5 I will argue that the cases cited as involving "long-distance control" of PRO (or "Super Equi"; see Grinder (1970, 1971), Kimball (1971), and Wasow (1979) for extensive discussion of these kinds of examples) are really instances of pragmatic control.

25. A comment on the alphabetical indices i and j is also in order. Since there can easily be sentences with more than 26 instances of indexing, the grammar must have access to more than the 26 unique indices the alphabet provides. Perhaps, as R. M. Harnish has pointed out to me, numbers should more properly be used. Though the point is well taken, I will continue to use alphabetical indices, because it is standard linguistic usage. Since all instances of i and j can be reinterpreted as 1 and 2, this practice should make no difference in the discussion.

26. I will not go into the categorial affiliation of words like *wounded*. Not having settled on an inventory of categories and finding the X-bar inventories to be inadequate, I put this question aside. For the purpose of this discussion, I will call *wounded* a "verb," not intending to engender a new category "verb."

27. *BY* will indicate that the subject argument is "bound."

28. See Steele (1981), Hasegawa (1981), and Bresnan (1982) for what appear to be analyses similar to this one, though the theoretical paradigms are quite different.

29. Perhaps V + *able* is another case where the "logical object" becomes the "surface subject." For a discussion of just such an approach, see Akmajian, Demers, and Harnish (1979, chap. 7).

30. Recall that we are assuming that clauses do not have to have case in order to be evaluated. Because of this assumption, we will have to stipulate a well-formedness condition that in effect requires clauses to have some kind of interpretive index. Sentences like (i) will have to be ruled out:
(i)
*John ran that Bill was a creep.

The verb *ran* does not lexically sanction the clause *that Bill was a creep*, which therefore cannot receive an interpretation.

31. This appears to have the same function as Chomsky's Subjacency Condition on Move α and Bresnan and Kaplan's Functional Locality Principle.

32. Linking the NP_j with the leftmost internal argument is accomplished by way of "matching" the NP_j, category-wise, to the argument slot that is specified as being associated with an NP. I have not included this categorial information directly in the PAS, simply to avoid confusion; that is, I don't want to give the misleading impression that argument slots *are* NPs. Recall also the earlier statement that argument slots may be associated with θ-roles in the sense of Hale (1983); though this is not to say that argument slots *are* θ-roles (as was claimed in Farmer (1980)).

33. See Wilkins (1981) for an alternative account of NOC verbs.

34. See Williams (1980, 218) for discussion of examples similar to this one.

35. There is another interpretation of *together* that may render the string grammatical; but under the interpretation that *together* means something like a group, this sentence is definitely odd.

36. This is different from the example where *seem* was odd, (4.49). That sentence had neither a syntactic nor a lexical "subject" to assign an index to.

37. Chisato Kitagawa has pointed out the following example to me:
(i)
I wanted to try to promote $\begin{Bmatrix} \text{ourselves} \\ \text{*themselves} \end{Bmatrix}$.

Kitagawa has made some suggestions concerning this example that entail both positing different types of indices and that *want*, essentially, always assigns an index. His suggestion is in part based on the Pragmatic Inference rule P5, to be discussed in chapter 5 (roughly, if an NP binds a pronoun, then the pragmatic inference must be made that there is at least overlapping reference). Kitagawa observes that these *want* sentences appear to involve this situation in which two NPs are "bound" (i.e., coindexed). I leave this question for future research, however.

38. Supporting his view of the treatment of Japanese topic-*wa*, Chisato Kitagawa has suggested (personal communication) that the condition that *John*, for example, must be construed with an argument slot be carried over to the case of Japanese Topic, NP-*wa* (and NP-*ga*), since in both English and Japanese indexing so far only involves the grammar and not pragmatics.

39. See Bresnan (1982), Visser (1963–1973, part III 2. 2118), Bach (1979), Jacobson (1982). Note, however, that this generalization appears to be true only if control actually enters into the analysis of the sentence. Bresnan (1982) discusses sentences where control is not involved and the passive is fine (example from Bresnan (1982, 404)):

(i)
Mary was never promised that she would be allowed to leave.

40. See Hasegawa (1981, 121) for a theory of "raising" and "equi" using a notion of predication.

41. This appears to be essentially equivalent to saying that S is a projection of INFL. We could simply say, as Chomsky does (1981b and elsewhere), that INFL is a constituent of S, but we must be careful about what we mean by "constituent." (See Bresnan (1982) and references cited there for discussion of similar misgivings.) It is not the spirit of MG theory to posit a phonologically null syntactic constituent or to invoke "Affix Hopping." Following Stowell (1981, 266), I will assume that the ". . . categorial status of the S-system is directly linked to the tense feature . . ." The relevant feature, be it tense or modality (drawing on work in Steele (1981)), may reside in the verb or in one of the auxiliary elements (i.e., a modal, *have*, or *be*. The category V is not the relevant notion for identifying or talking about S. Therefore, I should not be construed as claiming that auxiliary elements are verbs; recall that S is not a projection of V. (The "auxiliaries as main verbs" controversy is an old one. For arguments in favor of that position, see Ross (1967), Pullum and Wilson (1977). For the opposite view, see Steele (1981) and Akmajian, Steele, and Wasow (1979).) Rather, I will say that S involves the following situation: the subject of the verb is syntactically present (i.e., nominative case is assigned to the subject). Recall that we have adopted Chomsky's position that the entity that assigns case may not necessarily be the same one that "assigns the θ-role" or, in MG terms, provides the argument slot. For example, it may be that "INFL" resides in the modal; that is, the modal harbors the "element" that syntactically sanctions the subject, and not the verb.

42. Gazdar, Pullum, and Sag (GPS) (1982) appeared just as this book was in the final stages of preparation. Therefore, I cannot compare GPS's approach with mine in any detail. Briefly though, I assume, as GPS do, that the Affix Hopping rule plays no role in the grammar. Also, like GPS, I rely on "subcategorization" to account for the verbal morphology of the following (complement) verb.

43. Ken Hale (personal communication) takes the same position with respect to the status of S.

44. It is interesting to note that in Harnish's (1983) work on interpreting the function of utterances like "Go," it is not necessary to posit an S boundary; that is, reference to V^2 suffices for identifying "Go" as a directive (Harnish uses Akmajian, Steele, and Wasow's category system). The present theory would not involve the construal of a syntactic S, but this does not appear to be a deficiency when it comes to determining the function of an utterance like "Go!"

45. I would like to thank Susan Steele for discussing the material in this present section.

Also see Steele (1981, chap. 4) for the source of some of the ideas expressed in the next section, 4.3.2.

46. There are also verbs like *help* that take "bare infinitivals," as in *John helped him go*.

This analysis of *to* as a complement-taking element is another feature common to both the system developed here and Gazdar, Pullum, and Sag's system.

47. This is basically the same approach adopted by Gazdar, Pullum, and Sag.

48. Ken Hale (personal communication) takes an approach to subject-aux inversion similar to the one to be outlined here; that is, it has no transformation that inverts the subject and the aux element. The two approaches do not coincide exactly, however, and I will note differences in the text. Gazdar, Pullum, and Sag's analysis also does without an inversion transformation.

49. Stowell (1981) develops a version of case theory that incorporates an adjacency condition. Stowell concludes (p. 106) that ". . . X-bar theory turns out to play no role whatsoever in determining the fixed order of complements in languages such as English . . ."

Chapter 5

1. Chomsky (1982, 78) has made a similar move: "I have been discussing some consequences of the more principled approach to ECs [empty categories] in chapter 6 of Chomsky [1981b], which replaces an interpretation in terms of intrinsic content by a functional interpretation." For Chomsky, once the EC is identified under the functional definition as an NP-trace, it falls under the Binding Condition A (see (5.4a) of the text). If an EC is identified as a PRO, then it falls under none of the Binding Conditions. In the theory adopted here, the notion PRO versus NP-trace plays no role—a claim that will be defended in sections 5.3 and 5.4.

2. Concerning anaphors, pronouns, and R-expressions, see for example Chomsky (1981a,b, 1982), Aoun (1982), Jaeggli (1980). Concerning movement rules, see Dresher and Hornstein (1979).

3. This case of stipulated noncoreference or disjoint reference raises some interesting questions. Chomsky (personal communication) says that examples like (5.3) are not cases of semantic disjointness, since one can replace either NP with the phrase *the average man*, which doesn't denote anything, and the "reading" remains disjoint.

4. It appears that we are left with the problem of just how the indices are to be interpreted. What is meant by *noncoreferential?* It has been suggested (by Chomsky and others) that there is a domain D of mental entities to which a reference-like relation holds and that it is at this level and in this domain that disjointness is captured. That is, in (5.6) each NP is associated with a mental entity, and these entities are distinct in domain D. It may very well turn out that, say, two of these mental entities end up referring to one entity in the world.

5. Example (5.14a) is from Chomsky (1981b, 285), (5.15) is from Chomsky (1981b, 288), and (5.16) is from Lasnik (1976, 16).

6. It is the job of an adequate semantics to say what this relation consists of.

7. The Binding Mechanism given here is in part adopted from Reinhart (1980, 34, (54)).

Minimal governing category must be redefined to yield V''' as a governing category. This is necessary because instances of "infinitival" complements do not have an "S" intervening between the upstairs verb and the downstairs verb, and yet examples like (i) must satisfy the structural description of the Binding Mechanism:

(i)
John$_i$ wants Mary to love him$_i$.

8. I put quotation marks around S (i.e., "S") as a reminder that I do not assume "S" to be a separate system (see chapter 4). I will use the S node with the understanding that it stands for V''', M''', etc.

9. P3 and P5 appear to be redundant in this case. I hesitate to eliminate P3, since it may still play a role in sentences like *Carter voted for every Democrat*. In Farmer (in preparation) P5 is modified with the result that P3 and P5 are not redundant. The modification also has consequences for sentences like (5.13).

10. The tree is slightly abbreviated; that is, the N''s are not extended all the way down. This does not affect the conclusions in this discussion, however.

11. An obvious point arises concerning ambiguity. So far the proposed analysis treats (5.23) as though it were ambiguous—a consequence of M1's being optional. Intuitively this does not seem to be a proper characterization. This issue is discussed more extensively in Farmer and Harnish (in preparation). In Farmer (in preparation) M1 is dispensed with altogether; thus the question of ambiguity does not arise.

12. Farmer and Harnish (in preparation) discuss the possibility of "replacing" *him* with *himself* even though the N'' dominating *him* does not appear to be an argument of *believe*.

Notes to Pages 177–184   219

13. This and related issues on the interaction of semantic principles versus pragmatic principles will be taken up in more detail in Farmer and Harnish (in preparation).

14. The following examples are discussed in Chomsky (1981b) where he notes that they constitute a paradox for GB theory.

Also, concerning this kind of construction, the following example comes to mind. Notice that (i) is clearly odd, but it isn't obvious what kind of oddity is involved:

(i)
Ann lost my way.

Since the semantics of the predicate fixes $x = y$ (by P2) and since F2 states that if *my* is being used to refer, then the speaker is referring to the speaker, then the subject must also be satisfied by an expression that refers to the speaker. If the speaker is named Ann, then an entity denoted by the word *Ann* is the speaker; thus, a semantic explanation for the oddity of this sentence is not obvious. Harnish (personal communication) has suggested that perhaps a general pragmatic principle exists, requiring that if a speaker is going to refer to him/herself, the appropriate pronoun (*I, my, mine, our, we*) must be used. This is purely speculative, of course.

15. See Lasnik (1980) for discussion of this kind of case in defense of an "On Binding"-type of account.

16. The condition that NP α not be referential was added so that P5 would not counterintuitively designate cases like *John saw himself* as involving disjoint reference.

17. For example, I have not accounted for reflexives in picture NP contexts. I am not striving for a unified account of reflexives; in fact, there is good reason to believe that a unified account is problematic and not optimal. See especially Bach (1977), Jackendoff (1972).

18. This section is independent of the conclusions reached in the previous one, but it should be of particular interest to readers familiar with GB theory.

19. It is an open question whether all instances of ECs receive their indices freely or not. Chomsky (1981b, 186) notes,

Apart from trace, I have been assuming that indexing is free; in fact, we might assume that traces and moved elements are also freely indexed, say at S-structure, but for convenience of exposition I will continue to suppose that the rule Move-α coindexes in the manner already indicated.

20. Recall the question raised in notes 3 and 4 of the interpretation of these "referential" indices when they are indicating disjointness.

21. A θ-position is an argument position (A-position) that also has an independent thematic role (θ-role) associated with it. A $\bar{\theta}$-position is an A-position that does not have a θ-role associated with it. For example, subject, [NP, S], is an A-position that may or may not be a θ-position. In (i) the subject is an A-position *and* a θ-position, whereas in (ii) it is an A-position that is a $\bar{\theta}$-position.

(i)
John likes baseball.

(ii)
John seems to like baseball.

22. For example, imagine a wedding scene where Nancy and Bill are the bride and groom. They are all dressed up and can hardly move. Mary is the photographer. The guests are all standing around the wedding cake waiting for Nancy and Bill to cut the first slice. Mary wants the traditional picture of the bride and groom feeding each other cake. But Bill is nervous, considering all the wedding finery. He says, "I think that to feed each other (feeding each other) would be (rather) difficult." Mary doesn't take the traditional photo. Later, remarking on the fact that Mary didn't insist on taking the picture, a speaker reports that "Mary thought that Bill said that to feed each other would be difficult."

23. This is not to say that there are no phenomena that are sensitive to θ-position versus $\bar{\theta}$-position. For example, Chomsky (1981b, 61) gives the following examples (his (15) and (16)) that are supposed to illustrate yet another difference between PRO and trace:

(i)
a. they assigned one interpreter each to the visiting diplomats
b. one interpreter each was assigned t to the visiting diplomats
c. one interpreter each seems [t to have been assigned t to the visiting diplomats]

(ii)
*one interpreter each tried [PRO to be assigned t to the visiting diplomats]

Chomsky notes that "[(ii)] is ungrammatical though it differs from [(ic)], which is grammatical, only in replacement of trace by PRO." As a result of this "replacement," the antecedent, which includes *each*, is now in a θ-position. The domain for *each* interpretation seems to be determined by the argument slot it is most directly associated with (cf. Chomsky's discussion on function chains (1981b, 62)). But this does not argue that PRO and trace differ in fundamental respects.

24. Definition of *c-command* from Chomsky (1981b, 166):

α c-commands β if and only if

(i)
α does not contain β

(ii)
Suppose that $\gamma_1,...,\gamma_n$ is the maximal sequence such that
(a) $\gamma_n = \alpha$
(b) $\gamma_i = \alpha^j$
(c) γ_i immediately dominates γ_{i+1}
Then if δ dominates α, then either (I) δ dominates β, or (II) $\delta = \gamma_i$ and γ_1 dominates β

25. Though the structure for passive constructions in GB theory suggests one exception to this generalization. Also, in Chomsky (1982) there are hints that this view toward subcategorization may be changing.

26. According to Jaeggli (1980, 16), "A 'minimal governing category' is a governing category which properly contains no other governing category. We will assume that NP and S or S̄ [S'] are governing categories." Notice that this is a slightly different version of *minimal governing category* from the one used in section 5.2.

In looking at structure (5.56), recall that "S" is a projection of Tense/Modality and that this may be realized on a verb or Aux element.

Chapter 6

1. Kenneth Hale, most notably, is concerned with these kinds of questions. In Hale (1983, 10) he poses the question ". . . is there a parameter, clearly definable within a general theory of language, from which the observed differences between the two linguistic types follow straightforwardly?" Specifically, I would like to explore the possibility that the typological distinction in question originates not in phrase structure itself, but rather in the nature of the relationship between phrase structure (PS) and lexical structure(LS). I agree with Hale that therein may lie the secrets, but the proposal that Hale offers, the Configurationality Parameter (CP), cannot be the answer in MG theory *if* this entails positing phonologically null entities at the PS level:

(i)
Configurationality Parameter (Hale (1983, (28)))
a. In configurational languages, the Projection Principle holds of the pair (LS, PS).
b. In nonconfigurational languages, the Projection Principle holds of LS alone.

Hale assumes that PS is identical to LS. Strictly speaking, if this is true in Hale's theory, then MG theory has no analogue to LS or PS. These and related questions are raised in Farmer (in preparation).

2. See Hale (1983) for his account of this difference. Also, see Farmer (in preparation) for more extensive discussion of Hale's point than is presented here.

3. Recall that this interpretation of "missing" is not assumed by Chomsky (1981b, 1982) and references cited there. Hale (1983) appears to concur with Chomsky on this point.

4. Of course, there are instances where the object is "missing" even when there is case: for example, instances of WH-movement. But in these types of examples, the object is to be found somewhere in the syntax.

References

Akmajian, A., R. Demers, and R. M. Harnish (1979). *Linguistics: An introduction to language and communication.* Cambridge, Mass.: The MIT Press.

Akmajian, A., R. Demers, and R. M. Harnish (1983). *Linguistics: An introduction to language and communication.* 2nd ed. Cambridge, Mass.: The MIT Press.

Akmajian, A., and C. Kitagawa (1976). Deep-structure binding of pronouns and anaphoric bleeding. *Language* 52, 61–77.

Akmajian, A., S. Steele, and T. Wasow (1979). The category AUX in universal grammar. *Linguistic Inquiry* 10, 1–64.

Aoun, J. (1982). The formal nature of anaphoric relations. Doctoral dissertation, Massachusetts Institute of Technology.

Aronoff, M. (1976). *Word formation in generative grammar.* Linguistic Inquiry Monograph 1. Cambridge, Mass.: The MIT Press.

Bach, E. (1970). Problominalization. *Linguistic Inquiry* 1, 121–122.

Bach, E. (1977). Comments on the paper by Chomsky. In P. Culicover, T. Wasow, and A. Akmajian, eds., *Formal syntax,* 133–155. New York: Academic Press.

Bach, E. (1979). Control in Montague grammar. *Linguistic Inquiry* 10, 515–531.

Bach, E., and B. H. Partee (1980). Anaphora and semantic structure. In J. Kreiman and A. E. Ojeda, eds., *Papers from the parasessions on pronouns and anaphora,* 1–28. University of Chicago, Chicago, Ill.

Bach, K., and R. M. Harnish (1979). *Linguistic communication and speech acts.* Cambridge, Mass.: The MIT Press.

Bedell, G. (1973). On certain bathroom expressions. In M. Shibatani, ed., *Papers in Japanese Linguistics* 2, 170–173. University of California, Berkeley, Calif.

Bever, T., J. Katz, and D. T. Langendoen, eds. (1976). *An integrated theory of linguistic ability.* New York: Crowell.

References

Brame, M. (1976). *Conjectures and refutations in syntax and semantics*. New York: Elsevier.

Brame, M. (1979). Chomsky/Lasnik filters are special cases of functional deviance. Paper presented at the Sloan Workshop, Stanford University, January 1979.

Bresnan, J. (1970). An argument against pronominalization. *Linguistic Inquiry* 1, 122–123.

Bresnan, J. (1971). Sentence stress and syntactic transformations. *Language* 47, 257–297.

Bresnan, J. (1978). A realistic transformational grammar. In M. Halle, J. Bresnan, and G. A. Miller, eds. (1978), 1–59.

Bresnan, J. (1982). Control and complementation. *Linguistic Inquiry* 13, 343–434.

Chomsky, N. (1957). *Syntactic structures*. The Hague: Mouton.

Chomsky, N. (1965). *Aspects of the theory of syntax*. Cambridge, Mass.: The MIT Press.

Chomsky, N. (1970). Remarks on nominalization. In R. Jacobs and P. Rosenbaum, eds., *Readings in English transformational grammar*, 184–221. Waltham, Mass.: Ginn.

Chomsky, N. (1971). Topics in the theory of generative grammar. In J. R. Searle, ed., *The Philosophy of Language*, 71–100. Oxford: Oxford University Press.

Chomsky, N. (1975). *Reflections on language*. New York: Pantheon Books.

Chomsky, N. (1981a). On the representation of form and function. *Linguistic Review* 1, 3–40.

Chomsky, N. (1981b). *Lectures on Government and Binding*. Dordrecht: Foris.

Chomsky, N. (1982). *Some concepts and consequences of the theory of government and binding*. Linguistic Inquiry Monograph 6. Cambridge, Mass.: The MIT Press.

Culicover, P. (1976). *Syntax*. New York: Academic Press.

Culicover, P., T. Wasow, and A. Akmajian (1977). *Formal syntax*. New York: Academic Press.

Dougherty, R. (1969). An interpretive theory of pronominal reference. *Foundations of Language* 5, 488–518.

Dresher, B. E., and N. Hornstein (1979). Trace theory and NP-movement rules. *Linguistic Inquiry* 10, 65–82.

Evans, G. (1980). Pronouns. *Linguistic Inquiry* 11, 337–362.

References

Farmer, A. K. (1980). On the interaction of morphology and syntax. Doctoral dissertation, Massachusetts Institute of Technology.

Farmer, A. K. (1981a). Modularity. In A. K. Farmer and C. Kitagawa, eds. (1981b), 9–24.

Farmer, A. K. (1981b). The absence of scrambling in Japanese and its relation to modularity. In *Metropolitan Linguistics* 4, 137–148. Linguistics Circle of Tokyo, Metropolitan University, Tokyo.

Farmer, A. K. (in preparation). Consequences of the Configurationality Parameter: A reply to Hale.

Farmer, A. K., and R. M. Harnish (in preparation). The modularity of anaphora: Formal and pragmatic constraints.

Farmer, A. K., and C. Kitagawa (1981a). Introduction. In A. K. Farmer and C. Kitagawa, eds. (1981b), 3–7.

Farmer, A. K., and C. Kitagawa, eds. (1981b). *Proceedings of the Arizona conference on Japanese linguistics*. Coyote Papers, Vol. 2. Department of Linguistics, University of Arizona, Tucson, Ariz.

Fiengo, R. (1974). Semantic conditions on surface structure. Doctoral dissertation, Massachusetts Institute of Technology.

Fodor, J., and J. Katz (1964). *The structure of language*. Englewood Cliffs, N.J.: Prentice-Hall.

Gazdar, G. (1981). Unbounded dependencies and coordinate structure. *Linguistic Inquiry* 12, 155–184.

Gazdar, G., G. K. Pullum, and I. Sag (1982). Auxiliaries and related phenomena in a restrictive theory of grammar. *Language* 58, 591–638.

Grinder, J. (1970). Super equi-NP deletion. In *Papers from the Sixth Regional Meeting of the Chicago Linguistic Society*, 297–317. University of Chicago, Chicago, Ill.

Grinder, J. (1971). A reply to "Super equi-NP deletion as dative deletion." In *Papers from the Seventh Regional Meeting of the Chicago Linguistic Society*, 101–111. University of Chicago, Chicago, Ill.

Hale, K. (1980). Remarks on Japanese phrase structure: Comments on the papers on Japanese syntax. In Y. Otsu and A. K. Farmer, eds. (1980), 185–203.

Hale, K. (1981a). *On the position of Warlpiri in a typology of the base*. Bloomington, Ind.: Indiana University Linguistics Club.

Hale, K. (1981b). Preliminary remarks on configurationality. In J. Pustejovsky and P. Sells, eds., *Proceedings of the Twelfth Annual Meeting of the Northeastern Linguistic Society* [NELS], 86–96. Massachusetts Institute of Technology, Cambridge, Mass.

Hale, K. (1983). Warlpiri and the grammar of non-configurational languages. *Natural Language and Linguistic Theory* 1.1.

Halle, M., J. Bresnan, and G. A. Miller (1978). *Linguistic theory and psychological reality*. Cambridge, Mass.: The MIT Press.

Harada, S. I. (1973). Counter equi NP deletion. *Annual Bulletin*, Research Laboratory of Logopedics and Phoniatrics, 113–147. University of Tokyo, Tokyo.

Harada, S. I. (1976). Honorifics. In M. Shibatani, ed. (1976), 449–571.

Harnish, R. M. (1975). The argument from *lurk*. *Linguistic Inquiry* 6, 145–154.

Harnish, R. M. (1976). Logical form and implicature. In T. Bever, J. Katz, and D. T. Langendoen, eds. (1976).

Harnish, R. M. (1982). *Four lectures on inferential pragmatics*. Studies in the Cognitive Sciences 13. University of California, Irvine.

Harnish, R. M. (1983). Pragmatic derivations. *Synthese*, March.

Hasegawa, N. (1981). A lexical interpretive theory with emphasis on the role of subject. Doctoral dissertation, University of Washington.

Helke, M. (1973). On reflexives in English. *Linguistics* 106, 5–23.

Higginbotham, J. (1980). Pronouns and bound variables. *Linguistic Inquiry* 11, 679–708.

Hinds, J., and I. Howard, eds. (1978). *Problems in Japanese syntax and semantics*. Tokyo: Kaitakusa.

Hornstein, N. (1977). S and the $\bar{X}$ convention. *Linguistic Analysis* 3, 137–176.

Howard, I., and A. M. Niyekawa-Howard (1976). Passivization. In M. Shibatani, ed. (1976), 201–234.

Huang, J. (1982). Logical relations in Chinese and the theory of grammar. Doctoral dissertation, Massachusetts Institute of Technology.

Inoue, K. (1976). Reflexivization: An interpretive approach. In M. Shibatani, ed. (1976).

Inoue, K. (1981). Transformational versus lexical analysis of Japanese complex predicates. Ms., International Christian University, Tokyo.

Iwakura, K. (1982). On government. *Linguistic Analysis* 9, 135–159.

Jackendoff, R. (1972). *Semantic interpretation in generative grammar*. Cambridge, Mass.: The MIT Press.

Jackendoff, R. (1977). $\bar{X}$ *syntax: A study of phrase structure*. Linguistic Inquiry Monograph 2. Cambridge, Mass.: The MIT Press.

Jacobs, R., and P. Rosenbaum, eds. (1970). *Readings in English transformational grammar*. Waltham, Mass.: Ginn.

Jacobson, P. (1982). "Visser revisited" in generalized phrase structure grammar. In *Papers from the Eighteenth Regional Meeting of the Chicago Linguistic Society*, 218–243. University of Chicago, Chicago, Ill.

Jaeggli, O. (1980). On some phonologically-null elements in syntax. Doctoral dissertation, Massachusetts Institute of Technology.

Jaeggli, O. (1981). A modular approach to "passives." In A. K. Farmer and C. Kitagawa, eds. (1981b), 41–59.

Kimball, J. (1971). Super equi-NP deletion as dative deletion. In *Papers from the Seventh Regional Meeting of the Chicago Linguistic Society*, 142–148. University of Chicago, Chicago, Ill.

Kitagawa, C. (1980). Hinds and Howard (eds.): Problems in Japanese syntax and semantics. Review in *Language* 56, 435–439.

Kitagawa, C. (1981). Anaphora in Japanese: *Kare* and *zibun*. In A. K. Farmer and C. Kitagawa, eds. (1981b), 61–75.

Kitagawa, C. (1982). Topic constructions in Japanese. *Lingua* 57, 175–214.

Klima, E. S. (1964). Negation in English. In J. Fodor and J. Katz, eds. (1964), 246–323.

Koster, J. (1978). *Locality principles in syntax*. Dordrecht: Foris.

Koster, J., and R. May (1982). On the constituency of infinitives. *Language* 58, 116–143.

Kuno, S. (1973). *The structure of the Japanese language*. Cambridge, Mass.: The MIT Press.

Kuno, S. (1978). Theoretical perspectives on Japanese linguistics. In J. Hinds and I. Howard, eds. (1978), 213–285.

Kuno, S. (1980). A note on Ostler's nontransformational analysis of Japanese case-marking. In Y. Otsu and A. K. Farmer, eds. (1980), 93–114.

Kuno, S., and S. Tonoike (1980). Kuno and Tonoike exchanges. In Y. Otsu and A. K. Farmer, eds. (1980), 149–171.

Kuroda, S.-Y. (1965). Generative grammatical studies in the Japanese language. Doctoral dissertation, Massachusetts Institute of Technology.

Kuroda, S.-Y. (1978). Case marking, canonical sentence patterns, and counter equi in Japanese (a preliminary survey). In J. Hinds and I. Howard, eds. (1978), 30–51.

Kuroda, S.-Y. (1981). Some recent trends in syntactic theory and the Japanese language. In A. K. Farmer and C. Kitagawa, eds. (1981b), 103–121.

Lakoff, G. (1968). Pronouns and reference. Bloomington, Ind.: Indiana University Linguistics Club.

Lakoff, G. (1970). Pronominalization, negation, and the analysis of adverbs. In R. Jacobs and P. Rosenbaum, eds. (1970), 145–165.

Langacker, R. W. (1969). On pronominalization and the chain of command. In D. A. Reibel and S. A. Schane, eds. (1969), 169–200.

Lapointe, S. G. (1980). A theory of grammatical agreement. Doctoral dissertation, University of Massachusetts at Amherst.

Lasnik, H. (1976). Remarks on coreference. *Linguistic Analysis* 2, 1–22.

Lasnik, H. (1980). On two treatments of disjoint reference. *Journal of Linguistic Research* 1, 48–58.

Lees, R. B., and E. S. Klima (1963). Rules for English pronominalization. *Language* 39, 17–28. Reprinted in D. A. Reibel and S. A. Schane, eds. (1969).

Lekach, A. F. (A. K. Farmer) (1978). Speculations on the interaction of morphology and syntax: A look at complex verbs in Japanese. In E. Battistella, ed., *Proceedings of the Ninth Annual Meeting of the North East Linguistic Society* [NELS], 76–87. *CUNY Forum. Papers in Linguistics*, Nos. 5–6. Queens, N.Y.: Queens College Press. Reprinted in Y. Otsu and A. K. Farmer, eds. (1980), 29–40.

Lieber, R. (1980). On the organization of the lexicon. Doctoral dissertation, Massachusetts Institute of Technology.

Littel, R. (1979). *The debriefing*. New York: Dell.

McCawley, J. (1968). The role of semantics in a grammar. In E. Bach and R. Harms, eds., *Universals in linguistic theory*. New York: Holt, Rinehart and Winston.

McCawley, N. W. (1972). On the treatment of Japanese passives. In P. M. Peranteau, J. Levi, and G. C. Phares, eds., *Papers from the Eighth Regional Meeting of the Chicago Linguistic Society*, 256–270. University of Chicago, Chicago, Ill.

McCawley, N. W. (1976). Reflexivization: A transformational approach. In M. Shibatani, ed. (1976), 51–115.

McCloskey, J. (1979). *Transformational syntax and model theoretic semantics: A case study in modern Irish*. Dordrecht: Reidel.

Marantz, A. (1980). English S is the maximal projection of V. In J. Jensen, ed., *Proceedings of the Tenth Annual Meeting of the North East Linguistic Society* [NELS], 303–314. *Cahiers Linguistiques d'Ottawa* 9. University of Ottowa.

Marantz, A. (1981a). On the nature of grammatical relations. Doctoral dissertation, Massachusetts Institute of Technology.

Marantz, A. (1981b). Grammatical relations, lexical rules, and Japanese syntax. In A. K. Farmer and C. Kitagawa, eds. (1981b), 123–144.

Marantz, A., and T. Stowell, eds. (1982). *Papers in Syntax*. MIT Working Papers in Linguistics, Vol. 4. Department of Linguistics and Philosophy, Massachusetts Institute of Technology, Cambridge, Mass.

Martin, S. E. (1962). *Essential Japanese: An introduction to the standard colloquial language*. Rutland, Vt.: Charles E. Tuttle.

Martin, S. E. (1975). *Reference grammar of Japanese*. New Haven, Conn.: Yale University Press.

Mikami, A. (1972). *Zoku: Gendai gohō zyosetu*. Tokyo: Kuroshio.

Miyagawa, S. (1980). *Complex verbs and the lexicon*. Coyote Papers, Vol. 1. Department of Linguistics, University of Arizona, Tucson, Ariz.

Morin, J.-Y., and E. Wehrli (1978). Wh-movement in $\overline{\text{VP}}$: Infinitival interrogatives. In E. Battistella, ed., *Proceedings of the Ninth Annual Meeting of the North East Linguistic Society* [NELS], 103–111. *CUNY Forum. Papers in Linguistics*, Nos. 5–6. Queens, N.Y.: Queens College Press.

Newmeyer, F. J. (1980). *Linguistic theory in America*. New York: Academic Press.

Nishio, H. (1982). Multiple nominative and adversity constructions in Japanese. Doctoral dissertation, University of Arizona.

Oehrle, R. T., and H. Nishio (1981). Adversity. In A. K. Farmer and C. Kitagawa, eds. (1981b), 163–185.

Oshima, S. (1979). Conditions of rules: Anaphora in Japanese. In G. Bedell, E. Kobayashi, and M. Muraki, eds., *Explorations in Linguistics: Papers in Honor of Kazuko Inoue*. Kenkyusha.

Ostler, N. (1979). Case linking: A theory of case and verb diathesis applied to classical Sanskrit. Doctoral dissertation, Massachusetts Institute of Technology.

Otsu, Y., and A. K. Farmer, eds. (1980). *Theoretical issues in Japanese linguistics*. MIT Working Papers in Linguistics, Vol. 2. Department of Linguistics and Philosophy, Massachusetts Institute of Technology, Cambridge, Mass.

Perlmutter, D. M. (1978). Impersonal passives and the unaccusative hypothesis. In J. J. Jaeger et al., eds., *Proceedings of the Fourth Annual Meeting of the Berkeley Linguistics Society*, 157–189. Berkeley Linguistics Society, University of California, Berkeley, Calif.

Perlmutter, D. M., and P. Postal (1977). Toward a universal characterization of passivization. In K. Whistler et al., eds., *Proceedings of the Third Annual Meeting of the Berkeley Linguistics Society*, 394–417. Berkeley Linguistics Society, University of California, Berkeley, Calif.

Postal, P. (1970). On coreferential complement subject deletion. *Linguistic Inquiry* 1, 439–500.

Pullum, G., and D. Wilson (1977). Autonomous syntax and the analysis of auxiliaries. *Language* 53, 741–788.

Pylyshyn, Z. (1980). Computation and cognition. *The Behavioral and Brain Sciences* 3, 111–169.

Quine, W. V. O. (1953). Two dogmas of empiricism. In *From a logical point of view*. Cambridge, Mass.: Harvard University Press.

Radford, A. (1981). *Transformational syntax: A student's guide to Chomsky's extended standard theory.* Cambridge: Cambridge University Press.

Reibel, D. A., and S. A. Schane, eds. (1969). *Modern studies in English.* Englewood Cliffs, N.J.: Prentice-Hall.

Reinhart, T. (1976). The syntactic domain of anaphora. Doctoral dissertation, Massachusetts Institute of Technology.

Reinhart, T. (1980). Coreference and bound anaphora: A restatement of the anaphora questions. Ms., Tel Aviv University.

Ross, J. R. (1967). Auxiliaries as main verbs. In W. Todd, ed., *Studies in philosophical linguistics.* Evanston, Ill.: Great Expectations Press.

Ross, J. R. (1969). On the cyclic nature of English pronominalization. In D. A. Reibel and S. A. Schane, eds. (1969).

Saito, M. (1981). A case of lexically induced topic in Japanese. Ms., Massachusetts Institute of Technology.

Searle, J. R., ed. (1971). *The philosophy of language.* Readings in Philosophy. Oxford: Oxford University Press.

Shibatani, M., ed. (1976). *Japanese generative grammar.* Syntax and Semantics, Vol. 5. New York: Academic Press.

Shibatani, M. (1977). Grammatical relations and surface cases. *Language* 53, 789-809.

Shibatani, M. (1978). Mikami Akira and the notion of "subject" in Japanese grammar. In J. Hinds and I. Howard, eds. (1978), 52-67.

Steele, S. (with A. Akmajian, R. Demers, E. Jelinek, C. Kitagawa, R. Oehrle, T. Wasow) (1981). *An encyclopedia of AUX: A study in cross-linguistic equivalence.* Linguistic Inquiry Monograph 5. Cambridge, Mass.: The MIT Press.

Stowell, T. (1981). Origins of phrase structure. Doctoral dissertation, Massachusetts Institute of Techology.

Stowell, T. (to appear). Subjects across categories. *Linguistic Review.*

Taylor, H. M. (1971). *Case in Japanese.* South Orange, N.J.: Seaton Hall University Press.

Tomoda, S. (1982). "Tough" construction in Japanese. Ms., University of Arizona.

Tonoike, S. (1979). Complementation and case particles in Japanese. Doctoral dissertation, University of Hawaii.

Tonoike, S. (1980). Intra-subjectivization. In Y. Otsu and A. K. Farmer, eds. (1980), 137-148.

Ueda, M. (1981). On the notion "surface filter" in Japanese. Otaru Shōka Daigaku, Jinbun kenkyū. Vol. 62, December 1981.

Vergnaud, J.-R., and M.-L. Zubizarreta (1982). On virtual categories. In A. Marantz and T. Stowell, eds. (1982), 293–303.

Visser, F. (1963–1973). *An historical syntax of the English language.* Leiden: E. J. Brill.

Washio, R. (1981). Towards a mixed theory of lexical grammar. Master's thesis, International Christian University, Tokyo.

Wasow, T. (1973). Anaphoric pronouns and bound variables. *Language* 51, 368–383.

Wasow, T. (1979). *Anaphora in generative grammar.* Studies in Generative Linguistic Analysis 2. Ghent: E. Story-Scientia.

Whitman, J. (1979). Scrambled, over easy, or sunny side up? In P. R. Clyne, W. F. Hanks, and C. L. Hofbauer, eds., *Papers from the Fifteenth Regional Meeting of the Chicago Linguistic Society,* 342–352. University of Chicago, Chicago, Ill.

Wilkins, W. (1981). Deep structure predication. Social Sciences Research Reports 89. School of Social Sciences, University of California, Irvine.

Williams, E. (1980). Predication. *Linguistic Inquiry* 11, 203–238.

Williams, E. (1981a). On the notions "lexically related" and "head of a word." *Linguistic Inquiry* 12, 245–274.

Williams, E. (1981b). Morphology and argument structures. *Linguistic Review* 1, 81–114.

Index

Adversity Passive. *See* Passive, Indirect
Akmajian, Adrian, 4, 87, 153, 210n10, 215n29, 216n41, 217n44
Ambiguity, 4–6, 93–94. *See also* Zibun
  and the binding mechanism, 218n11
  structural, 199n1
Anaphora, 6, 99, 161
  bound, 164–165, 194
  coindexing procedure (Reinhart), 164
  conditions, 163
  and coreference, 6, 162–163
  modular account of, 104, 165–169, 173–182
  null-, 99, 103–104, 195, 197
  "pronominalization," 161–162
  three-valued indexing systems, 162–163
Anaphors
  binding of, 163–164
  reflexives, 168
Aoun, J., 213n15, 217n2
Argument
  dative argument slot, 51
  external, 119, 143
  internal, 144
  NP-, 112
  slot, 47, 71
  subject slot, 47
  unevaluated, (def.) 72, 111, 206n30
Aronoff, Mark, 205n26
Auxiliary Elements, 156–158
  subcategorization of, 159
  tense, 156

Bach, E., 21, 162, 216n39, 219n17
Bach, Kent, xv, 87, 166
Base, 7. *See also* Phrase Structure Component

Bedell, George, 203n10
Binding
  conditions, (def.) 163, 182
  mechanism (MG theory), 168, 218n7
  and NP-trace and PRO, 161
  of pronouns, 164–165
  topic-, 88, 209–210n8
  of unevaluated argument slot, 121, 124
Brame, Michael, 200n7, 202n17, 212n2, 213n14
Bresnan, Joan W., 9, 162, 200n7, 202n17, 202n20, 205n27, 212n2, 213n8, 213nn13–15, 215n28, 215n31, 216n39, 216n41

Carter, Richard, 52
Case
  array filters, 37, 56
  arrays, 45–47
  assigner, 110
  canonical sentence patterns, 35
  case-marking and the cycle, 50, 56–63
  cyclic/noncyclic case marking, 59–63
  linking register, 48, 50, 121
  linking rules, 48–50
  marking, 33–37
  marking transformations, 34, 56
  particles: ga, ni, o, 27–28
  regular case linking, 50, 66, 70–71, 80, 84, 89
  semantic, (def.) 51
Categorial Component, 8. *See also* Base
Category-Neutral Theory. *See also* Phrase Structure (PS) Rules
  English phrase structure, 18
  Japanese phrase structure, 11–17

Category-Neutral Theory (cont.)
  ramifications of, 19–24
  rules and principles, 18–19
Causative, 25–26, 42–43, 52–54
  dative noun phrases in, 30–31
Chomsky, Noam, xvi, 7–11, 19–20,
    23–24, 66, 72, 109–114, 122, 132–133,
    147, 151–152, 161–162, 182, 186–191,
    199nn2–3, 207n7, 200n14, 202nn17–18,
    202nn20–21, 212n4, 213n9, 213n12,
    214n17, 214n21, 215n31, 216n41,
    217nn1–2, 218nn3–5, 219n14, 219n19,
    220nn23–25, 221n3
Command, 4, 6
  c-command condition, 151, 199n2,
    220n24
  in construction with, 199n2
  kommand, 199n2
  precede and command condition, 6–7
Communication, inferential theories of,
    166
Communicative Intent, 166–167
Complex Verbs in Japanese, 25–27,
    72–74. See also Causative;
    Passive
Configurational/Nonconfigurational, 196
Configurationality Parameter (CP), 221n1
Control. See also Evaluation, direct and
    indirect
  generalized, 115
  "long distance," 214n24
  nonobligatory (NOC), 144, 146
  object, 118, 127, 143
  pragmatic, 150, 186, 188
  of PRO, 146
  revised, 123, 140
  role of, 120
  rule of, (def.) 117
  subjacency, 122, 188
  subject, 118
  verb(s) in MG theory, 123, 126, 128
Culicover, Peter, 155–156

Deletion Rules
  counter equi, 36–37, 62
  equi, 36–37, 62
  S'-deletion in GB theory, 190
Demers, Richard, 4, 210n10, 215n29
Domain D, 200–201n14, 218n4
Dougherty, Ray, 162
Dresher, B. E., 151, 217n2

Empty Categories. See also "Gaps";
    NP-trace; PRO
  indexing of, 219n19
  status of, 24, 182–183, 193, 217n1
Empty Cateogory Principle (ECP), (def.)
    190, 191
Evaluation, 48–49, 110. See also
    Sanctioning, lexical and syntactic
  and case particles, 71
  direct, 82, 84–86, 95, 111, (def.) 117,
    140
  indirect, 82, 85, (def.) 91, 111, (def.)
    117, 140
  nature of, 196
  of postpositional phrases, 91–92
  procedure, 49
  unevaluated argument slot, 72
Evans, Gareth, 104, 162
Exocentric Structures, 8, 9
Extended Standard Theory, 72, 151
  status of "scrambling" rules, 21

Farmer, Ann K., 10, 20–21, 23, 49, 52,
    54, 56, 60–61, 66, 72, 94, 103–104,
    173, 180, 193, 195, 200n7, 203n2,
    203n8, 204nn17–18, 204n20, 205n21,
    205n24, 205nn27–28, 206–207n2,
    207–208n3, 209n8, 211n19, 215n32,
    218n9, 218nn11–12, 219n13, 221nn1–2
Feature Percolation, 14, 77, 153. See also
    Node Labeling
  procedure of, 15
Fiengo, Robert, 151

"Gaps," 23, 187. See also Empty
    Categories; NP-trace; PRO
Gazdar, Gerald, 153, 202n17, 216n42,
    217nn46–48
Government, 114, (def.) 189
  proper, (def.) 189, 190
Government Binding Theory, 7, 23, 72,
    113–114, 133–134, 139, 189
  move α in, 187–188
  S-structure in, 182, 202n21
  status of "referential" index in, 182
  subcategorization in, 191
Governor
  as case assigner, 110
  c-command requirement, 110
  proper, 190
Grammatical Case Linking, 77–78,
    80–81. See also Case linking rules

Index

Grammatical Relations, consequences of the Category-Neutral theory for, 21
Grinder, J., 214n24

Hale, Kenneth, xvi, 11, 20–21, 32, 52, 54, 60, 65–66, 77, 158, 195, 200nn6–7, 205n27–28, 206n30, 212nn1–3, 213n8, 213n11, 215n32, 217n43, 217n48, 221nn1–3
Harada, S. I., 32, 35, 65
Harnish, Robert M., xv, 4, 20, 87, 105, 166, 169, 173, 179, 193, 199n1, 210n10, 214n25, 215n29, 217n44, 218nn11–12, 219nn13–14
Hasegawa, Nobuko, 204n16, 212nn2–3, 212n7, 214n19, 215n28, 216n40
Head. *See also* X-Bar Theory
  definition of, 9, 11
Helke, Michael, 162
Hierarchical Structure, 3–7
Higginbotham, James, 193
Hinds, J., 203n2
Hornstein, Norbert, 151–152, 217n2
Howard, I., 38, 39, 40, 42, 44, 45, 93, 203n2, 203n15
Huang, James, 193

Imperative, 169
Index, 182. *See also* Evaluation; Binding
Infinitival Complements, 154
INFL, 110, 132, 212n5
Inoue, K., 32, 63, 100–101, 204n16, 210–211n15
Interpretation
  literal and direct, xv, 87
  nonliteral, 101
  of passive, 124
  of unevaluated argument slots, 116
Iwakura, K., 213n15

Jackendoff, Ray, 9–10, 152, 162, 200nn4–5, 219n17
Jacobson, P., 216n39
Jaeggli, Osvaldo, 20, 189, 202n18, 202n20, 205n25, 217n2, 221n26

Kaplan, R., 215n31
Kimball, J., 214n24
Kitagawa, Chisato, 63, 84, 87–88, 93, 96, 195, 203n2, 203n11, 205n24, 209n5, 209–210n8, 211n17, 215n37
Klima, E. S., 161, 199n2

Koster, J., 163, 202n17, 213n14
Kuno, Susumo, 21–22, 28–35, 38–40, 42, 44–45, 56–57, 59–64, 67–68, 72, 88, 98–99, 200n13, 203n14
Kuroda, S.-Y., 27, 32–33, 35–37, 42, 44–45, 49, 56, 61, 63, 72, 202n16

Lakoff, George, 162
Langacker, R., 6, 161
Language, Theory of. *See* Language System
Language System, xv, 87, 161, 165
Lasnik, Howard, 162, 181, 199n2, 218n5, 219n15
Lees, R. B., 161
Lekach, A. F., 76
Lexical Insertion
  context-free, 13, 18, 77–78
  matching format, 7–8
  substitution format, 7–8
  as a transformation, 13
Lexical Item
  idiosyncratic properties of, 71
  role of, 12
  subcategorization frames, 10
Lexicon, 71
  "permanent," 54
Lexicosyntactic Rules, 111, 115–116, 122, 129, 139. *See also* Evaluation, direct and indirect
Lieber, Rochelle, 205n26
Linking. *See also* Case linking rules
  register, 121

McCawley, James, 199n1
McCawley, N., 29
McCloskey, J., 152
Marantz, Alec, 9, 152, 200n9, 205n27, 206n1, 210n13
Martin, S. E., 33
May, Robert, 163, 202n17, 213n14
Mikami, Akira, 63
Minimal Governing Category, 168, 218n7, 221n26
Miyagawa, Shigeru, 72, 204n16
Modular Grammar (MG)
  analogue to PRO and NP-trace, 113, 115
  assumptions of, 20, 76, 116, 160, 173
  consequences of, 132–133
  move α relation in, 187
  NP-movement in, 115, 146

Modular Grammar (MG) (cont.)
  obligatoriness of [NP,S], 113–115
  "raising," 125
  role of pleonastic elements, 112
  S-structure in, 182, 202–203n21
  status of INFL in, 212n5
  status of NP-trace and PRO in, 161, 182, 192
  status of subjacency in, 122, 189
  status of S'-deletion in, 191
  θ (theta) criterion in, 112, 147, 149, 189, 213n10
Morin, J.-Y., 202n17, 213n14
Morphologically Complex Verbs in Japanese
  status of, 22
  syntax of, 25–28
Move α
  analogue to, 97
  as a condition on antecedent/gap relation, 187–188
  subjacency, 147

Newmeyer, F., 200n4
Nishio, Hiroko, 94–96, 99, 209n7
Niyekawa-Howard, A. M., 38–40, 42, 45, 93, 203n15
Node Labeling, 14, 77. *See also* Feature Percolation
Node-Markers, 11–12
Nonconfigurational Language
  Japanese as a, 22
Nonliterality, 92
NP-Movement
  in MG theory, 115, 118
  in "nonconfigurational" languages, 196
  left/right asymmetry of, 151
NP-trace, 23–24. *See also* "Gaps"; Empty Categories
  as an anaphor, 151
  in GB theory, 183–186
  in MG theory, 113, 132

Oddity
  due to conflict, 179
  involving inversion, 159
  involving passive, 150
  involving PRO, 139
  pragmatic, 88, 177
  semantic, 101
Oehrle, Richard T., 94–96, 209n7
Oshima, Shin, 103, 211n19

Overgeneration, 17, 20, 33, 35, 45, 49, 60–61, 92, 105
  instances of, 37

Partee, B. H., 162
Passive, 38–42, 54–55, 57, 63–71, 187
  dative, 67
  direct, 26, 29–30
  global constraint, 68
  indirect, 26–27, 29–30, 38, 81, 84, 93–94, 97, 197
  in MG theory, 66–71, 79
  promise, 150
  rule, 57
  uniform and nonuniform account, 38–42, 64, 93
  word formation, 122
  and *zibun*, 38–42 (*see also* Zibun)
Perlmutter, David, 213n8
Phrase Structure Component, 77
Phrase Structure (PS) Rules, 7. *See also* Category-Neutral Theory
  consequences of, (GB theory), 114
  as redundancy rules, 10, 19
  role of (in GB theory), 10
  role of (in MG theory), 10, 21, 31, 43
  stripping categorial content from, 10
  two functions of, 8
Pleonastic Elements, 133
  anaphorically related to S', 136
  behavior of, 23
  role of, 112, 114
Poser, William, 206n1, 206–207n2
Postal, Paul, 162, 213n8
Pragmatic Inference Rule, 87–88, 93, 95, 97
Pragmatics
  inferential system, role of, 87
  modular, xv, xvi, 87
  pragmatic control, 151
  role of, 82
Predication
  English, 111, (def.) 117, (def.) 140
  Japanese, 82, 85–86, 90, 95, 97
  role of, 119
  Williams's version, 151
Predicate Argument Structure (PAS), 20, 47–48, 50–51, 66, 77
Presumptions, referential, 104

Index

Principles (MG theory)
  coreference/disjoint reference, 168
  co-satisfaction (P2), 168
  co-satisfaction (P4), 168
  disjoint reference, 168
  imperative, 169
  predicate argument, 168
  X-bar, 152
PRO, 23–24, 72, 103, 139. See also "Gaps"; Empty Categories
  in GB theory, 183–186
  "long distance" control of, 214n24
  in MG theory, 113, 132
Projection Principle, 10, 112, 200n14, 213n12
  extended projection principle, 190
Pronouns
  bound variable interpretation of, 164
  as indexicals, 165, 173
  indexing of, 168
Pullum, G., 153, 216nn41–42, 217nn46–48
Pylyshyn, Z., xv

Quine, W. V. O., 211n16

Radford, Andrew, 4–5
Reference
  disjoint (English), 163
  disjoint (Japanese), 103
  pragmatic (speaker) versus semantic, 167
  role of linguistic structure, 166, 182
  speaker, 104, 163, 181–182
Referential Index, 163, 165. See also Binding; Anaphora
Reflexivization, 22, 28. See also Zibun
Reinhart, Tanya, 161–164, 194, 199n2, 218n7
Rewrite Rules. See Phrase Structure (PS) Rules
Ross, John R., 40, 162, 216n41

Sag, Ivan, 153, 216n42, 217nn46–48
Saito, Mamoru, 97, 209n6, 210n11
Sanctioning, 112
  by case, 112
  lexical, 110, 133
  overlap, 112
  syntactic, 110, 129, 154, 156

Scrambling, 21, 31–32, 43–44, 78
  context-free lexical insertion, 78 (see also Lexical Insertion)
'S' Diacritic, 102
  interaction with passive, 69
  'S' assignment, 66, 77–78
Self, semantics of, 168, 177
Semantic Linking, 50–55, 71, 80–81
  NI-Linking, 52, 54, 61, 89
  "residue" case markings, 50, 89
S(entence) Node
  projection of INFL, 152
  projection of V, 9, 15, 19
  status of, in MG theory, 152–154
Shibatani, M., 27, 29, 32, 63
S-structure, status of, 24. See also Modular Grammar, S-structure in
Stative Verbs, 28
Steele, Susan, 153, 159, 202n17, 213n14, 215n28, 216n41, 217nn44–45
Stowell, Timothy, 9, 10, 18, 152, 160, 195, 200n11, 202n19, 213n15, 214n20, 216n41, 217n49
Subjacency, (def.) 188. See also Control
  bounding nodes, 147
  and NP-movement, 147
  and NP-trace, 186–187
  violations of, 149
Subject, 63–65
  AUX inversion, 155–159
  definition of (English), 109
  diacritic, ('S'), 63, 65
  domain of, 78
  of an infinitival, 133
  multiple subject (Japanese), 98–99
  obligatoriness of, 19, 23, 113–115
  phonologically-null, 23
  properties of, 33
  role of, 22
  'S' assignment, 66–67, 69–70
  slot, 47
Syntactic Level of Representation, 200–201n14

Taylor, H. M., 200n8
Terminal Node, Δ, 13, 20, 72
Thematic Hierarchy, 204n20
θ (theta) criterion
  analogue in MG theory, 112
  violations of, 111
θ (theta) theory, 114
Tomoda, Shizuko, 89, 209n6, 210nn11–14

Tonoike, Shigeo, 31–32, 43–44, 72, 203n14
Topic Construction (Japanese), 81–88, 196
Tough Sentences (Japanese), 81, 83, 88–93, 97, 197
Transformations
 global constraint, 68
 pure passive formation, 65
 summary of Kuno's transformations for Japanese, 58
Tsugihara, Sachiko, 211n21
Tsujimura, Natsuko, 206n31, 211n21

Ueda, M., 81, 206–207n2, 207n3

Vergnaud, J.-R., 205n27
Visser, F., 216n39

Washio, R., 103–104, 211n18, 211n21
Wasow, Tom, 153, 162, 214n24, 216n41, 217n44
Wehrli, Eric, 202n17, 213n14
Whitman, John, 21
Wilkins, Wendy, 212n7, 215n33
Williams, Edwin, 14, 82, 109, 144, 151, 205n27, 208n4, 213n8, 214n23, 215n34
Wilson, D., 216n41
Word order, 195–196
 preferred, 45

X-Bar Theory, 8, 9

Yes/No Questions, 155–159. *See also* Subject, AUX inversion

Zibun, 29–30, 38–42, 63–65
 antecedent of, 29, 63–64, 78
 cases of ambiguity, 29–30, 64, 94
 interpretation rule, 100, 210–211n15
 reflexive coreference constraint (RCC), 40–42
 review of previous accounts, 99–101
Zubizarreta, M.-L., 205n27

www.ingramcontent.com/pod-product-compliance
Lightning Source LLC
Chambersburg PA
CBHW060948230426
43665CB00015B/2111